SEARCH
FOR THE
ABSENT GOD

SEARCH
FOR THE
ABSENT GOD

*Tradition and Modernity
in Religious Understanding*

WILLIAM J. HILL

EDITED BY
MARY CATHERINE HILKERT

CROSSROAD • NEW YORK

1992

The Crossroad Publishing Company
370 Lexington Avenue, New York, NY 10017

Printed in the United States of America

Library of Congress Cataloging-in-Publication Data

Hill William J., 1924–
    Search for the absent God : tradition and modernity in religious
understanding / William J. Hill ; edited by Mary Catherine Hilkert
        p. cm.
    ISBN 0-8245-1114-X
    1. God 2. Philosophical theology. 3. Preaching. I. Hilkert,
Mary Catherine. II. Title.
BT102.H54 1992
231—dc20   91-30773
                                                                  CIP

The enduring element of thought is the way. And the ways of thought conceal within themselves the mystery that we can walk on them both forward and backward, that even the way backward is what first leads us forward. — Martin Heidegger

It is when from the uttermost depths of our being we need a sound which does mean something — when we cry out for an answer and it is not granted — it is then that we touch the silence of God. — Simone Weil

Contents

Acknowledgements

My gratitude is due, and hereby tendered, to all who contributed in various ways to the origin of this volume: to my colleagues and students in the department of theology at Catholic University and to my confreres in the Dominican House of Studies in Washington, D.C., especially to Romanus Cessario.

My special thanks are owed to Mary Catherine Hilkert of Aquinas Institute of Theology in St. Louis who encouraged the project and served as its general editor; also to Karen Reiniger for typing the notes, to Mary Ducey for preparing the index, and to Justus George Lawler and Frank Oveis of Crossroad Publishing Company for their professional advice.

I am grateful as well for the cooperation of the following publications: *The Thomist, Theological Studies, Journal of Religion, Heythrop Journal, Proceedings of the Catholic Theological Society of America, New Scholasticism, Homiletic and Pastoral Review*, Liturgical Press, Paragon House Publishers, Michael Glazier, Inc., University Press of America, and *Listening*.

Preface

As Christianity prepares to enter its third millennium it is increasingly acknowledged that theology is on the verge of an epochal change. This heralds the end of the modern world and the advent of post-modernity in the search for the meaning and the truth of what is believed. Two obvious characteristics of this new age of thought are a marked reaction against the rationalism of the Enlightenment and its premise of pure objectivity and second, against the emphasis upon subjectivity remotely deriving from Descartes but proximately owed to transcendental thought (including the move from classical Thomism to the primacy of the subject in the transcendental Thomism initiated by Joseph Marechal and consolidated by Karl Rahner, Bernard Lonergan, and others). The more positive stance of this new thinking has been illumined by Fergus Kerr in his *Theology After Wittgenstein* and by Claude Geffré in his essay on "Non-Metaphysical Theology" in *A New Age in Theology*. Also instructive of how post-modern theology will function is George Lindbeck's *The Nature of Doctrine*. This radical revision is congenial to Heidegger's dismissal of metaphysics and thus of its providing foundations for theology. Metaphysics is looked upon as an intrusion of Hellenic thought into Christian revelation. The shift is thus easily made to the so-called linguistic turn enabling theology to view itself neither as science of God (the classical tradition), nor as a hermeneutics of Christian experience (the legacy of modernity), but as critical reflection upon the phenomenon of language which "brackets" the question of any ontological referent to such language. This has prompted the *bon mot* from the Italian novelist, Umberto Eco, that theologians will soon be back with Homer!

This present volume seeks to explore, in a non-systematic way,the crisis of the God question in contemporary theology, that is to say, in the living tradition as it engages modernity and stands on the threshold of what awaits it in the rethinking of post-modernity. The consequences of this engagement for theology are considerable. If one asks what theology today is, as distinct from what it once was or what it should now be, the search for an answer can begin only with a reflection upon what practic-

ing theologians are actually doing. There it immediately becomes evident
that dogmatics has given way to hermeneutics, science to linguistics, nature
to history, eternity to temporality, the past/present to the present/future,
metaphysics to epistemology, theology proper to Christian anthropology,
unity to pluralism, continuity to discontinuity, theory to praxis, being to
becoming, analogical thinking to dialectical thinking — the list could go
on. Eberhard Jüngel is perhaps right in locating the neuralgic point in this
one-sided shift in the sphere of philosophical theology. Here the domi-
nating concern is no longer the atheist question (not since the demise of
the "God is dead" movement of the sixties), i.e., the question of whether
or not God exists, but the bypassing of the whole theistic tradition. The
maintenance of a critical distance from that inheritance underscores the
"rethinkability" (E. Jüngel) of God, that is to say, far from closing off debate about God, it in fact opens up the question on a new level and with
a new urgency.

One positive gain in this confrontation with modernity has been the
finding of place for religious pluralism. But accompanying that advance is
the specter of relativism, of a pluralism that is random and arbitrary. Also
deserving of re-examination is the assumption that the theistic concept of
God is an intrusion of Hellenic rationalism into the domain of faith. Does
this not neglect the ambiance of the Old Testament conviction of God as
creator *ex nihilo?*

The central concern in what follows is a recovery for theology of the
lost metaphysical dimension. Employing at once a method of discovery
(*via inventionis*) starting from experience, and a method of learning (*via
disciplinae*) starting from what is prior in the subject engaged, i.e., in deity itself, theology remains a metaphysical venture in at least one respect,
namely that it concerns itself with reality transcendent to the categorical realities of our spatio-temporal world. We cannot talk about God in
the way we talk about objects in our everyday world. Nevertheless, theology has traditionally remained a metaphysical venture in a more radical
and integral sense than this. I should like to suggest that this is a heritage not to be abandoned lightly especially in this age of theological
pluralism.

It is legitimate to ask if the question of God can be dealt with satis-
factorily by appealing to a theology that employs exclusively an historical
method. Heidegger's alleged overthrow of metaphysics, which is perhaps
the most trenchant and influential negative critique, indicts all of theology
in the Christian tradition as being in fact an onto-theo-logic — that is a
grounding of Being in *a* being, *a primum ens.* Usurping the revealed God
of the Gospels is the notion of Absolute Being postulated out of the immanence of thought as the ground of the beings. This is, for Heidegger and
his followers, an instance of representational thinking in which theology
seeks its own foundations and ends by conceiving God as an object over

which it can exercise cognitive control. This is seen as an importation into Christian thought of pagan Greek rationalism.

But this is natural theology in the pejorative sense it acquired in Enlightenment thinking, one heightened in the nineteenth century when theologians after Kant entered upon a tactical withdrawal from the God question, abandoning it to the philosophers. For Thomas Aquinas, by contrast, theology is an inquiry that presupposes faith, i.e., that originates within faith even as it is, first, a reflection upon the presuppositions of faith (what Aquinas calls the *preambula fidei*), and, second, a clarification of belief. It does not constitute of itself a neutral zone which is the prerogative of pure reason unillumined by faith. The late Dominic Dubarle has written that in questions 2–26 of St. Thomas's *Summa Theologiae*, "the Christian religion is constantly present" as both the authorities cited and certain issues raised make clear. For Aquinas, it is always faith grounding metaphysical reflection and not vice versa. The *quinque viae* are thus theological products, giving logical formulation in a reflective way to what is already believed. The metaphysics at work here is thus rooted in experience, but experience to which faith gives *entre*, as it does to subsequent understanding and ultimately to liberating practice. This is to call into question Karl Barth's contention that revelation is emptied of all significance if knowledge of God is possible any place other than in that revelation to which the Scriptures bear witness. But if all philosophical theology is to be abandoned, what justification is there for continuing to maintain and believe what Jesus says about God? Seemingly, only the human authority of Jesus. But in truth, Jesus authority comes from his proclamation that the kingdom of God has drawn near to us and is in fact inaugurated in himself, which already assumes a preliminary notion of God both on Jesus' part and our own. For us this preliminary notion may take the form of a question about deity; further, the question as first posed by us is radically transformed in light of the answer given by Christ. True enough, the Bible does not propose any natural theology, but it practices a kind of natural theology which it takes simply as a matter of course. YHWH who speaks through the prophets is already acknowledged in the creation accounts as the beginning and end of everything. Thus, the metaphysical presuppositions at issue here derive less from Hellenic philosophy than from religious consciousness witnessed to in the Old and New Testaments.

Moreover, the metaphysics employed by Aquinas in the conceptual clarification of belief is not essentialistic. It does not seek to answer questions about the natures of the things that make up this world. It arises from the far more primal question "Why are there beings rather than nothing at all?" The answer for Thomas, of course, lies in his conviction that God's essence is his very act of existence, and in his original insight that existence is not another kind of essence, nor a matter of mere facticity, but something on another level of intelligibility entirely, namely the *act* of "to be." He is "extra ordinem omnium entium existens" (In *Peri hermenias*, I,14,197). Thus creatures *are* in virtue of a real relation of dependence upon Be-ing that subsists of itself. The ontological dimension appealed to here does not ignore the role of modern historical consciousness — thus to be true to itself it must open out onto the contingencies of history, and find meaning not in spite of contingency, but in that very contingency itself. Also, the prevailing role of faith enables the believer to recognize Subsistent Be-ing as analogous to what is experienced as personal in the finite order, as answering to the God of the prophets and to the *Abba* of Jesus.

Perhaps the major issue in all this today focuses on the possibilities for a genuine panentheism, that is for a reciprocity between God and creation. Where lies the greater religious value — in the belief that we are totally unnecessary to God and cannot affect God or contribute to the divine life in any way? Or that God wills to need a universe of finitely free creatures capable of responding in free and determining ways? Luther in an oft quoted sermon of 1534 made it clear that he sought not the deity in itself (*Deus in se*) but a God of and for humankind (*Deus pro nobis*), a God of salvation, a gracious God. The question about God has become the question about God's presence in human life and thus the question about the meaning and destiny of human history, both individual and social. Bonhoeffer radicalized this in proclaiming that "only a suffering God can help." J. Moltmann and E. Jüngel have worked out the theological justification for this position, arguing that God does not suffer by any necessity of nature but as something freely willed as logically entailed in his love for a suffering humanity. They make abundantly clear that it does not do justice to the Christian claim to understand this as merely a suffering of God in his assumed humanity, explained by recourse to the traditional formula of "communication of idioms," whereby the attributes of Christ's human nature are transferred to his divine nature by virtue of the hypostatic union, and vice versa. What is clearly meant is that God suffers in his very divinity. But is this not to introduce a cryptic commonality between God and world, and in effect to sacrifice his transcendence? Is not God's immutability, his incapacity for change, the formal reason for his total immanence to the world? God thus alleviates suffering not by taking it upon himself and sharing it with its human victims in a willed impotence, but by opposing it in the most intimate, intense and efficacious ways through his loving omnipotence. Herbert McCabe suggests as a motive for the doctrine of a suffering God a weakened understanding of the incarnation, of the confession that God has become man in Jesus of Nazareth and truly suffers in his humanity.

Most promising of all perhaps for the recovery of the idea of God is the richness available in the doctrine of the Trinity. Can this dynamism within deity, which knows neither before nor after, be analogous to what in the created universe is perceived as change? Can God be more richly conceived as event than as substance? The trinitarian relations have always been looked upon as the source of creation and the economy of salvation, especially if the processions be viewed as genuine actions rather than as emanations, and the central structural element of personhood be relatedness.

Lastly, the volume will conclude with some efforts at a theory of communicating these mysteries of God, i.e., with the mystery of proclamation.

INTRODUCTION

Sacra Doctrina in the Twentieth Century: The Theological Project of William J. Hill

At the center of theological discourse in the United States today are fundamental questions about the discipline itself — the nature, method, and very possibility of "doing theology." Is theology a ministry within the community of faith, an academic science, or an art? Can theology be done after "the death of metaphysics"? Can we speak of the very mystery of God or only of human faith experience? Can religious language make a claim to meaning, let alone truth? Is a world theology possible? How do fundamental, systematic, and practical theology interrelate? What are the appropriate sources for theology? Whose experience counts in the formation and interpretation of the tradition? Who does theology and in what context? Is it necessary that the theologian be a believer?

The predominant focus on questions of method within theological discourse has been criticized however by John B. Cobb and Gordon Kaufman among others. Addressing the faculty and students at his alma mater, the University of Chicago, rather pointedly, Cobb charged that

> Theological faculties have, on the whole, moved from the center to the periphery of the thought life of the church.... There are a not inconsiderable number who find the meaning of their vocation, if not of their lives as a whole, in the service of their disciplines.... I think it is time to name this stance for what it is, disciplinolatry.... Theology now seeks to define its subject matter and method without taking responsibility for shaping the faith of the church or its mission. It seeks to be a discipline. It does not claim the center.[1]

1

In an essay in which he describes theology as a public vocation Kaufman also used the language of idolatry to describe the temptations facing contemporary theologians. Naming some of the more subtle idols before which theologians bow, Kaufman included serving the needs of the Church as an institution, holding academic positions, editing journals, writing books and articles, and furthering the interests of the university.[2] Granting the relative value of each of these pursuits, Kaufman, too, summoned theologians to reclaim their central responsibility: "that of dealing seriously and critically with the question of God."[3] At root the crisis facing theologians is one of vocation. Will we, and how will we, "claim the center"?

In his creative retrieval of the Thomistic tradition of doing theology as a share in *sacra doctrina* — God's holy teaching — William J. Hill has provided his own answer to that question. Clearly Hill has claimed the center of the theological endeavor, focusing his life's work on what Schubert Ogden has called "the only problem there is"[4] — the problem of God. At the same time he has engaged profoundly human and pastoral questions, thus contributing his share to the faith of the Church and its mission.

Describing his own understanding of the task facing the theologian, Hill has cited more than once a favorite quotation from Maurice Merleau-Ponty: One must at once "remain faithful to what one has been and take up everything again from the beginning."[5] It is in that sense that Hill can be described as a Thomist. He stands within a living tradition, not repeating or defending Thomas Aquinas, but rather doing in the twentieth century what Aquinas did in the thirteenth: seeking a creative and critical, but ultimately limited, understanding of faith in the context of the contemporary culture. There are, of course, fundamental Thomistic distinctions and insights to which Hill repeatedly returns in his own work: Aquinas's understanding of God as pure act, i.e., dynamic be-ing; the autonomy of creation and the conviction that God and the human do not compete; the reminder that faith ends not in propositions, but in reality; the trust that faith and reason cannot ultimately conflict; and an understanding of analogy that preserves both the utter transcendence of God and the possibility of doing theology at all, to name some of the more central ones. Hill's appropriation of those key insights, however, is not based merely on the authority of his mentor in the tradition who himself described the argument from authority as the weakest ground for truth.[6] Rather the search for truth wherever it is to be found is a commitment Hill shares with Aquinas, *veritas* being the very motto of their common Dominican tradition. In the pursuit of truth, Hill has felt free to reject or rework the conclusions of recognized authorities who have gone before him (as did Aquinas) and compelled to explore the questions and disputes of his own day with the freedom of spirit described by Aquinas in his commentary on Aristotle's *Metaphysics*:

One should love both, namely: those whose opinions we follow and those whose opinions we repudiate, because the one and the other have been at pains to seek out the truth, and have helped us in that quest.[7]

Hill has given a creative and original interpretation to a number of Thomistic insights, most notably in his work on analogy, his efforts to incorporate history and subjectivity in a serious way into the Thomistic project, and his retrieval of an understanding of the Trinity as "the Three-Personed God." What characterizes him most deeply as a theologian in the Thomistic tradition, however, is the way in which he has understood and engaged in the theological task, the way in which he has embraced his vocation as a theologian, a vocation he himself has described as precarious. Preaching during the Eucharist at the 1985 convention of the Catholic Theological Society of America, he announced:

"It is an awesome thing to fall into the hands of the living God." These warning words of St. Paul are stark ones indeed... for one thing they suggest more may be required of us than we are prepared to give. But they are doubly awesome to those of us who are summoned to that ministry of the Word proper to the theologian, to we who are called upon to speak and write meaningfully of such a God to our contemporaries. Difficult and challenging enough in ordinary times, this attempt to show who God will be for us and what humankind must be for God, becomes nothing less than precarious in these days of cultural sea-changes.[8]

The life project of the theologian is clearly a vocation for Hill — a ministry of the Word which involves rigorous intellectual pursuit, but which is in the end far more than an academic career. Aquinas's discussion of *sacra doctrina* in the opening question of the *Summa Theologiae* sets the backdrop for Hill's own twentieth-century pursuit of the theological task.

The fourteen chapters of this book serve as contemporary examples of the kind of wisdom which Aquinas described as primarily speculative, but eminently practical. Even in its most profoundly speculative reflection on the mystery of the inner-trinitarian relations, Hill's theology of God is intended ultimately (as was Aquinas's theology) "for salvation." On the other hand, Hill's lesser known work on a theology of preaching is a clear example of a form of pastoral theology which brings serious and sustained systematic reflection to bear on a ministry at the very center of the Church's mission.

Sacra Doctrina in a New Cultural Context

An understanding of theology in the Thomistic tradition as a participation in *sacra doctrina*,[9] the revelatory process by which God shares
God's own life with humanity, provides the context from which Hill responds to questions facing both classical and contemporary theologians
in the studies collected here. Thomistic concerns of explicit interest in
Hill's foundational writings are questions of whether theology is a science,
whether theology is or can be metaphysical, and whether and how religious
language can speak of God.

Though Aquinas was vitally interested in establishing theology as a
science in the Aristotelian sense of *epistēmē*, the discursive dimension of
theology was always subsumed into a higher wisdom. According to Aquinas the theologian shares in this wisdom of revelation — ultimately God's
own self-knowledge — through the discursive discipline of study, but the
fullest understanding of the mystery of God and of all of reality in relation to God comes from a higher wisdom — the gift of the Holy Spirit
that flows from charity. As John of St. Thomas described this connatural
experiential knowledge of God, the gift of wisdom which enables the theologian to judge through sympathy rather than scientific instruction, "the
human mind no longer merely walks by its own deliberations, but takes the
wings of love — and surpassing our notions about divine things, is gathered
into them."[10] While emphasis in Aquinas's theology is usually put on the
logos dimension, the search for the intelligibility in things as they stand
in relation to God, the affective and pneumatological dimension in Aquinas's project, what Thomas Gilby has called "the dialectic of love in the
Summa"[11] is too often overlooked or ignored.

Here Hill is clearly faithful to the heritage of Thomas: not only is theology a matter of *faith* seeking understanding, but further, the deepest
understanding emerges from a living faith that requires love. A trinitarian
perspective is operative not only throughout his writings on the theology
of God, but in his very understanding of the theological task. The theologian is drawn into "holy teaching" by which God shares God's own
self-knowledge with the believer through the missions of the Trinity —
the Word spoken in history and the Spirit who draws all of creation back
to its source in love. To "do theology" is ultimately to be drawn into the
dynamic life of the Trinity, or as Hill has said, "the theological act gradually moves from discursive thinking to mystical intuition, from analogical
understanding to anagogical union."[12]

To emphasize, however, that theology is preeminently a form of wisdom
is not to say that it is not a science. One of the unfortunate dichotomies on
the contemporary theological scene is reflected in the question of whether
theology is a confessional hermeneutic or whether it is an academic science
which can claim respectability in the public arena. For Hill, in the tradition

of Aquinas, it is both. While the community of faith is the matrix in which revelation occurs since all experience is interpreted, still faith claims to speak about ultimate reality. Hence Hill argues that theology is a science in that it is a rational, public discourse that critically employs criteria for meaning and truth. As for its confessional nature, he notes that all thought involves commitment as Michael Polanyi and the sociologists of knowledge have persuasively shown.[13]

Ultimately Hill shares Aquinas's conviction as expressed by Marie-Dominique Chenu: "Theology is the happy result of a daring trust in the coherence of faith and reason."[14] The contemporary claim that theology is a science obviously means something quite different from Aristotle's *epistēmē*, certain and evident knowledge known in a causal demonstrated way after the model of the natural sciences. Rather in the context of historical consciousness, Hill notes that the truth theology seeks is the truth proper to the human person's being rooted in freedom; hence it is indigenously historical and linguistic.[15]

The crucial issue here is, of course, the contingency of history. The lack of historical consciousness which Congar, among others, has identified as the major weakness of medieval thought[16] is at the core of the critique which any theologian who claims to speak about the ultimate meaning of history and reality must face today. Can one speak of intelligibility in history? Here Hill parts company with the Dominican theologian who has had such a marked influence on his recent thinking — Edward Schillebeeckx.

In his earlier writings Schillebeeckx, relying on the work of his Louvain philosophy mentor, Dominic De Petter, grounded knowledge of reality in a non-conceptual dimension to the cognitive act, an implicit intuition of being which finds its source in the participationist structure of creation.[17] In his *Jesus* book, however, Schillebeeckx explicitly breaks with the claims of both classical metaphysics and De Petter's phenomenology in this identification of an implicit intuition of meaning-totality in every particular experience of meaning. Rather he now asserts that concrete human history remains fundamentally ambiguous: "*logos* and facticity stand in irresolvable tension."[18] No universal meaning is available before history has reached its conclusion both because of the utter non-intelligibility of evil and excessive human suffering and because individual events and periods of history take on their full significance only in light of history's final outcome. Hence Schillebeeckx turns to a narrative-practical anticipation of the meaning-totality of the Christian story, but rejects the possibility of an undergirding metaphysical explanation of reality that grounds that eschatological hope.

Hill, on the other hand, insists that to speak theologically, to speak of God in history, requires metaphysics. He argues not for a particular form of metaphysics (admitting that a critical realism of post-Kantian origin remains a rich and vital alternative to his own moderate realism),[19] but rather that if theology is to speak with any depth or consistency, it must penetrate to the level of reality undergirding history. The theologian must make some informed metaphysical option precisely because theology is a public discourse which makes claims not only to meaning, but also to truth. Thus Hill remains dissatisfied with various forms of narrative or aesthetic theology (including Schillebeeckx's narrative-practical approach). Granting that the *pneuma*-dimension of theology which emerges in symbol, myth, and silence extends beyond the *logos* dimension which seeks intelligibility and meaning, Hill still defends the *logos* dimension as one dimension of God's being in our midst.

In the foundational essays in Part I, Hill argues for a dialectical relationship between history and nature if history is to be more than random and arbitrary. The God who is author of creation *is* the God who acts in history. The creative summons of divine love inviting humanity toward a future which remains open is rooted in the wisdom of God that was active at creation. The intelligibility which the theologian seeks in history is that of *revelabilitas*, the truth history bears in relation to God, but the basic horizon for understanding all that the transcendent and free God has done and will do is to be found in the fundamental intelligibility of being and some sort of isomorphic relationship between consciousness and reality. That metaphysical undergirding provides the very possibility for human beings to interpret and experience God's historical revelation.

The Thomistic metaphysical scaffolding which Hill describes as a necessary foundation for faith is an existential metaphysics (a judgmental grasp of the real) rather than an essentialist one (which unifies plurality conceptually). Hill moves beyond Aquinas's metaphysics, however, in proposing a fusion of horizons which incorporates Heidegger's crucial awareness of subjectivity at the core of reality. From an explicitly trinitarian faith perspective, Hill further describes the mysterious dynamism at the heart of reality as intersubjectivity, God's self-presencing in the twofold modality of Word and Spirit. One sees here the deeper roots of Hill's claim that it is the *logos* dimension of reality which grounds the theologian's search for meaning and truth.

Hill's defense of the *logos* dimension of intelligibility which faith spontaneously seeks, however, is itself limited by Aquinas's understanding of God as pure dynamic act of be-ing. The coincidence of essence and existence in God places God beyond all human understanding. Hence even this highly metaphysical theology remains ultimately apophatic. While the participationist structure of creation allows for the possibility of naming the divine (speaking of God *in se* and not only of human experience of God in faith), it is precisely God's utter transcendence that necessitates that all theology end finally in silence and worship.

More than once Hill has described Aquinas's doctrine of analogy as "the nerve" of the theological project. In the face of the prevalent neo-

Scholastic conceptualist interpretations of Aquinas's theory of analogy and the turn of contemporary analysts of religious language to symbol, Hill's own careful study and creative retrieval of Aquinas's question 13 in the *prima pars* of the *Summa*[20] has clearly made a major contribution to contemporary theological discussion of religious language and the very possibility of doing theology. At once more apophatic than the conceptualists who dominated the earlier Thomistic tradition of interpretation and more kataphatic than the growing number of theologians who would restrict theological language to speech about the depth dimension of human experience, Hill, in his *Knowing the Unknown God*, has retrieved an understanding of analogy that asserts the possibility of speaking of God *in se* while admitting that the unknown God remains beyond the reach of human concepts as the mystery intended, but never grasped. Here the metaphysical scaffolding reaches its limits; the science of theology returns to mystery; faith's search for understanding gives way to love.

This Thomistic vision of theology as the scientific dimension to *sacra doctrina*, as simultaneously speculative and practical (each in an eminent mode), is demonstrated well in the two major areas of Hill's work that are the focus of study in this volume: theology of God (Part II) and theology of preaching (Part III).

The Mystery of God: Faith Seeking Understanding

The central focus of Hill's lifetime of research, writing, teaching, and preaching has been the "affair" that Christopher Fry described as "soul-size": exploration into God.[21] He has addressed not only the most basic question of the very possibility of speaking about God in *Knowing the Unknown God* and the most profound mystery of the Christian faith (the only mystery that there is according to Karl Rahner) in *The Three-Personed God*, but also the radical challenges to, and critiques of, classical theism that have arisen from such diverse thinkers as Karl Marx and Karl Barth, Martin Heidegger and Alfred North Whitehead, Jürgen Moltmann and Karl Rahner. Other conversation partners whose critiques and questions have repeatedly engaged Hill's thinking have included Wolfhart Pannenberg, Edward Schillebeeckx, Hans Urs von Balthasar, Walter Kasper, Bernard Lonergan, John Macquarrie, Louis Dupré, Langdon Gilkey, Schubert Ogden, J. B. Metz, and Lewis Ford. These same questions are being newly surfaced today in theology after Wittgenstein, called by some "post-modern theology."

Hill's basic project could be characterized as a retrieval of the tradition — the tradition of classical theism as it was forged in a highly original way in the thought of Thomas Aquinas (though often misrepresented and even unwittingly betrayed by the lesser minds that followed), but more importantly the retrieval of the Judaeo-Christian tradition of revelation in a new age and culture. More than once Hill has repeated that the Thomistic tradition is only one among other viable options in the arena of contemporary theology. Still it is clear from his writings and teaching that his own conviction is that fundamental Thomistic insights rethought in the contemporary context can offer the most adequate response to some of the crucial questions of our day. One might dispute the adequacy of Aquinas's concepts to describe the God revealed in the Scriptures and most profoundly in the concrete history of Jesus of Nazareth, but it is important to note that Hill adopts and creatively develops those concepts precisely because he sees them, when properly understood, to guard and express aspects of the mystery of revelation which might otherwise be lost. The tradition Hill attempts to retrieve is not the Thomistic tradition in the sense of what Thomas said or wrote, but the experience of the living God as encountered in the community of faith, an experience which has been handed on to us through the symbols and texts of the lived history of the Christian tradition.

Hence Hill's exploration of the mystery of the "Three-Personed God" for example, neither begins nor ends with Aquinas. The starting point is religious experience (the experience of the primitive Christian community as reflected in the symbolic language of the Scriptures) and the final move is a return to religious experience — contemporary ecclesial experience and genuine religious experience outside Christianity. In the hermeneutics of tradition which constitutes the major section of Hill's *The Three-Personed God* Aquinas is situated in the historical development of the larger Christian tradition. Hill highlights Aquinas's contribution of offering ontological density to Augustine's psychological understanding of person as relation through a metaphysics of notional act, but he also admits that that contribution is baffling and misunderstood by the contemporary religious mind. Only after exploring the broad spectrum of reformulations of the doctrine of the Trinity in the ongoing history of the tradition which eventually led to the relegation of that doctrine to a postscript to the Christian faith or a mere mental construct, does Hill offer his own proposal. Though indebted to Aquinas's metaphysical understanding of person, Hill incorporates further insights into the mystery of the Trinity which derive precisely from a contemporary psychological understanding of person, namely the extension of the concept to incorporate consciousness of self and others, a greater emphasis on relationality, and a new focus on intersubjectivity.[22]

What is clearly evidenced in that book, as in the studies collected here, is that it is the history of the entire Christian tradition including the present moment of ecclesial experience, not only the Thomistic contribution to that tradition, that Hill is committed to reappropriating. Still, convinced that Aquinas is a classic resource too often misunderstood or ignored in contemporary theology, Hill looks for forgotten traces ("latent intelligibilities," he would say) in the Thomistic tradition which as an "open system" offers room for creative contemporary development.

If the classic insights of Aquinas are to have a hearing in the modern world, however, they must be reappropriated in the context of historical consciousness and subjectivity. Hill's contributions toward a more profound theology of God in our day all attempt in one way or another to expand the Thomistic horizon through a fusion with the contemporary horizon of historicity and freedom. Hill grapples seriously with modern questions which demand a response that a medieval worldview cannot offer. In chapter 7 Hill probes the question "Does the World Make a Difference to God?" and writes:

> If God is indeed the Lord of history so that the human project is somehow his [God's] project and if that project in its genuine historicity and precariousness is contingent and can fail, then what the world is and becomes must of necessity affect God.

Chapter 10 asks, "Is it possible any longer, after several holocausts, to discern the presence of God in universal human progress?" The question that recurs in his ongoing dialogue with process thought (chapters 7 to 9), "Is God really related to the world?" takes on a poignant urgency in his later work when it is reechoed anew in the context of radical human suffering. In dialogue with Moltmann, Schillebeeckx, and liberation theologians, Hill wrestles in chapter 11 with the question: "Does Divine Love Entail Suffering in God?"

While Hill's response in each case is, in one sense, a creative retrieval of the Thomistic tradition, it should be noted that the retrieval is more one of the Thomistic theological process, than of content. What is perhaps most like Thomas, and most unlike his neo-Scholastic interpreters, is that Hill not only seriously engages the questions of his day, but also grasps the inadequacy of traditionally formulated answers to those questions. Realizing for example that "somehow or other, God with a creation and God without it are not entirely the same thing," Hill admits in chapter 7 that "it appears overly facile to dismiss this as exclusively on the side of the creature." As in chapter 4, he questions seriously whether Aquinas's preservation of the transcendence of God can be reconciled with a *genuine* notion of human freedom.

Further, Hill notes that not only the contemporary context, but also the biblical claims of revelation call into question the tenability of the Thomistic system. Thus he grants the strength of process theologians' attempt to envision God as the "fellow-sufferer who understands" in that they take seriously the Christian belief that the humanity of Jesus is the humanity of God. In Jesus, suffering has been brought into the very mystery of God — a truth, Hill reminds us, that finds its strongest warrant in the cross of Christ and a mystery, he acknowledges in chapters 5 and 9, that the traditional doctrine of the *communicatio idiomatum* is inadequate to express. In engaging the claims of modernity and biblical revelation as well as the perspectives of other theologians, Hill has been willing to rethink not only Aquinas's answers, but also his own, in the kind of self-correcting process of learning that he observed in Aquinas's development of thought on questions of analogy or grace.

Beyond the process of listening seriously both to the tradition and to new questions and perspectives, however, Hill has made his own creative contributions to the dialogue, often through a process remarkably like Aquinas's of making new distinctions. From the modern context of history and subjectivity particularly as explored by Heidegger in the distinction of the ontological from the ontic order, Hill looks back and detects what he calls "some faint premonition" within the *theological* corpus of Aquinas of the modern "turn to the subject" (chapter 7). Using Aquinas's formal distinction between the entitative order (of objective being-there-ness) and the intentional order (of knowing and loving) Hill finds the basis for probing the irreducible distinction between person and nature in God in such a way as to be able to speak in the contemporary context of God as really related to the world and hence as genuinely affected in some way by the creature's response in the dialogic partnership between God and humanity (chapters 3, 4, 5, 6, 7, 8, and 10), of God's suffering in and with humanity (in Jesus) (chapters 9 and 11), and of historicity in God (chapter 5). What has been verbally denied by Aquinas in the medieval metaphysical consideration of God's nature can be explicitly affirmed by Hill from the perspective of trinitarian theology and a contemporary understanding of person.

Similarly the medieval debate about God's foreknowledge, if transposed into the modern question of the relationship between human freedom and divine transcendence, can be rethought, Hill suggests in chapter 7, in light of a Christian understanding of freedom as radically constituting personhood, thus placing the discussion in a context which surmounts the former Greek categories of contingency and necessity. In terms of the question of temporality in God, Hill points out that while the scholastic notion of eternity (often misunderstood as a motionless now) excludes the past and future of cosmological time, that the system remains open to new interpretation in light of a contemporary understanding of "historic time" of self-creating decision. Thus Hill proposes a simultaneity of history's past, present, and future in God, but that future is freely created by human beings who introduce genuine novelty into the historical process. Hill does not pretend that Aquinas's notion of eternity is really the same as Heidegger's understanding of primal temporality, but rather suggests in chapter 5 that Aquinas's thinking does not exclude Heidegger's understanding and that through a fusion of horizons the two projects might prove mutually illuminating.

In some cases, such as the question of whether divine love entails suffering in God, Hill suggests that the Thomistic understanding of love is actually richer than the possibilities discussed in contemporary debates. Moving beyond the self-fulfilling *eros* of a God who needs the world and even the divine *pathos* which Abraham Heschel and Jürgen Moltmann have so powerfully described, Hill concludes in chapters 9 and 11 that the concepts of *agape* and *amicitia* do greater justice to the God of biblical revelation and promise ultimately greater hope for suffering humanity.

Even this quick survey of some of the major questions Hill has addressed in his soul-size exploration of the mystery of God reveals the depth and breadth of his speculative thinking. What is not so immediately obvious is that this speculative endeavor also remains profoundly pastoral or as Aquinas would say, "eminently practical." Ultimately theology, for Hill as for Aquinas, is "for salvation" as even the subtitle of his book on the Trinity suggests: *The Three-Personed God: A Mystery of Salvation*. Further the very questions he has engaged in his serious academic work on the theology of God are deeply pastoral ones: Does God act in history? How is God related to our world, especially to suffering humanity? What are the implications and dimensions of genuine human freedom? Can we speak at all of God in a nuclear, post-holocaust age in which even believers experience the silence and absence of God? Hill would rarely be described as a pastoral theologian, yet it is another aspect of his fidelity to the Thomistic tradition to have achieved a profound integration of deep pastoral concern with serious speculative reflection as is reflected in the final section of this book.

The Mystery of Preaching: Faith-Praxis Seeking Understanding

Viewing theology as a participation in *sacra doctrina* challenges yet another unfortunate dichotomy in the contemporary context: the split between academic and pastoral theology. The Protestant tradition has more easily preserved the relationship between pastor and theologian, yet Catholic theologians of the stature of Karl Rahner and Edward Schillebeeckx as well as the growing numbers of liberation theologians have also described their theology as pastoral. In its own way Hill's theological work has also challenged that false dichotomy. Not only has his contribution to the theological understanding of the trinitarian God been constantly directed toward questions of human salvation, but also his essays toward a theology of proclamation, a more obviously pastoral topic, have made a distinctive contribution precisely because of their speculative insight and depth. It is fitting that as a theologian in the Dominican and Thomistic tradition, Hill's work in an explicitly pastoral area should be in the area of preaching since preaching was an integral part of the role of the Master of theology in the medieval context.[23]

In his work on a theology of proclamation, Hill is engaged in the Thomistic enterprise of *sacra doctrina* which is at once speculative and practical. It is precisely his understanding of theology that allows Hill to describe the proclamatory act as more than a practical adjunct to, or application of, theology. Rather, as he explains in chapter 13, preaching is a genuine moment in the revelatory process, the final moment in the theological process if theology is understood as the expression of God's word in history terminating in present experience.

Describing the field of pastoral theology as a *"terra incognita"* which stands in serious need of development, Hill suggests in chapter 12 that he is engaged more properly in a "theology of practice" — theological reflection not on texts or doctrines, but on what believers actually do by way of bringing their faith to authentic expression." While the art of preaching demands serious theological reflection on the part of the preacher, the ministry of preaching also serves as a very real source for systematic reflection.

In responding to the demanding questions which the ministry of preaching poses to the systematic theologian, Hill brings to bear the resources of speculative theology, but more importantly the habit of thinking which seeks intelligibility and makes connections. Hence the rich resources of his more obviously speculative work in hermeneutics, metaphysics, and trinitarian theology, as well as his creative retrieval of key insights of Aquinas, all reappear in his essays on preaching.

Heidegger's understanding of hermeneutics and Gadamer's "fusion of horizons" are drawn upon to explain the task that faces the preacher — bridging the gap between the New Testament kerygma and contemporary human experience. For Hill, however, a theology of preaching cannot rest at the level of hermeneutics or discussions of Word-event rooted in the work of the later Heidegger or Gadamer. Pushing his reflection on preaching to an explicitly metaphysical level, Hill remarks that the Scriptures themselves initiate us into a dialogue with their own subject matter: the living God. Even in his most recent writing on the theology of preaching (chapter 14) in which Hill discusses revelation as occurring in the depth dimension of ordinary human experience as interpreted-experienced in faith (thinking explicitly indebted to Edward Schillebeeckx), he continues to place an emphasis on the notion that revelation occurs "not because of the experiencing as such, but because of *what is experienced* in its objectivity over and against all activity of human subjectivity." Interpretation which is essential to the revelation event is always, for Hill, a response in faith to the God who is disclosed through the realities of history and the creation.

While most theologies of preaching focus largely or even exclusively on the power of the Word, Hill's work preserves the trinitarian dimensions of the mystery of proclamation and conversion through a retrieval of the Thomistic insight that faith has both an exterior cause ("faith comes from hearing") and an interior cause (the anointing of the Holy Spirit). Further he suggests that the process of conversion might be rethought and developed in terms of Aquinas's understanding of the intellectual gifts of the Holy Spirit perhaps reexpressed in Lonerganian categories as the experience of grace which occasions a radical shift of horizons.

This emerging form of pastoral theology which begins and ends with Christian experience (here, the ministry of preaching which is clearly central to the mission of the Church), but which requires serious systematic reflection, illustrates the kind of integration of speculative and practical theology which a full retrieval of the Thomistic vision of *sacra doctrina* in our day demands.

To characterize William Hill as a Thomist is, in one sense, far too narrow an understanding of his theological project. Nonetheless, one of his major contributions to theology in the twentieth century has been to preserve the Thomistic tradition as a living tradition — discovering lost and overlooked insights in Aquinas's writings, probing unexplored texts and implications of Thomas's thought, searching for the deeper spirituality that undergirds Aquinas's individual works, and finally making his own original contribution in our times. As Hill himself summarized his efforts at creative retrieval of the tradition during his 1980 presidential address to the Catholic Theological Society of America (see chapter 10): "This is no plea to repudiate the past; more a plea to be genuinely true to that past by giving it a future in the present."

MARY CATHERINE HILKERT, O.P.

PART I

FOUNDATIONS

ONE

Seeking Foundations for Faith: Symbolism of Person or Metaphysics of Being?

"Theology is the happy result of a daring trust in the coherence of faith and reason."[1] Much of the uneasiness posed for the contemporary critical thinker by the phenomenon of Christianity stems from the awareness that Christian existence is predicated on a commitment that seemingly breaks continuity with secular existence in the dipolar domain of nature and history that human beings have humanized in the mode of contemporary culture. Somewhat surprisingly, this discomfiture does not so easily surface in any study of the period of antiquity or the medieval era, and one can but wonder why. These earlier epochs of Christianity emphasized the transcendence of God more readily and more radically than do we, and they thematized that transcendence from within an exacting intellectualism. True enough, this was done prior to the rise of historical consciousness and preceded today's all-pervasive secularity. But the feeling persists that this goes only part way toward explaining why and how earlier modes of Christian thought were able to maintain faith and reason in such a delicate balance.

One clue lies in the refusal of early Christian thought to allow the transcendence of God to collapse into what the Stoics meant by *apatheia*, in which God remained at an ontological remove from the world, impassive and indifferent to its plight. The stress upon God's utter transcendence of the world was always complemented with an insistence upon his creating, knowing, loving and saving action in that world even to the point of assuming its history as his own in the human life of Christ and in the Spirit-directed life of the believing community. The real theological question was how the two — the transcendence and the immanence of God — were brought together. The answer usually lay in viewing God as the *Pantocrator* whose transcendence was such that he planned and carried out all

17

things (moral evil excepted) in the *oikonomia*. In the patristic period the categories used were Christian adaptations of sometimes Stoic, but more usually Platonic, notions. The advantage they offered is that they possessed a symbolic power that enabled believers to speak of the world as a vast sacrament of God everywhere present and operative in the depths of creation. All reality, nature and history, bespoke the transcendent because the metaphysics at work nurtured within itself a symbolism. What was uncovered to the human spirit was a *logos* structure *and* a mysterious dynamism of symbol — both of which pointed the way to God. The thought forms borrowed from Platonism engendered a rich symbolic vision in Gregory of Nyssa, Augustine, and (less successfully) Dionysius. The statements of belief worked out in the early councils were called *symbola* because they were intended as a locus of encounter with God. For the Greek Fathers, the world and the Bible were two differing symbolic forms of the *Logos* of God from which the soul began its mystical ascent to God. For Bonaventure in the Middle Ages, the Word is the supreme exemplar cause containing all divine ideas, and moreover is present within the soul as the illuminating ground of all the truth to which it attains.[2]

But, if medieval theology vindicated its foundations by discovering the isomorphism between the *Logos* of God that came to expression in his historical revelation addressed to faith, and the *logos*-structure of the real as God's creation that lay open to reason, it can be questioned whether this is any longer an option for theology in the post-Enlightenment, post-critical period. On the contemporary scene this has been thrown into further jeopardy by Heidegger's "overcoming" of metaphysics in uncovering the "onto-theo-logical" character of Western thought. The influence of this on foundational questions in contemporary theology has been massive. Its implication is that the Greek discovery of *logos* was a mixed blessing — on the one hand, it led to a concern for existents; on the other, it resulted in a neglect of being itself. Both Plato and Aristotle were philosophers of essence: the former sought the pure forms reflected in things, the latter focused on *ousia* to discover the being and intelligibility inherent within things. With Descartes, in the modern era, this forgetfulness of being was furthered to where it culminated in the introduction of a dichotomy between the existent and its representation in the mind. The Cartesian fissure between soul and body as *substantia cogitans* and *substantia corporea* meant isolating an abstract realm of ideas from a concrete world of sensations; it set a whole new problem for philosophy in seeking the origins of thought from within a radical subject-object dichotomy. Its immediate implication for theology was that religious faith could no longer find its anchorage in reason's encountering of the real. Subsequent theology had the option of casting its lot with Descartes and Spinoza and treating the content of faith rationalistically, or traveling the distinct route that leads from the restrictive empiricism of Hume to the fideism of Kant. Reason, at any rate, was loosened from all experiential contact with the real, and theology could only repudiate experience and its symbolic modes of expression entirely, or accept the limitations of an empiricism that deems the object of theology unknowable and so only postulated by practical reason (Kant) or by feeling (Schleiermacher's *Gefühl*).

Heidegger, however, viewed his own project as overthrowing what had previously been a neglect of Being (*Sein*) in the pursuit of the beingness (*Seiendenheit*) of the beings. His urging of the "ontological difference" found surprising confirmation in the concerns of the later Wittgenstein who writes of originating language in a way that suggests Heidegger's Being itself at least in this that both possess an ontological priority over the natures and being of things. Religious language, for Wittgenstein, has a meaningfulness of its own that derives from nothing more basic than language itself as a phenomenon of life. The meaning in question arises solely from the use of language in the particular "language game" being played. It does not reflect a prior intelligible structure to reality itself; the truth factor then is not embedded in any correspondence of what is said to some actual state of affairs (as if knowing were analogous to seeing), but solely in its adequacy to meet and deal with an ever changing state of affairs (so that knowing is more adequately grasped as analogous to acting).

What Heidegger and Wittgenstein seem compelled to say is that any search for the foundations of religious faith in the structure of the real is not only impossible but ill-advised. They repudiate all metaphysical underpinnings of faith; Barth and Bultmann represent a differently nuanced version of this basic stance in repudiating all historical foundations for Christian faith, the former by appeal to an ahistorical *Urgeschichte*, the latter by recourse to existential "decision." In all these cases, we are a long way indeed from the Greek Fathers in the third and fourth centuries, and from Bonaventure and Aquinas in the thirteenth. It is Aquinas who finally offers a conceptual clue as to what was at work all along in the Classical achievement, namely the distinction between faith and reason which allows to the latter in principle the capacity to grasp the causal relation of the world to its creative cause. By contrast, Heidegger and Wittgenstein would have us believe that the search for theological foundations is illegitimate to begin with. It may be so. The Medievals never exaggerated the distinction between faith and reason into a separation, much less an opposition. Christian theologians today find it next to impossible to appropriate that distinction otherwise than in the misleading light of the divorce of faith from reason that is the history of modern religious thought. What may well explain the medieval accomplishment is a common rooting of both faith and metaphysics in experience; something alien to modern thinkers. For the Medievals it was an experience that went unthematized into a theory of experience, partly because there was no felt need to do so, and partly because the resources with which to do it were lacking at this time.

The Consequences for Foundational Theology

Once thought (by which is meant ultimately some form of metaphysics) is precluded as affording a grounding for religious belief, the sole alternative is recourse to some form of experience. But experience by itself is ambiguous and its meaning turns on interpretation. To avoid a subtle reentry of reflective thought in grounding faith, contemporary theology has chosen rather to risk a great deal on personal commitment of the subject. This assumes many forms: some variation on Kant's postulate of practical reason, or on Schleiermacher's *Gefühl* (e.g., Tillich's ultimate concern), or response to a divine word that escapes history, as in Barth's *Urgeschichte*, or Bultmann's *Geschichte* as a demythologized interpretation by the believer of his summons to authentic existence. It can legitimately be asked, too, if Lonergan's "conversion" does not reduce to this also, since intellectual conversion, though critically mediated, is itself sublated by the religious conversion. This latter is explained only as "the love of God flooding the heart" and its occurrence does not observe the axiom *nihil amatum nisi praecognitum*.[3] This is not entirely clear of the aura of voluntarism, in spite of the fact that the language of faculty psychology gives way to that of horizon analysis. Thus, for Lonergan, meaning (including that which might undergird belief) is an act of the subject who intends it (in the drive to self-transcendence) rather than something embedded in the objects experienced. Rahner's *Vorgriff* makes his thought cognate to that of Lonergan in that the intellect's pregrasp of infinite being ultimately derives from an ontologically prior surrender of love.[4]

There is an alternative, it is true, to grounding faith in the commitment of the subject; it lies in the objectivity of a radical historicity. Gadamer's *Truth and Method* has shown the impossibility of pursuing Husserl's earlier defense of presuppositionless thought, and has convincingly argued that human beings come to awareness from within an historical tradition and a culture-bearing language. But Gadamer's vision is not without theological problems of its own. The interpreter's preunderstanding, delivered by the tradition in which one stands, does supply to some degree the bases for the act of faith. Also, the fact that the horizon of the investigator is a moving one that alters as it "fuses" with the alien horizon of the historical text may explain that the hermeneutical circle is not a vicious one. But there is no escaping the finitude and temporality of the understanding that emerges from all this (even Gadamer himself insists upon it), and so the history of which the investigator-believer becomes part remains always radically relative and can have no absolute point of reference. The vector into the open future, while ever transcending present history, can never intend anything beyond the finite and the temporal, even asymptotically.

Pannenberg attempts to supply this lack in Gadamer by grounding the hermeneutical act in the unity of world history (*Universalgeschichte*).

To Gadamer's objection that this marks a return to Hegel, to the absorption of history into philosophy, Pannenberg replies that this can be avoided by the awareness that history can be one and universal only in its end that is not yet realized. This, we do not yet know such history in its universality and will not know it before its consummation. This final consummation of things cannot be derived from the present course of history, nor is it some *telos* toward which history is tending. Paradoxically, without being itself actual, it comes to us out of the future which thus enjoys ontological priority over the present, and determines that present retroactively. We know the unity of world history only provisionally, in anticipating its end; it is the event of the resurrection of Jesus that vouchsafes to us that anticipation, by lifting as it were the veil of history. Pannenberg is quite sanguine on the objectivity, and so public availability of this understanding, for all: "because this future is not alien to reason, but is rather its origin from which it implicitly always derives, faith cannot stand in opposition to reason."[5] For all its impressiveness, this theological adaptation of Gadamer's thought suffers two difficulties: (1) first, it is an idiosyncratic view of history that seemingly distinguishes between history in itself that is somehow finished and so can determine the present, and history as it concretely comes to actualization within the parameters of our time, and (2) second, it amounts in the end to an ontologizing of history.

In summary, the two consequences for foundational theology of the overcoming of metaphysics are the two flights to personal commitment on the one hand, and to a radical historicity on the other. In the former, there seems missing an element of objectivity, one that is cognitive in kind (the subjective experience of human knowing replaces the objective experience of what is known); in the latter, history is transformed covertly into ontology, a move in which it is difficult to see how history is any longer historical.

The Positive Gain: A Symbolism of Person

Whereas Heidegger is clear that his thought says nothing for or against the theological question, which is the question of God, he does observe in *Identity and Difference* that his critique of the onto-theo-logical structure of Western thought is meant to open human beings to at least the possibility of the true God as opposed to the idols of thought.[6] Here his project is not unlike that of Kant in disallowing knowledge in order to make room for "faith." Heidegger spells this out by way of the analogy he suggests for theological thinking: namely, that theology is to God as philosophy is to Being (*Sein*).[7] The turning aside from the existents to make room for Being's coming to pass in the beings it lights up is not too far removed from what the believer intends with the category of divine revelation. Indeed, Heidegger's *Sein* is described in terms traditionally reserved for the divine: it casts itself into *Dasein* in a gift-like (fate-like?) fashion; in itself it lies beyond the grasp of *Dasein* and can be experienced only as it makes known the beings, yet it ever transcends them without assuming any thing-like identity as *the* Transcendent, as itself a being. Wittgenstein's thought (as noted earlier) bears surprising parallels to this line of thinking, in a quite different context.

What cannot be gainsaid is that there have been positive gains for Christian theology in this new direction given to speculative thinking. For one thing, it does check a rationalism which, while not running rampant in theology, must be acknowledged to have been at work covertly at least in some quarters. For modern Catholic theology this was most evident in the method (largely developed in the wake of the Baroque theologian, Christian Wolff) of using propositions of faith as premises for reaching new conclusions through the rigorous application of a formal logic, both deductive and inductive. Looking back from a present vantage point, one can see that the neo-Scholastic revival was not free from a certain conceptualism that gave epistemological underpinnings to this rationalistic emphasis. More importantly and positively, however, the new way of posing the being-question drew explicit attention to the phenomenon of historical consciousness, to the rooting of meaning in experience. It pointed the way to a recovery of literature (especially sacred literature) and its symbolic modes of expression from its absorption by philosophy. On similar grounds, it obviated the temptation to confuse religious beliefs with their theological understandings.

Heidegger, moreover, believed himself to be reversing a direction first taken as early as Socrates and Plato; his retrieval (*Wiederholung*) of the origins of genuine thought is meant to be, not another metaphysics, but the overthrow of all metaphysics. This, if it be taken seriously, means something radical where the search for foundations to religious faith is entered upon. If it need not mean that faith lacks all foundations, or even such as are publicly verifiable, it does mean that it is vain to seek such in any *logos*-structure to the ontic (the "onto-theo-logical") order, in the realm of the beingness of the beings. Rather, if there be any such foundations, they come unbidden to consciousness out of the unknown (*das Nichts*) assuming forms of temporality and historical finitude which are ever being transcended as humanity is released into the future.

This shift in thought from a metaphysics of being or becoming to an ontology of existence, with its transcendental dimension and the marked turn to the subject, is well caught by Thomas Munson; his expression "A symbolism of person" comes close to the mark as a descriptive phrase.[8] This conveys that what is being explored is the domain of consciousness, with obvious centrality given to experience wherein the context of life, history, and culture prevail over the forms and structures of reason. The implication, for theology, is one of the origins of religion lying beyond the ordered intelligibility to which reason has access. Theology, in so reflecting, is able to break out of the Platonic mold in which it came to birth culturally and to which traditionally it has been beholden; that is, it is not restricted to what it can know in and as idea. Some major consequences of this are: an acceptance of love as capable of taking the human spirit beyond what it is capable of when love is viewed as always measured and limited by prior cognitive achievement; an allowance for novelty and unpredictability *beyond* the phenomenon of order; an awareness of the priority of the future over the past whereby the present is appropriated less as determined by the past than as something continuously being recreated in the light of a projected future. The play of consciousness here is markedly creative in kind and more closely approximates aesthetic activity than that proper to science. The resulting expressions, both cognitive and linguistic, are symbolic rather than literal in kind, leaning toward the image rather than the concept. The stance of consciousness is one that puts into relief its receptivity toward reality as it gives itself to human beings, as over and against the concupiscence of reason to control and manipulate. At least the sublating of knowledge by love at work here bespeaks our being drawn into the place of encounter where we are not only less concerned with imposing our ideas on reality, but even less concerned with registering what has already come to appearance than with being gifted with a new and deepened awareness of the richness of reality. Speaking metaphorically, Munson suggests that it is more a matter of hearing than of seeing, something closer to the experience of music than of painting.[9] The sort of knowledge that comes to the fore is one that resists absolutizing; it helps explain the random element in things and events; it coheres with the human sense of our own rootedness in freedom. The source of this pre-logical knowing is itself mystery, but in the positive rather than negative sense of the term; only the believer is able to name it "God." The ambiance that best nurtures the human enriching encounter with it is less thought than silence; its most proper language is not science but prayer. The Christian, caught up in this kind of awareness that expresses itself as a symbolism of person, understands that knowing God is something more than knowing about God.

The Need for a Recovery of Metaphysics

The positive gains of this cannot be gainsaid, above all that heightened sense of the divine transcendence (recommended to us by Kierkegaard's insistence upon the "infinite qualitative difference"). But insofar as what is mysteriously encountered is thematized by way of a phenomenology of

consciousness and expressed in a symbolism of person, there is some problem as to how this "given" can be dealt with in the objective domain of
public discourse — where surely the theological enterprise belongs. This is
not to suggest that whatever foundations for faith can be articulated by way
of a symbolism of person can be dismissed as entirely subjective — not at
any rate in the sense in which Heidegger speaks of "subjectity" since Descartes. Still, the objective, scientific examination to which they are open
is a qualified one that ultimately cannot get beyond the flight to commitment, or contents itself with pointing out (with Wittgenstein) what sort of
language game is being played and what are the corresponding rules of
grammar to be observed. If something can be said for the meaningfulness
of such language, usually on the basis of usage, little can be done to verify truth-claims. This raises the problem of the cognitive character of the
theological act; theology's statements are truly acknowledged to be "expressive," but it is not so clear that they are genuinely "assertive." This calls
into question whether or not a symbolism of person by itself can uncover
adequately the foundations of faith, since the affirmations of the believer
clearly intend to assert something about a real state of affairs over and
against the subject and human language.

One clue to the inadequacy of any symbolism of person lies in the elu-
siveness of the very term "person." To protect it from collapsing into pure
randomness it is commonly conceived in conjunction with "nature" as its
correlate. The distinction — person/nature — would appear to be an irreducible one; it is for example unnegotiable in any talk about the Trinity that
would avoid dissolving the doctrine. The notion "person" even as taken
metaphysically is of itself relational. Psychologically taken, it is rooted in
the exercise of freedom wherein one makes oneself to be the sort of person one is on the basis of one's free decisions, one's chosen relationality
to others. But within the human sphere this self-positing is tethered down
to within the ambit of human nature, to the finite range of relationships
the latter makes possible. Even within divinity, Christian tradition speaks
of three persons of one nature (though that nature is not to be thought
of as a fourth element in the godhead behind the persons, as both Aquinas and Karl Barth are at pains to insist). It is the nature that accounts for
the structure or range of intelligibility within which the person achieves itself in free self-relating. If the latter is the domain of freedom, the former
bespeaks the realm of what is not contingent and could not be otherwise
than it is even (conceptually speaking) in God, where the divine nature
means that the trinitarian relations cannot be finite or temporal, cannot
be meaningless or loveless, etc.

But if natures are laid hold of in concepts (so that it is the *logos*-
structure of the real that is isomorphic to the ideas of the mind), this
excludes the divine nature which cannot be circumscribed by any finite
concept and so remains conceptually unknown and unknowable. More-

over, as long as one remains within a metaphysics that sees being in terms of essence, it is not clear how even the intelligibility within the transcendental concepts (goodness, truth, life, knowledge, love, etc.) can offer a cognitive perspective onto God. Thus, of themselves, neither Platonic *eidos* nor Aristotelian *ousia* bespeaks the divine. But need this mean the jettisoning of all metaphysical knowledge in the interest of the creative free-play that characterizes knowing by way of a symbolism of person? If the remote origins of the forgetfulness of Being to which Heidegger's "ontological difference" calls attention lie with Plato's *idea* (reducing knowledge to remembrance) and with Aristotle's *ousia* (reducing knowledge to abstraction of form) — is not an alternative approach possible?

Being Not as Essence, nor Facticity, but as Act

Another route, at any rate, was first suggested by the Arabic commentators on Aristotle, whose Islamic faith led them into a misinterpretation of Aristotle.[10] Much later, Aquinas's Christian faith was able to supply him with an insight into the character of existence as something other than mere "givenness" explained as the will of Allah. The origin of this was his Christian belief in God as the transcendent one who is not part of the world but the ground of the world which he summons out of nothingness and sustains in being. This initiated the move in thought from concern with a domain of essence (grasped in the concept) to that of existence (achieved in the judgment); the latter understood as manifesting a different level of intelligibility entirely. Theology was then able to thematize its understanding of God in terms of the pure act of be-ing, once the mystery of finite being was grasped, not as mere facticity, but as the exercise by existents of an act whereby they participated in the unparticipating pure act of "to be" (*esse*). Such a move surmounted the immanentism of Aristotelian naturalism on the one hand, and the mere positing of a realm of transcendent forms in Platonic symbolic thinking (which reduces to a form of "faith") on the other. Here faith is finding its foundations — and so capable of verifying the meaning and truth claims of its language by way of public discourse — in an act that is truly metaphysical. But not, it must be noted, with any version of the metaphysics that Heidegger set himself to overcome, i.e., the metaphysics of subjectivity deriving from Descartes in which reason in effect imposes its own structures upon the real order. It is rather a metaphysics that has its origins in concrete historical experience, experience wherein finite being, in its very otherness from the knowing subject, reveals itself as neither groundless, nor as grounding itself, but as real only in its grounding in the pure subsisting act of "to be."

Metaphysics Rooted in Experience: The Intuition of Being

Heidegger's *Sein*, while not the Transcendent, is transhistorical and so transcending, and comes gift-like (fate-like?) to *Dasein* as a primal thinking out
of which originates all subsequent thinking about entities in their ontic (ex-
istentiell) state. Rahner's *Vorgriff* plays a similar role, supplying what the
philosopher knows as the horizon of being, and what the believer names
God, as the absolute mystery toward which the human spirit strives; it is
the background and *telos* against which all categorical knowing and loving
occurs as a limited thematization of what is seized non-objectively in the
pregrasp. Cognate to this, also, is Lonergan's "insight" into the phantasm
which, in the context of the dynamic structure of consciousness in its drive
toward self-transcendence, releases the inexhaustible intelligibility of the
transcendental "notions" (being, truth, goodness, etc.) of which categorical
concepts are particularized expressions.

What this serves to draw attention to is that in some sense conceptual thinking is a derivative from a prior state of preconceptual awareness,
rooted in the immediacy of life experience. But — as an alternative to
Heidegger's "primal thinking," Rahner's *Vorgriff* and Lonergan's "transcendental notions" — what is here suggested is simply the intellect's
intuition of real existence in a non-conceptual dimension to the single
unified act of knowing that always includes the conceptual.[11] What this
implies, however, is the priority of existence over essence, not solely in the
sense of being more ultimate in the ontological order, but also in the sense
of being the first thing understood by the intellect. Aquinas makes very
clear that being is what first of all comes to be in the human intellect.[12]
He literally calls this awareness "intuition," identifying it as the mode of
knowing proper to spirit; that the human spirit is incarnate spirit seemingly
demands the qualification that the connatural mode of knowing in the case
of human beings is "abstractive intuition."[13] This is so because all intellectual contact with the real is mediated by way of sensing the entities of this
spatio-temporal world, but as long as one is speaking of synthetic knowing,
i.e., of an awareness of existence in the conceptual grasp of essences that
are really existent, such contact with the real is operative from the very beginning and constitutes the intellect's intending of the real order — thus
retaining an intuitional character. This occurs only on the pre-reflective
level, and amounts to an implicit intuition of finite being in its dynamic
origin from and *telos* toward the unparticipating act of being.

Exactly how this occurs epistemologically is a question that lies beyond
the confines of this brief reflection. Suffice it to say for present purposes
that prior to the grasp of being in its formal structures in a reflective abstractive act (yielding the concept of essence) there is a grasp of things in
their existential reality by way of a pre-reflective judgmental act that spontaneously consummates the sense intuition of spatio-temporal entities, in

which the act of "to be" of the entities of the world is lived intentionally by the intelligence as its own act of "to know." Only subsequently is this thematized as the idea of being that is achieved reflectively in the science of metaphysics. Rahner, of course, attempts to say something very much like this but in the differing philosophical categories of his "pre-grasp." The differences (and, as I think, advantages) to the alternate explanation offered here is that it does not demand recourse to an *a priori*, though non-objective, grasp of infinite being as the transcendental condition of knowing categorical realities, but can content itself with allowing an intuitional dimension to *a posteriori* knowing in which finite being is grasped in its analogical unity relative to a pure act of be-ing as its source and ground. The only *a priori* element lies in the very structure of intelligence itself as isomorphic with reality so as to allow for that intentional identity which constitutes the mystery of knowing, and not in any "content" to intelligence, even non-objective and pre-conceptual in kind. Thus, ultimately, the dynamism at work here is that of the being which is known rather than of the knowing itself; it is an objective and cognitive dynamism, not a subjective and conative one. What the two explanations have in common is an anthropological, and so experiential, rooting of a genuine metaphysics.

A Reservation: the Objectification of God

Granting an implicit intuition of being, however, requires understanding that all human knowledge is at the same time conceptual. If the former remains the wellspring of what has here been called a symbolism of person, the latter dimension calls for an extension of thought into a metaphysics of being. This suggests that theology, in using the resources of metaphysics, does in fact objectify God in the concepts it uses and in so doing reduces God to within the world of finitude. In dealing with this objection, it should be noted at the very outset that the being which is primordially intuited, and then elaborated into the metaphysician's idea of being in all its analogical range, is *finite* being. The intelligible content then of all our concepts, including the transcendentals, remains finite, and so there is no question of their circumscribing or representing properly the divine. What they do provide is a perspective from which it is possible to discourse meaningfully and truthfully about the divine; their finite intelligibilities offer us a means of naming God in the judgment that he is the source and ground of the perfection or value in question in lieu of any proper concept representing God.

Still and all, this does depend upon an exercise of thought that only occurs by way of a subject-object dichotomy. Yet Heidegger's search was for a primal thinking that was precisely antecedent to all differentiation of subject and object. There is one serious warning in this objection for the metaphysical tradition that views being as act: it cautions against the encroachments of conceptualism from which that tradition needs constantly to purge itself. Nonetheless, it needs to be noted that on the reflective level thought cannot occur otherwise than by a process of objectification. This is not to reduce everything that is known either to the status of a thing, or of an idea subject to the intellect's manipulative control. It is rather rooted in knowing reality as other than oneself as the knower, and constitutes consciousness's act of throwing (from *ob-jicere*) the intelligibility it seeks in relief over against its horizon of understanding. As Pannenberg has noted, all explicit knowledge is objective "since every definite content is grasped in distinction from one's own subjectivity and other contents."[14] All talk about the "non-objectifiability" of God, then, is merely a way of noting that the concept used is not subject to manipulation by reason. It is not meant to imply another sort of autonomous, privileged experience and language that is immediate and so escapes objectification. Where our knowledge of God is concerned, at any rate, it is naive to suppose that one can escape the limitations of objectifying thinking by fleeing to a realm of existential thinking; to speak of the divine in such existential terms is seemingly only a way of conveying that God does not exist in reality as finitized by the mind's objectifications of him.

Foundations for Faith

Where does all this lead us where the question of foundations to faith is concerned? The overcoming of metaphysics has had as its effect the attempt to seek such foundations either in the personal commitment of the subject or in the objectivity of language that has no ontological ground beyond itself (language is here seen as a mode of life, in the sense of an acting that sets its own norms rather than finding them in reality as antecedently known). But the religious knowledge which arises in these ways, and which perhaps can best be characterized as a symbolism of person, for all its richness and even indispensability, needs to be complemented by, and tethered down in, a metaphysics of being. It is misleading to suggest that the categories of being, seized in a genuine metaphysics, block off the personal act of "listening" to the ultimately real that lies beyond concepts, or impede the facing of a future that is fully such in remaining open and unforeseen. Were this the case, it would imply that human beings are open to the mystery of things only in their personhood and not in their nature; it would equate freedom with irrationality suggesting that the latter can be gained only by jettisoning a major function of intellect; it would tend somehow to disjoin spirit from bodiliness and from concrete existence in the spatio-temporal cosmos.

Heidegger's analysis of *Dasein* shows that the very ontological structure of human beings involves a relationship to Being and its summons, in virtue of which the human person is the shepherd of Being. True enough, Being always unveils itself out of nothingness (*das Nichts*), so that it conceals itself even as it unveils itself; thus Being itself never appears as such, is rather "no thing," but only the horizon in which the beings appear. Rahner transforms this, however, to where the *Vorgriff* terminates at the absolute and the holy which is the divine. Still, for both thinkers, human beings are in the stance of openness toward Being out of which there occurs an originating manifestation of the ultimately real, and so of the sacred (literally and religiously for Rahner, metaphorically and in a profane sense for Heidegger).

A certain uneasiness with the degree to which this emphasizes the *a priori* element, exaggerating the pre-conceptual aspect in knowing to the detriment of reason's *a posteriori* contact with real existents — one is like a pilot in an airplane at night or in fog, laying by controls[15] — had led to espousing a somewhat different metaphysics in this essay. It is one in which a conceptual grasp of the essences of existing things includes an implicit non-conceptual intuition of the being of things (their *actus essendi*) as participating in a subsisting act of Be-ing. It is cognate to the thinking that has come into prominence since Heidegger, however, in that it views Being as the ultimately real that makes its claim upon human beings; moreover, it does so in a way that precedes reflective knowledge and also retains an ontological priority over all conceptual thinking, thus bespeaking the original unity of the subject and object of knowledge.

Concretely considered, this call of Being to humanity through the beings is nothing less than the summons of God. It is God inviting the human community to believe through the structures of nature and the events of history. Formally speaking, the distinction between nature and grace, has to be maintained, i.e., between what we are capable of on our own resources (not without God, it should be noted, but apart from God's self-communication), and what we become capable of in virtue of God's self-communication. As freely coming from God, the former benefits are given to us as our own; the latter are bestowed on as a sharing in what in itself remains proper to God, and so come only through the saving events of concrete history as a transformation and transfinalization of our natural existence. The revelatory intelligibility of these events is manifest, of course, only to the "light" of faith, but that is something formal by itself that demands the events themselves as supplying "content." Still, nature and grace are but two inseparable dimensions to one concrete and integral order of human existence. Human nature exists only historically, and God's will to save, which is universal, has sublated all of history into salvation history. The truth is that God would not have created us had he not intended to destine us for real union with himself. Thus, we can echo Tertullian's phrase, *anima humana naturaliter Christiana est;* or with others

among the Fathers understand that "the *Logos* Incarnate walked on earth
in his own footprints." It is God's claim upon humankind, then, that is the
ontological root of the "natural" desire for God. The reality of this appetite
within consciousness and so within experience (though not necessarily reflectively so), founds the basic human stance vis-à-vis God which is one of
openness to revelation — whether such revelation, which is thereby universal, be heeded or not. But that revelation is real only as mediated through
the cosmos on the one hand (in a "natural" revelation wherein God retains a certain anonymity), and through salvation history on the other (in
a covenantal revelation wherein God both manifests and communicates
himself as Trinity). But the former so-called "natural" revelation in actual
fact takes place only within the ambiance of grace — because it does not
occur apart from God's offer of salvation addressed to human freedom, by
way for example of moral choices implicitly regarding ultimates. When it
occurs, however, among those who are explicit believers, then (and in all
probability only then) it affords the foundations for eliciting an act that is
properly called "natural theology." What is affirmed thereby — formally
speaking as an act of reason but from within an ambiance of faith — is,
on different levels, at once something believed and something that functions as the rational ground for believing in the triune God of a historical
revelation. As so functioning, faith is illuminating reason so as to free
the latter for its proper role of discerning the meaning of what faith con-
fesses, including the grounds for believing itself, without collapsing the act
of faith itself into a rational act. The advantage to a theology that proceeds in this way is that it allows faith to reach into the domain proper
to metaphysics. It does so only insofar as the latter illumines the ground
of existence that the believer alone names God. Moreover, it does so for
its own (i.e., theology's) purposes and so transposes metaphysical thinking into the perspective of another wisdom, but it does so by leaving intact
and not violating the methods and procedures proper to the discipline it
enlists in its own cause. Metaphysics is thereby left a rational discipline
which rationally grounds the act of believing in historical revelation.

    Thus, if theology is to seek the foundations of faith, seemingly knowl-
edge by way of a symbolism of person needs the complementarity provided
by a metaphysics of being. This is only to say that, against Ritschl's hope,
"theology cannot dispense from, or be construed in isolation from, some
overall metaphysical scheme."[16] There are other ways of saying this: that
faith needs a juncture within the human person to be the place of its inser-
tion, of its donation, one which it elevates and transforms but which itself
can only be in the domain of reason; or that history, concerned with events
that are by definition contingent, needs structures that are not arbitrary
and which are supplied by nature — if history is not to collapse into mere
randomness. This complementarity of the historical and the natural (by
which is meant not the physical alone but the metaphysical also) means

that there is no need to ontologize history, making the future retroactive, as Pannenberg appears to do; nor to hypostasize tradition as is suggested by Gadamer's project. Another advantage to this mode of thinking is that it clearly leaves history free of all covert implication of necessity. This latter remains a suspicion that persists in all systems of thought that bear a Hegelian stamp. Even Rahner's theology, while explicitly defending the freedom of the incarnation and so the eternal utterance of the Word in God, is not without the suggestion that, by the very nature of things, that Word is eternally spoken in order to be uttered in time to humankind, as a sort of divine self-enactment.

Insisting upon the dialectical relationship between history and nature (thus between a symbolism of person and a metaphysics of being, as modes of knowing) makes it clearer that God's revelation reaches into both domains. Langdon Gilkey has pointed out the curious tendency to think of nature as the sphere of the scientist, and history as the sphere of the theologian.[17] Yet the meaning of God's acting in history finds at least a point of reference in his acting as the author of creation. History is saved thereby from being reduced to the interpretation of human events. The *Logos* becomes flesh (as St. John tells us) and not data for human interiority as it is constitutive of meaning (which is at least an implication of Lonergan's thought). None of this need imply that the occurrence of meaning is anything other than an immanent act of consciousness. But it does mean allowing history to be precisely history, with the consequence that the events of God's acting in the world assume the character of what Walter Kasper calls an underivable historical event of love.[18] By this is meant God's love which is always creative and summons us to a future that remains open, but which is rooted in God's being and wisdom and so avoids arbitrariness and all decline into voluntarism.

What God has definitively done within history in raising Christ from the dead has set the omega point for history. But the way to that eschatological consummation lies across a vast uncharted and still open, worldly future in which God's love responds creatively to human freedom. But the basic horizon for understanding all that God has done and will do in transcendent freedom lies in the intelligibility of being seized by the intellect in its finite modes as providing a true cognitive perspective onto the divine ground in which alone it is actual. Here Christian faith finds the rational foundations for its own believing in the God who is confessed on the basis of his self-manifestation and self-communication — and beyond this the conceptual resources for a deepening understanding of that confession. But this is by no means adequate for the restless search for understanding unleashed by the act of faith. Beyond this lies an appeal to that mode of knowing indigenous to faith that we have characterized in a most general way as a symbolism of person, a knowing which finds expression in the evocative language of symbol and myth. The kind of knowledge that faith puts one in pursuit of looks at once to silence and to speech. Plato's absorption with the forms to be contemplated, or in Aristotle's case to be abstracted from things, began a tradition that did not tend to give place to the former. Munson, at any rate, is quite right in noting that for both Hume and Descartes silence is disqualified as rational experience, whereas for the Medievals it was a necessary component of thought.[19] The silence to which one is brought by faith, however, is not empty but a silence in which there sounds the word. If this be so, it calls into question James Mackey's suggestion that theologians should set aside the category of revelation and content themselves with that of faith.[20] Perhaps a contrary suggestion is not out of order: has not the time come to repudiate Kant's doing away with knowledge in order to make room for faith, or in its contemporary versions to make room for commitment or for language as ultimates? One argument for this is the belief in two modes of God's presence in our midst — as *Pneuma* and as *Logos*.

TWO

Rescuing Theism:
A Bridge between
Aquinas and Heidegger

The Destruction of Theism: Heidegger

It has become commonplace in philosophical theology to acknowledge that what was formerly the Archimedean point in theology — namely, the reality of God as the one truth unassailable in itself and from which everything else stems — has eroded away and no longer holds. Thus, the task of vindicating the starting point in systematic theology has fallen to the theologian. Previously, this was not the case; even the "five ways" which inaugurate the *Summa Theologiae* of Thomas Aquinas were precisely that, "ways" of the mind in its quest for God rather than proofs or demonstrations. If the remote reasons for this stem from the success of the atheist critique launched by Feuerbach, a more proximate and graphic reason is to be found in Martin Heidegger's supposed "overcoming" of metaphysics and the theism it undergirded. In spite of his declared neutrality toward the God-question, there is no denying the import of Heidegger's familiar words:

> It is the time of the gods that have fled *and* of the god that is coming.
> It is the time of *need* because it lies under a double Not; the No-more
> of the gods that have fled and the Not-yet of the god that is coming.[1]

Previous encounters with the divine are over and done with; the gods of Greece, of Judaism, and of Christianity now absent themselves. What theology has concerned itself with in the past, then, is not what is truly ultimate, namely that e-vent (*Ereignis*) behind which it is impossible to go, that pure happening — itself ungrounded and the ground of everything else — explaining the sheer givenness of the world, the fact that there are beings rather than no beings at all (in answer to Leibniz's question). Rather, theology in the past has engaged itself with but one historical epoch of Being that comes to appearance as the Uncaused Cause (Heidegger actually writes *causa sui* and so casts the fate of Western thought about God as an instance of "onto-theo-logic," of concern with one temporal manifestation of Being to the neglect of Being itself. What theology has forgotten is the Being-process that lets the beings be, that casts itself into *Dasein* by way of the beings; what it neglects is what the thinker thinks in primal thinking, what the poet names, and even what the theologian can invest with the aura of divinity, in spite of Heidegger's insistence that *Sein* is finite and ungodly.

The Defense of Thomism: Being as Act

Impressive attempts have been made to challenge this overthrow of metaphysics and the concomitant undermining of classical theism.[2] The more significant among them are perhaps those that seek to do so by maintaining that the philosophical theology of Aquinas escapes this deconstruction of metaphysics. A basic contention in that defense is that in the thought of Aquinas the doctrine of creation *ex nihilo* functions as a Christian version of Heidegger's *Ereignis* as the e-vent of Being, and of the unconcealment of Being (*aletheia*) by way of the coming to be of the beings. This Thomistic understanding of creation is itself rooted in an insight, original with Thomas but inspired by Avicenna's religious (i.e., Islamic) reading of Aristotle, notably the *Posterior Analytics*. Avicenna there misreads Aristotle as making the distinction between essence and existence to be real in things themselves, whereas Aristotle was simply noting a distinction in the way we speak about things, i.e., in the difference between stating that a substance is a particular kind of thing and merely saying that it is something.[3] This raises the question in Avicenna's mind as to how the two are related. His solution is that essences are necessary (triangles must have three sides, fire must be hot, etc.), whereas their existence or non-existence is a mere accident of the essence; as such it is a matter of pure givenness or facticity explained only by the will of Allah.[4] One simply encounters or comes across an instance of some nature or essence as "there." This doctrine of Avicenna triggered in the mind of Aquinas an interpretive re-reading that owed everything to the Christian tradition in which he stood. It amounted to a highly original hermeneutics which was to constitute the very heart of his metaphysical system, namely the discovery that existence is not the mere accident of essence but its act. Existence was seen as the actuality of what enjoys existence, as *actus essendi;* thus the existent was understood to exist as analogously the runner runs or the singer sings, etc. As act, indeed the act of all acts (*actualitas omnium actuum*),[5] existence is a surging up out of the Void into being; it is not a mere state but a *dynamis*, the primal instance of energy (*energeia*). It explains the emergence of something into beingness in an active overcoming of nothingness. Expressed grammatically as an infinitive, *esse* is not mere facticity or "thereness" but a process of continuing achievement. From this it follows that, as act, existence is limited only by the receptive capacities of the nature it brings to actualization. Of itself it bespeaks only illimitation; of itself it is pure actuality that is only trimmed to some modality of being by the suppositum or first substance upon which it bestows existence that is thus finite in kind. Here there comes to the fore the distinction between Being existing in its own right, *Ipsum Esse Subsistens*, and being by participation in such subsisting Being. The former is pure actuality or Being *a se* (not merely *per se* as opposed to *in alio*), and answers to a Thomistic description of what a believer means by "God." It explains the existence of everything other than itself in terms of such finite entities receiving passively a share in itself as unreceived *Esse*. Such entities *have* being without being identified with their own act of being. They are suspended, as it were, over the *Nihil*, held out of nothingness whence they continue to be drawn by the creative act of their pure source that is God. The creature is thus a finite and limited coming to manifestation of God as a mysterious abyss that cannot be fully revealed. In Heidegger's vocabulary, Being ever remains concealed in its very act of unconcealment. But for Thomas, unlike Heidegger, this does not mean a negative action on the part of Being withdrawing itself, but simply that its own superintelligibility can only come to appearance in partial and deficient, i.e., creaturely, ways.

The upshot of all this is the claim that Thomistic existentialism — in which existence (*esse*) belongs to a realm of intelligibility radically other than that of essence, with the consequence that such intelligibility is grasped by the mind, not in a process of conceptualization but in the differing process of judgment, wherein the intellect "lives" in its own intentional mode the extra-mental beingness of the known — enables Aquinas's thought to escape Heidegger's charge of forgetting Being in its absorption with the beings.

Demurral: Being as Aletheia

Recently, this defense of Aquinas against the general accusation by Heidegger of leaving Being in oblivion (*Seinvergessenheit*) has itself been called into question. John Caputo, in a careful and convincing study, has surveyed much of the pertinent literature and concluded that Heidegger's "ontological difference" goes beyond and in fact says more than what is conveyed in Thomas's distinction between subsistent being and participated being, between *Esse* as pure act and *esse* as the finite actualization of some limiting mode of being.[6] The reason lies in seeing that what Aquinas means by being is, in the end, after all, *actuality*, in the sense of *energeia*. The understanding then is a causal one; actuality is what makes something to be, bestowing upon it a perduring state of beingness outside of nothingness and outside of its own causes. Being, in short, is the act that constitutes something as real. This causal view of being characterizes it as markedly objectivistic in kind. In spite of its dynamism as act, being still signifies what is objectively "there" with a persisting mode of presence. This objectivism gives to Thomistic being a certain realistic autonomy; it signifies what exists apart from any phenomenality, in so far as the latter concerns itself with what comes to appearance within human consciousness, and so bespeaks a dependence upon thinking.

All of this is in contrast to Heidegger's vision of Being as *aletheia*, as the process or event of unveiling, of unconcealment. If this is what Being truly means then the thought of Aquinas is really not immune to Heidegger's accusation of a forgetfulness of Being (*Sein*) due to a preoccupation with the beings (*die Seienden*). Indeed, if Heidegger's *aletheia* be rendered as truth, it is something prior to the beingness of the beings, whereas the very opposite is the case with Aquinas for whom truth (*veritas*) is logically subsequent to being as a property of being, as the transcendental relation of being to intelligence. For Thomas, it is because something *is* that it can manifest itself.

The conclusion to which all this leads is that the two views of Being, the Thomistic and the Heideggerian, are radically disparate and at bottom irreconcilable. This, at any rate, is the conclusion to which Caputo is led by his study, and his argument cannot be easily dismissed. On the one hand, is Being as *esse*, meaning actuality (from the Latin *agere*) with implications of causality and productivity. On the other hand, is Being as *aletheia* with its implications of manifestness, of the pure process that "lets be" the beings. Caputo's resolution is an uncompromising one:

> The case of St. Thomas is clearly included within the range of what Heidegger calls the metaphysical oblivion of Being, the failure to think Being itself and on its terms. One cannot subscribe to Heidegger's *Seinsdenken* and hold too that it is practiced by St. Thomas. One cannot accept Heidegger's criteria and think that St. Thomas meets them. One must stand with either one or the other. The competing claims are forever at odds with each other.[7]

Aquinas's view, in short, remains a participationist one, which precisely leaves it open to Heidegger's charge of remaining a "onto-theo-logic." Such a notion is alien to Heidegger's step back from metaphysics, and more primal insight into the mystery of Being as "presencing" (*Anwesen*). His focus on emergence into presence, with its connotation of approach and withdrawal, is something that comes to pass, by way of the beings, within *Dasein* — as the "there" where Being as the lighting-up process occurs. As such, it is totally other than the beings in a more radical way than anything envisaged by Aquinas. Heidegger's awareness goes back to the pre-Socratics (Caputo here has express recourse to the Heideggerian reconstruction of the thought of Anaximander, Heraclitus, and especially Parmenides), to the beginnings of thought prior to its dominance by Plato's discovery (invention?) of *eidos* and Aristotle's recourse to *ousia*.

Being as E-vent: Some Reservations

To maintain that Heidegger's "ontological difference" with its corresponding view of Being as (in Caputo's words) epiphanic and alethiological is something quite different from Aquinas's grasp of Being as *esse* and so as causal and reducible to objective presence (what Heidegger would call *Vorhandenheit*) is one thing. To maintain, however, that Heidegger's thought represents an unqualified and positive advance beyond Thomas in the history of Western thought is something else again. Such a thesis would have to be established on its own grounds. This is not to contest Caputo's contention that Heidegger is saying something different from Thomas, but rather the assumption that what he says is a profounder penetration into the nature of reality. Some reservations that such is the case merit mentioning at this point.

Ontological Priority of Possibility

Caputo observes in the last line of this study that " . . . possibility is always higher than actuality, *sicut Martinus dixit*." This states what is in fact a decisive problem with Heidegger's view of Being as event, reversing as it does the traditional order between potentiality and act, and giving ontological priority to the former. Here Heidegger's thought runs directly counter to the metaphysics of Aquinas and the theism it undergirds. Heidegger's starting point is his analysis of *Dasein* which thus stands revealed as the "there" (*Da*) where Being occurs. Such "coming to pass" (*Geschehnis*) of Being appears at first to be grounded in nothing more ultimate than *Dasein's* own structure and facticity, its "thrownness" (*Geworfenheit*) in the world. It is not grounded in a prior realm of subsisting forms (as for Plato), nor in substance as ultimate existent (as for Aristotle), nor in God (as for Aquinas), nor in the self on which is built a world of objects (as for the Cartesian *cogito*). Yet with the completion of *Being and Time*, Heidegger came to see that this leads directly to a subjectivism of its own: *Dasein* simply projects its own beingness upon things. At this point, the logical thrust of his thought dictates its own "reversal": as the process of unconcealment, Being is grounded in only the concealment out of which it issues. *Dasein's* anxiety in the face of death gives way to shyness before the historical appearances of Being. Yet in either case the process is one of the actualization of possibilities — whether the unlimited possibilities of *Dasein* itself (echoing the infinite human essence of Feuerbach), or the negative infinity of the Non-Being (*das Nichts*) which unveils itself in the Being process.

This latter view, which appears to hypostasize history and time as "fate-laden," still does not overcome the implication that Being is dependent upon human thought, upon the kind of nonconceptual thought available to *Dasein* that Heidegger calls "primal thinking." (This should not be interpreted as something narrowly cognitive in kind since by it Heidegger means to convey *Dasein's* global *way of being* in the world.) At any rate, it indicates that there is no escaping the finite point of view, and explains Heidegger's own neutrality vis-à-vis the God question. *Dasein* either "lets be" the event which is being and its unconcealment (not in total passivity but by way of its actual engagement in the world) as in the early Heidegger, or holds itself in openness to the mystery in its unnamability which comes to it, as in the later Heidegger who speaks thus of *Gelassenheit* ("releasement"). In either case Being (*Sein*) is a function of truth (*aletheia*), and what transpires is a process wherein the potentialities of *Dasein* are rendered actual, potentialities which are inexhaustible and possess ontological ultimacy. What is, in the final sense then, is simply the sheer phenomenon of giving without a giver, of fateful sending (*Geschickliche*) without a sender in which it is grounded. Understandably then, Heidegger has need for Non-Being as the complement to Being (not as its contrary), for untruth or concealment as the complement to truth or unconcealment (in which untruth is not falsity). Being as event is, in the end, the mysterious play of presence and absence.

All of this, of course, can be viewed as a defensible alternative to the traditional sense of being. All that is suggested here is that the consequences of such thinking are indeed radical. Of most significance is the acknowledgement that what is ultimately real cannot be anything fully actual and thereby capable of grounding the beings and *Dasein* itself. What is ultimate is either *Dasein* itself in its own ungrounded structure, or a pre-grasp (*Vorgriff*) by *Dasein* of what comes to it unbidden as a realm of what is purely possible out of nothing. For Heidegger, reality is left forever in the realm of the historical and the temporal: there is nothing in which it can be grounded. Being as event-like cannot then take upon itself the character of personhood, in however an analogical or symbolic sense; it appears more as a mere principle of explanation, and a partial and mysterious one at that. Whether such a theory of reality can stand by itself unbolstered by any metaphysical system — since it claims to overthrow them all — is precisely the question which arises at this point. At least two correlates to Heidegger's point of view suggest its underlying vulnerability.

Theism as Onto-theo-logic

First, is the dismissal by Heidegger of theistic thought as an instance of what he calls "onto-theo-logic." This appears, however, as overly facile and unconvincing — at least if the charge be made against the genuine thought of Aquinas. To claim that God is conceived in the latter system as merely a being among the beings, albeit the first and all-perfect being, is simply an unwarranted assumption. True enough, Aquinas does not infrequently refer to God as *Primum Ens*. But he is not in such instances formally addressing the question raised here, and clearly intends the designation to be taken analogously: God is "a being" but not one "among the beings." The reason for this is that the *ens* in question is quidditatively the very act of being as self-subsistent, something that is not true of anything of the finite order. There is not — as Question 13, Article 5, of the *prima pars* insists — any question of a common predicate which would allow God and creatures to be compared to one another in virtue of their differing proportions to this one analogate. It was Scotus, arguing for the univocity of being, who ascribed it to God in an infinite manner and to the creature in finite manner — a position expressly rejected by Thomas. Deity for the latter is not the first being (*ens*) but the pure act of being (*esse*); this disqualifies his thought as an "onto-theo-logic." It also is the origin of reference to Aquinas's thought as "agnostic" — which really means not simply that, negatively, we fail to know God in any proper fashion, but that positively we *know* that we do not know God exactly because of his intrinsic unknowability by any finite intelligence.

Esse Subsistens as Causal and as Term of Objectivist Discourse

Paralleling this is Heidegger's contention that classical theism conceives being as causal (even *causa sui* in Heidegger's own phrase) and thereby amounts to an objectivist mode of discourse that fails to make the transition to being as *Ereignis*. A shortcoming in such an interpretation of Aquinas is the failure to note the latter's contention that efficient causality, taken in its pure formality as such and not in any of its finite modalities, is not some kind of *virtus* that goes out from the agent cause and enters into the effect, with the consequence that the agent and patient are reduced thereby to being two poles of an homogeneous order. The efficient cause as such does not assume some quality previously lacking to it, acquiring thereby some new actuation, and in the process undergoing mutation. Rather, its causation is nothing more than its own actuality in so far as some other entity is brought into its orbit, and acquires thereby a relation of dependence toward the cause. The alternation is entirely on the side of the effect. There is no real intrinsic alteration of the cause, except such as is due to the finitude of the causal entity apart from the pure formality of

causation. The log, for example, bursts into flame because it is brought into
contact with the fire, not because of some change in the being of the fire.
This should not, it might be noted, be misunderstood as a mere extrinsic
denomination of the agent as a cause. To say that the relationship of the
cause to the effect is not real but rational, is only to say, while not bespeaking any real dependence on the effect, that the relationship thereto is an
intrinsically intelligible one. This genuine understanding of what causality
means for Aquinas is, of course, of utmost significance in the issue at hand,
namely the causation of finite being itself by what subsists as the pure act
of being. It is in fact causation in an uniquely analogical use of the term;
it is efficiency of the transcendental order. Understanding this is not an
instance of "onto-theo-logic."

Aesthetic Language

Another reservation arises from the later Heidegger's flight, to aesthetic
language. Thinking (*Denken*) becomes thanking (*Danken*); the human person is "the shepherd of Being'; *physis* is (as it was for the Ionians, and
connoted by the Greek verb *phylein* meaning to engender) a "shining
forth"; *logos* is a "gathering together": primal thinking is the act of the poet
(especially Hölderlin for Heidegger) "naming the holy"; Being assumes
a stance of "shyness" as it encounters Being's concealment of itself; the
turn or reversal (*Kehre*) in Heidegger's thought is "repentance" or "conversion." Most graphic of all perhaps is Heidegger's imagery in depicting
his assembling of the square in which the jug is not experienced simply as
empty, or as full of air as the scientist would say, but as a receptacle for
wine drawn from the grapes that spring up from the earth *below*, nurtured
with the light and warmth of the sun *above*, to quench the thirst of mor-
tals *on one side*, and to be used in worship of the gods *on the other*.[8] The
mode of speech suggests not so much a going beyond metaphysics as a
by-passing of it. Linguistically, the thought marks "a rapprochement... to
poetry... hauntingly suggestive rather than conceptually explicit."[9] The
language is less that of the philosopher than that of the prophet, prompting Karl Löwith to remark that "Those who are nearest to understanding
it (*Sein*) are believers who think they find in... talk of "revelation" and
"unveiling" an access to the Christian revelation of a God who too is not
a being....[10]

Perhaps this assessment of Heidegger is overly negative. After all, a
parallel can be found in the theology of Aquinas, above all that developed in the *Summa Theologiae*. There, the thought marks a general move
from notional theology to mystical theology (which latter has little to do
with wonders such as visions and ecstasies). The notion of *sacra doctrina*,
worked out in the very first question, is that of a "holy teaching" which
terminates first in the assent of faith, second in the discursus proper to

theology as science, and third in the intuition of its subject which is the beatific vision. The move is that of a dynamic knowing process proceeding from belief, to an *intellectus fidei*, and thence to consummating intuition. The *secunda pars*, tracing the human journey back to God, unfolds itself from a consideration of acquired virtue, to infused virtue, and ultimately to that contemplative knowing made possible by the gifts of the Holy Spirit. The ambience of grace, never absent from the movement that the *Summa* traces out, is a living advance from created grace, characterizing human-kind's deliberative response to God's unexacted love, to uncreated grace, i.e., to docility toward the prompting of the indwelling Spirit. The impulse toward the latter state would seem to be not all that removed from Hei-degger's *Gelassenheit* as releasement to the Mystery in its unnamability. The very language of the *Summa* reflects this readiness to allow a concep-tual system to give way to a doxological articulation of prayer. Indeed, the mystical experience undergone in December, 1273, a few months before his death, which resulted in Aquinas's self-declared inability to continue his writings, may well reflect just such an urgency.

The difference, however, is that the Thomistic reach toward the dox-ological does not discredit the underpinnings provided by a conceptual system (one that is ontological in kind and remains as a sort of scaffolding) even as it declares the inadequacies of the latter and seeks to surmount them. The doxological language, in short, retains an analogical character, albeit one peculiarly its own. Heidegger's language, by contrast, assumes a more markedly mythological character. The mythology, moreover, seems not a matter of expression only, but of content of the thought. It signals a move wherein *logos* is repudiated in favor of *mythos*. Other seminal thinkers have taken a similar course; for example, Aristotle in his *De an-ima* suddenly abandons his thorough-going naturalism when attempting to explain how the intellect, whose knowing is receptive in kind, is activated, and appeals to *Nous* as *choristos* — which Avicenna interprets as a single separated intellect for all humankind. Such language is more suggestive of the Platonic Dialogues than of Aristotle's scientific treatises and recalls Aristotle's early tutelage under Plato. At any rate, Heidegger's recourse to aesthetic language can appear somewhat suspect as a flight from the more rigorous demands of philosophy. It can suggest that the "turn" (*Kehre*) in his thought is in fact a "conversion" to religious, or more likely, to mythic thinking.

An Alternative: Presencing at the Core of a Metaphysical Universe

In his *Truth and Method*, Hans-Georg Gadamer argues persuasively for fusing different horizons of understanding especially those of the past and the present in the ongoing search for meaning and truth. In this way, rather than collapsing one into the other, a bridge can be thrown between them, which thus becomes a third new horizon of historically developing understanding. In effect, this study seeks to explore such a path to a deepening of understanding — one which maintains that Heidegger's existential ontology cannot, on the one hand, sustain itself without a foundational metaphysics while, on the other hand, it can carry thought beyond the limits of such a metaphysical system. This is even to take a page from Heidegger himself who maintains that thinking (*Denken*) when "on the way" bears within itself just such enriching reversals of direction which are not so much repudiations of previous directions as sublimations of them. What this suggests is that Heidegger's *Anwesen* opens up an enriching, non-metaphysical dimension to a basically metaphysical universe. Heidegger himself looks upon metaphysics as a system of concepts which represents a chosen viewpoint and thus is paradoxically a form of subjectivism. But the metaphysics developed by Aquinas is not like this at all, but is a judgmental grasp of real being as act (*esse*) which points the way (without ever explicitly arriving there itself) to genuine subjectivity, as distinct from subjectivism. Being as causal and productive, in Thomas's authentic doctrine of creation, can be made to do what it does not expressly do in the latter's own thought, namely, lead the course of thinking by a vector of its own to an understanding of being as a process of self-presencing.

The Indispensability of Metaphysics

A first contention in an attempt to substantiate this view is the insistence upon metaphysics as underlying the theological (theistic) endeavor. A major reason for this has just been touched upon, namely the untoward consequences of giving ontic ultimacy to possibility rather than to actuality. Succinctly put, Heidegger's uncovering of *Dasein's* structure as self-transcendence itself demands an actual transcendent as the term of that transcendence. Nor is it adequate to do as Kant did earlier and merely posit the transcendent as a regulative idea. If the transcending process is real, then so too is the Absolute which is the consummation of that dynamism. This, of course, is what Karl Rahner, Emerich Coreth and others have done in transforming Heidegger's *Vorgriff* (which is an anticipation of *Dasein's* possibilities) into a pregrasp of the unlimited horizon, which is theologically described as absolute mystery. Heidegger's own starting point — the understanding of *Dasein* as being-in-the-world, and not as an epistemological ego capable of inspecting the world from a stance outside of it — leads to this. That is, it explains how *Dasein's* being already involved with beings results in forgetfulness of Being itself (*Seinvergessenheit*). This very forgetfulness leads in turn to a spontaneous movement to unify this plurality given to consciousness. Initially, this is sought conceptually — giving rise to the various sciences including metaphysics which is thereby essentialistic in looking upon the beings as objects, and thus the metaphysics Heidegger seeks to surmount. But beyond this is discernible a further drive of consciousness to unify, by reducing the many to the one, *existentially*. This enables one to say that the human person is simultaneously a being in the world and yet transcends the world in a *dynamis* toward a really existing Absolute. One explanation of this would allow for a non-conceptual dimension to the cognitive act; a subsequent appropriation of this in reflection would thereby constitute a genuine existential metaphysics.

Other attempts to circumvent metaphysics in the theological enterprise (other than that of Heidegger, that is) reveal upon examination a similar shortsightedness. Contemporary theology is not without its own version of an attitude articulated by the fourteenth-century Cambridge Dominican, Robert Holcot, to the effect that ordinary criteria of rationality do not apply in the sphere of faith. Perhaps the most subtle form this takes is that advocated by linguistic analysis which seeks a safe harbor from persisting metaphysical questions by appeal to theories such as that of Wittgenstein's autonomous language games. Narrative theology, too, for all its pastoral enrichment, can easily be a similar escape in its eschewing of truth claims. Certain theological usages of critical social theory confirm this tendency by granting that, while particular occurrences of human meaning may not actually participate in the unified and total meaning of reality, they at least anticipate such a meaning-totality.[11]

Subjectivity as the Presencing of Being

To plead thus for a basically metaphysical universe, to which humankind belongs by its very nature — a nature which simultaneously explains its being-in-the-world and its transcending of it — by no means implies a failure to acknowledge an advance in understanding achieved by Heidegger. What has emerged from such thinking as something genuinely new is the awareness of a subjectivity at the core of objective reality. This subjectivity, which is eventually revealed as an intersubjectivity, is less a pregrasp of Being by humans than a presencing of itself by Being, called by Heidegger *Anwesen*. Aquinas's thought does not go this far on the historical pathway to truth, even though there are not lacking virtualities in this thinking that point in this direction. Notably, there is the contention in IV *Contra gentiles*, chapter 11, that increasing levels of life bespeak increasing levels of interiority.

A first argument for this phenomenon of subjectivity underlying the causal order affirmed by metaphysics is a strictly theological one. It rests upon the Christian faith confession of there being three distinct hypostases or persons within the Godhead, theologically elaborated into the doctrine of intra-divine processions grounding really distinct relations (Father to Son, Spirator[s] to Spirit) which are not causal in kind. The correlates here are taken to be, in the trinitarian theology of Aquinas at any rate, self-subsisting relations which assume the prerogatives of personhood.[12] The Father, e.g., is formally his very relating to his Son/Word, which relating is a true action. This is to say, it is something achieved in what is analogously divine self-awareness and freedom, and not a mere emanation in the sense of a natural resultancy. Such action is obviously conceived as *actus perfecti*, not *actus imperfecti;* that is to say, it constitutes the immanent perfection of the subject and not the achieving of some perfection transitively in the effect. Moreover, it is not to be understood as a transitus from potency to act, but (if one may so speak) as a procession from act to act. What this can only mean is that the terminal act is not some new perfection lacking to the originating act, yet is posited by the originating act as subsisting in a really distinct fashion.

The implications of all this are highly speculative and can only be suggested in the most tentative of ways. But seemingly it implies that the Father freely relates to his Son and to their Spirit in such wise as to posit his own personal identity thereby. Such relating, called by Aquinas "notional act" as opposed to "essential act', is of course not anything temporal as if achieved once and for all, but is an eternal achievement. The actuality in which it is rooted is a pure actuality, which allows one to conceive of God as "new every moment" (Schillebeeckx). Personal existence thus assumes the characteristics of a self-constitution — not however in the domain of nature, but strictly in the sphere of personhood. This latter is understood as a distinct, i.e., subsisting relationality, non-causal in kind, within a common nature. Subjectivity is thus at once inter-subjectivity.

Human Existence as Self-Possession

Whatever can be made of the trinitarian theology at issue here — which cannot be further pursued at this point — the application to the question raised here is clear if still controversial. It means that at the very heart of Being (meaning the being of things and objects) there lies a process and a becoming which is not mere happening, not the mere phenomenon of unconcealment, but a self-constituting process which is the achievement of personhood. Thus is the reality of person an invitation to mystery, toward which the favored response is silence rather than speech, an openness toward self-communication and self-donation which is not a lack of awareness but the fullness of it. As noted in chapter 1, Thomas Munson has suggested here, and aptly so, that the richer analogy is that provided by music in contrast to painting; the succession of sound appears more evocative of personhood than does the simultaneity of what is represented in the picture — the person is more akin to the phenomenon of hearing than of looking. Significantly, the metaphor ordinarily used to express intellection is "seeing" rather than "hearing."

If this be plausible, it suggests one way of bridging the hiatus between realist thought (begun with Plato, revised by Aristotle, and Christianized by Aquinas) and thought that bears an idealist cast (inaugurated by Descartes, furthered by Kant, most clearly and vividly represented by Hegel, and reflected differently by Whitehead). It discerns a free and creative subjectivity at the core of reality which implies an inexhaustible process of ever newness — something not alien to Heidegger's notion of Being's presencing of itself, in a way that transcends the strictly causal. This non-causal dimension to the dynamism of reality is analogous to the non-conceptual dimension to intellection. Where this differs from Heidegger's vision is in its insistence upon the ultimacy of the giver behind not only the gift but the giving. In the end, the primordial giver is revealed as God, who is ultimate in an unqualified sense and the origin of the becoming which characterizes the universe of finite persons. So conceived, there is no negativity in God, as the nothingness (*das Nichts*) out of which the unconcealment (*aletheia*) comes to pass. The stress lies rather on the positivity of God which in its infinity is never exhausted. Heidegger's Being (*Sein*) as event (*Ereignis*) and as unveiling (*aletheia*) is itself grounded in Being as personhood — both that which participates in pure actuality and that which is itself pure actuality. The category of "person" — as a rendering of the Greek *hypostasis* and the Latin *subsistentia* — takes its origin in the early christological councils, where it is deployed in a Christian sense to signify what is unique about Jesus, namely his status as divine. It designates precisely not nature (as Chalcedon makes clear) but a subjectivity which is the self in its totality. The stress falls on the side of existence, with at first the connotation of concrete and objective presentation of some nature; much later the connotation of autonomy will come to the fore suggesting the achieving of self-possession. From the beginning, however, personal being is seen as the summit of beingness, so that infra-personal entities are only deficient approximations to this fullness of reality.

None of this is meant to imply that the finite person is an absolutely autonomous subject — as is the case for Sartre. Even the divine persons are radicated in the divine nature with which they are identified and on that level indistinguishable. The autonomy of the finite person is rather, paradoxically, constituted by its very dependence upon the Absolute. The existence of God, then, is not an obstacle to human freedom, rendering the latter an impossibility, but is the very condition of its possibility. This is strikingly articulated in Rahner's claim that the closer any creature is to God, the greater is its autonomy — an insight that Robert Hurd has paraphrased to read: "In my beholdenness I am radically free, and in my freedom I am radically beholden."[13]

The root of this presencing is freedom, not merely freedom of choice but freedom as a mode of being — i.e., that being which the subject "performs," not in choosing one object in preference to another but in deciding about the self, in disposing of itself regarding what is ultimate. This surmounting of liberty as *liberum arbitrium* avoids the either/or dilemma of intellectualism versus voluntarism that so engaged medieval thinkers. Freedom so conceived is a property of spirit, both pure spirit and incarnate spirit. Its existence in the latter case is due to the omnipotence of God which is great enough to enable him to bring into existence creatures who determine their own reality — not by way of escaping dependence upon God but precisely in virtue of that dependence. Being-for-itself (Sartre's *être pour soi*) is then Being as given over to itself by the Transcendent. Just such an awareness as this led Kierkegaard to observe that the mystery of mysteries is not that there are beings who are nothing in face of the creator, but beings that are truly *something* in relation to the creator.[14] In this same vein, Aquinas notes in the *De potentia* (Q.5, a.4) that God wills creatures ultimately not for his sake but for their sake. To suppose conflict then between divine causality (which is such only in an analogous and transcendental sense) and human freedom is at bottom a spurious problem. Created effects, in Thomas's words once again, are not partially from God and partially from secondary causes, but at once totally from both as two different levels of causation.[15] In light of this, there appears an alternative to the Scylla and Charybdis of total dependency on the one hand (in which God alone is cause) and on the other unbridled autonomy (in which the creature determines itself over and against God).

If this view of things be a plausible one, then the universe is basically as it is objectified in metaphysics, i.e., as a network of causes in which (in Caputo's phrase) reality "rises up into objective presence, as mute being in itself, prior to phenomenality."[16] But at the heart of that epiphanic world there lies the phenomenon of personal beings presencing themselves from within a causal scheme of things but in a formally non-causal way. The finite person then relates to other things and persons first of all in a causal way, acting through the faculties of its nature, and unavoidably being acted upon in the process. The fire, for example, is cooled by the environment it heats. But, at the interior of this exchange, the person unveils and communicates its very self, and not only some attribute of its nature, to another person or persons — a process wherein it establishes its own personal identity, becoming who (not what) it chooses to be.

Conclusion

The thesis advanced in this chapter has been argued for on two counts: the doctrine of the Trinity and the freedom indigenous to the human person. Perhaps no better conclusion is possible than that of drawing attention to one concrete illustration of both explanations. The trinitarian doctrine undergirds the confession that, more than any other, is distinctively Christian, namely that Jesus of Nazareth is the Word of the Father uttered into the world, by way of the embodiment of the Son of God for the reconciliation of humankind with God. This is only to say that he is the mode of God's presence to human existence. His humanity as such is created by God as is ours, granted that it is existent in the hypostasis of the Son as God's own humanity. All the events and activities of his human life are thus causally grounded in the first cause. But at the heart of this causal relationship is the personal presencing of the Logos by way of those human activities. The Logos acts humanly through the humanity as the ultimate subject of such activities. This free relating of the incarnate Son is, first of all, his relating to his Father — which is the correlate of the Father's prior relating to him. Jesus, for example, is enabled to call God "Abba" because of the Father's prior initiatives toward him as his unique Son. And because the Son is incarnate in our nature, this presencing becomes a reconciling and saving one, as God's chosen presence to humankind as a whole.

Because, however, the divine Person who renders himself present in our midst is the Son, his comportment is filial in kind. Its distinguishing mark is obedience to the Father. This chosen relating to God, founded on God's prior relating to Christ and to the world, assumes at first a heteronomous character. This is not, however, heteronomy in an unqualified sense; it is not something imposed from without in a coercive and alienating way. Rather it is a contemplative response to the beauty of the forms and structures of reality which gives itself to humankind. This is akin to what Heidegger calls *Gelassenheit*, as a releasement from manipulative thinking in order to make room for primal thinking in which Being gives itself to the human person, making the latter the "shepherd of Being." Augustine had expressed a similar understanding by distinguishing between *uti* as the desire to possess and control the real, and *frui* as the enjoyment of the beauty of the real as it enraptures human consciousness. Interestingly enough, the Greek word for beauty *kalon* is from the verb *kalein* which means to call or to summon. Here, too, is the basis for Hans Urs von Balthasar's conception of theology as a form of aesthetics, responding to the splendor (*Herrlichkeit*) of God's acting in nature and history.[17]

But it is the freedom of Christ's conforming himself to the divine will that most of all qualifies any suggestion of heteronomy here. With this, the mystery of personhood as a self-positing in radical freedom surmounts all semblance of causal determinism. At the same time, Jesus' correspondence to the Father's will mean that his personhood is not a self-positing in the sense of an unqualified autonomy either. A third possibility, neither heteronomy nor autonomy, is conceivable — one called by Paul Tillich "theonomy." By this is meant that Christ's free relating to the world, which is in fact the free communication of his very self to humankind, is not in contestation with the determining will of the Father but something made possible by it.

The implications of all this is that the phenomenon of presencing, of what Heidegger intends by *Anwesen*, is not on the one hand a pure self-assertion in which person is reduced to sheer will, nor is it on the other hand a direct function of totally objective factors in which person is eliminated in the face of an impersonal mechanism. The liberty congenial to the notion of person is not mere arbitrariness, because the person is not something subsisting of itself but is always the personification of a nature which is rational or, more accurately, intellectual in kind. (Even in God the persons subsist in virtue of their identity with the divine nature.) For this reason, created freedom is always a situated freedom submissive to the law of its own being. The freedom in question is something more radical than free choice, and the constitution of personhood in its exercise involves first of all receptivity toward reality — which receptivity is the origin and ground of the creative positing of the self. Openness to the world — and ultimately to the creator of the world — in a causally determining way, is thereby not the negation of finite freedom (Sartre) but the very ground of its possibility. The causal relationship, in short, makes room within itself for that achieving of personhood that is creative presencing. The latter is at once the constitution of the self in a relating to others and the free offer of the self in communication. As regards God's relationship to the world, the causal dimension rests upon the attribute of power, whereas the rendering of himself present to the world rather appeals to the attribute of love. The giving of gifts here shows itself as both expressing and mediating the giving of the self. Intriguingly, a common English word for gift is "present," suggesting that the person who gives something as a token of love is rendering himself or herself present to the other, the beloved. It is only a step beyond this to say that God presences himself in our midst in the twofold modality of the Son and the Holy Spirit — in what tradition has called the temporal missions of divine persons.

PART II

EXPLORATION INTO GOD

THREE

The Doctrine of God after Vatican II

The doctrine of God is in crisis. That now widely acknowledged claim is softened somewhat in discerning that this is less a crisis of faith itself than of the cultural mediation of faith. For some this is theological disaster, marking the loss of the traditional concept of God to the forces of atheism and secularism. To others it is a liberating factor in that it signals the displacement of an alienating idea of God that clears the way for a long overdue theological reconstruction. One undeniable benefit has been a return of the doctrine of God to its rightful place of centrality in theological discourse — a privileged position it occupied in the thirteenth-century thought of Aquinas and Bonaventure, in the sixteenth-century thought of Luther and Calvin, one retained by Schleiermacher in the nineteenth century and regained by Karl Barth in the twentieth century. Once again, God has become the focus of theological questioning. The difference lies in the way the question has shifted: now the burning issue is the absence or silence of God.

The New Way of Raising the Question of God

Heretofore the starting point for religion and theology was *Credo in unum Deum*, the creedal distillate of the Christian gospel. This was the Archimedean point of belief upon which depended anthropology, christology, ecclesiology, sacramentology, etc. Such is no longer the case due to the success of the atheist critique beginning with Feuerbach. The atheist challenge remains, either in the negative form of a massive indifference (here the very question of God's existence pales into insignificance, Sartre tells us, because it makes no difference whatsoever to the quality of life: believers kill one another just as do unbelievers, and even do so in the name of God), or in the positive form of a religious humanism, even in some

51

quarters of a theology without God. More radical still is what has been called "semantic atheism," i.e., the contention that the very word "God" is without meaning, any meaning, that is, that can be validated in the public forum. Nietzsche's cry "God is dead" gives way now to the assertion that the very term "God" has no referent other than that arbitrarily given to it by believers; no objectively real referent, that is.

What has occurred, in a spontaneous dialectic of history, whether for good or for bad, is the overthrow of classical theism, i.e., of that understanding in which God is the supreme being explaining the existence of everything else — a preunderstanding that precedes revelation and makes the latter credible. This Hellenic and medieval notion of God was called into question when the cultural world that gave it birth ceased to exist. What was rejected was an objectifying of God, cognitively, by way of metaphysics. This could no longer be the *point de départ* for the doctrine of God; it was no longer possible to begin with an idea that was then subsequently given content from the sources of revelation. This rendered suspect any demonstrating or verification of God's existence — though it must be said that the atheist premise was equally incapable of validation. This precipitated a radical shift in the question about God. No longer was the concern "Does God exist?", "Is God real?", but rather now "Is God present and operative in human life?", and "Does that presence make a difference?" This was in fact a return to the biblical question concerning God's role in human history both individual and social, a question especially urgent in the post-exilic period. God now meant, not "He who is" (*Ipsum Esse Subsistens*, nor even "He who is with us" (*mit-Sein*), but "He who will be who he will be toward humankind," "He who will be the God of our future." The new note being sounded is that of futurity; somewhat muted is the note of divine transcendence, at least in the sense that transcendence was being deferred.

The shift then was to the God of revelation, more concretely to the God encountered in Jesus of Nazareth. At the very origins of faith then was the attempt to set aside all endeavor to speak about God, in favor of being content to speak about Jesus and his summons to love. The difficulty with this was the impossibility of grounding belief in that God who was the Father of Jesus, in anything other than Jesus' own authority in proclaiming the nearness of that God and his kingdom. But the preaching of Jesus rests on nothing more than his human authority, unless he be recognized as of divine status. This latter confession, however, as to who Jesus is, implies some sort of preunderstanding of God that the believer brings to the encounter with Jesus. Thus does it seem that we can begin neither with a natural theology nor with a purely biblical faith.

Two resolutions to this aporia have emerged from within recent Catholic thought. One arises from rereading Aquinas through Kantian spectacles. The result is a transcendental Thomism — its practitioners are Karl

Rahner, Bernard Lonergan, Emerich Coreth, Joseph Lotz, and a host of disciples[1] — which reconceives human subjectivity as universally oriented toward the absolute, named at the start simply as holy mystery. In this anonymous affirmation of God, there is no prior seeking out of some objective concept of God (something humanly devised, then) with which to approach God. Rather, the human subject as such is always already standing before God. Human subjectivity is understood as intrinsically gifted with transcendence as God's unexacted gift (or at least offer) of himself. This transcendence is necessarily mediated by categorical reality, above all by concrete historical events, but within such mediation there is conscious experience of this orientation to God which in fact defines the human person as human. Nonetheless, it remains nonobjective, nonconceptual and unthematic. Categorical knowledge, by contrast, is precisely a thematizing, a focusing down as it were of this transcendental orientation, of this pregrasp (*Vorgriff*) of what is in fact the divine. The latter then constitutes a universal human experience which is subsequently given expression in the multiple and differing doctrines and beliefs which divide humankind. One common and universal experience is thus given varied expressions and articulations.

The alternative view finds this to give human subjectivity more weight than it can bear. Accordingly, it gives greater stress to the *object* of faith which is in fact the very person and deeds of Christ who is *within history* "the manifestation of the goodness and the loving kindness of God" (Titus 3:4). This position is represented by Hans Urs von Balthasar for one, who regards theology as more a matter of aesthetics than of science, as an intuition of the splendor and glory of God revealed in Christ.[2] Johann Baptist Metz advocates it, though differently in using memory as a theological category that stresses the primacy of genuine history over being, over what he would take to be only the illusion of history in transcendental Thomism; and in preference to the emphasis upon presentiality characteristic of existential thought, one markedly operative in Bultmannian theology.[3] Metz's own thought then is a reaction against the bias for what is individual and private in the interest of what pertains to the social and communitarian. Edward Schillebeeckx also leans in this direction, first by promoting the hermeneutic role in theology (as a reinterpretation of living tradition), but more recently by employing the social critical theory of the Frankfurt School wherein greater place is given to the discontinuities and the negativities in history. This allows him to give greater emphasis to actual occurrences in their uniqueness, which do not participate in a meaning totality otherwise than by anticipating it.[4] All these theologians are reserved toward the transcendental project of allowing for a common inner experience shaping subsequent expression. They prefer to begin with the given symbols of the community (scriptural, liturgical, sacramental) which then shape subsequent experiences.

The Church then preexists its members whom it forms by incorporating them into itself.

But this option, too, is not without difficulties of its own. Preeminent among them is the lack of some locus in the *humanum* which undergoes history, wherein humankind is open to and enabled to receive God's historical revelation. The only viable resolution of this dilemma seemingly is an even more radical fall back upon experience — not merely the experience of transcendence or of the Jesus-event — in all its contingency and secularity. This would seem to signal a retreat from metaphysics, and a natural theology built upon it, certainly from an essentialistic metaphysics. This then is an implicit acquiescence in Heidegger's charge that traditional theism is in fact an onto-theo-logic. Still, the doctrine of God has to be thought through, and it can be legitimately wondered if therefore all metaphysics can be abandoned. The language at work, for example, intends not only genuine meaning but also a real referent. The sole alternative to classical metaphysics need not be either linguistic analysis or biblical fundamentalism, nor may it mean collapse into uncritical belief or into action. The existence of a transsubjective referent to language here obviously cannot be verified empirically. So, at least in this minimal sense, the activity engaged in here is metaphysical, i.e., it is more than a purely empirical act. The rooting of such activity in experience means that the metaphysical dimension is an *a posteriori*, not an *a priori* one, But if, by and large, old certainties have been eroded away, the beginnings of a recovery can only lie someplace in the preconditions to thought, in the prerational, even visceral reaction to existence.

This lived experience may make it possible to mitigate any unvalidated presuppositions, especially since the experience at issue is an ordinary and universally accessible one, that is, not a specifically religious experience or encounter. Langdon Gilkey characterizes these as secular experiences in their very security, but occurring at a certain depth level that cannot fail to confront us with what is ultimate in life.[5] They are not direct experiences of God but experiences of ourselves, of our very humanity, which are experiences of God only covertly and negatively. They are experiences of such realities as the gift-like character of existence, of the unconditioned value of life even in the face of death suggesting that the latter is not mere disappearance into the void, of the transtemporal dimension to certain experiences of joy, of the awareness of being forgiven our betrayals, of the ambiguity of our freedom as rooting our capacity for love. These force upon us the question about God; the answers lie elsewhere, above all in the confessions of the positive religions.

What must be noted, however, is that all such experiences are interpreted ones. There are no such things as brute experiences which are value-free. From the very beginning then we are drawn up into the circle of faith. Philosophical anthropologies no longer acquiesce in the Enlightenment's "prejudice against prejudice." Unavoidably we bring a nexus of preunderstandings, of theories and conceptual systems, to our experiences. Thus a hermeneutical circle arises inevitably between present experiences on the one hand, and interpretive norms brought to them from the past on the other. Michael Polanyi has argued persuasively for the recognition that all human knowledge bears within itself a fiduciary element: "We must now recognize belief once more as the source of all knowledge, explaining the impulses which shape our vision of the nature of things. . . . "[6] Conceiving the problem somewhat differently, Hans-Georg Gadamer describes what happens as a "fusing of the horizons," i.e., as a bridging of the horizons of present experience with that forming the background of texts received from the tradition, to avoid either reading into the text something that is not there, or allowing the text to go uninterpreted.[7] The dialectical nature of this affirmation of God has been lucidly posed by Wolfhart Pannenberg: "Only if man, even outside the Christian message, is related in his being as man to the reality of God on which the message of Jesus is based, can fellowship with Jesus mean salvation to him."[8] This preliminary idea — which makes possible the question but not the answer about God — is radically transformed once it makes possible the encounter with Christ, not so much in the sense that the original "empty" concept is filled in and given content as that the very character of the question undergoes an enriching alteration. The faith encounter by way of the human life of Jesus, in other words, shapes the very question posed about God.

One confirmation of this way of asking about God is provided by Karl Marx who predicted that Marxist theorizers needn't worry about the reality of God, for once the revolution succeeded the very term itself would vanish as otiose. Events have proven him mistaken. The word refuses to go away and is raised today perhaps with greater urgency than ever. Even Marxist theorists, while explicitly denying any real referent to the term, resort to it as a means of forestalling any absolutizing of the socialist state. For them, the term has the function of invoking a transcendence that alone is unconditional and so can function in a regulatory way in thought; it appeals to a transcendence but denies a transcendent. For Ernst Bloch, "God" is a cipher or a code word for the limitless possibilities inherent in the human project.[9] Another atheist-Marxist from Czechoslovakia has entitled one of his books *God Is Not Quite Dead*, in which the theme of "God" is used to signify a liberating potentiality in challenging all arbitrarily closed historical and social horizons. This very word is necessary to any notion of humankind in its totality — so much so that the death of God means eventually the death of humankind as a bearer of meaning. Indeed, Rahner has written that without this word human beings remain but clever animals.[10]

But the enigmatic figure of Karl Marx has cast yet another shadow on contemporary theology. This derives from his well-known eleventh thesis on Feuerbach contending that the role of philosophy is not to construct one more theory about the world but to seek to change the world. This "second coming" of Marx "not in the dusty frock coat of the economist...[but]... as a philosopher and moral prophet with glad tidings about human freedom"[11] has obvious attractions for the contemporary theologian. If God breaks into our history, becoming human in Jesus, proclaiming the nearness of the kingdom, and summoning to salvation, this certainly intends an abrupt change in the direction our history has taken. The consequence is a new and pronounced emphasis upon orthopraxis as the indispensable means of establishing orthodoxy, that is, of rendering credible the mysteries confessed by the Christian. Praxis here means a dialectic between theory on the one hand and practice or behavior on the other. Any dichotomy between speculative and practical reason is thus seen to be a disastrous one. Edward Schillebeeckx indicated how such orthopraxis is at once operative in two domains: the mystical and the ethical.[12] The former is the approach to God in prayer, something that can assume a specifically Christian form but allows for non-Christian forms as well. The ethical assumes from the very beginning a universal character, marking a concern Christians share with all humankind. Praxis as such is not a norm for truth; Oscar Wilde once observed that willingness to die for a cause is no proof for the truthfulness or goodness of that cause. At the same time, praxis can have a cognitive dimension and function. *Metanoia* and the practice of God's kingdom are then the hermeneutical keys to interpreting Christian beliefs in the texts of the Bible, the Fathers and the teaching Church. It is in his own praxis of the kingdom — in his dealings with sinners, his miracles, his parables, his table fellowship with people, his attitude toward the Law — that Jesus comes to recognize God as *Abba*, caring for and offering a future to his children.[13]

From considerations such as these arises the centrality of hope in Christian existence. Recent reflection, even if allowing a temporal priority to faith, grants ontological primacy rather to hope. Christian life pivots on God's promises to us; if he is with us now, this "already" is the prolepsis of the "yet to come." If the kingdom is already inaugurated in Jesus' human life, its consummation lies ahead of us with the God who is to come as the future of humanity. Without succumbing to the myth of progress, we, like the Israelites of old, set out for the promised land — a land, however, that we ourselves must reclaim and cultivate, trusting in God's promises. Faith in a life to come, in the eschaton, can only ring true if our hope motivates us to seek a better future here and now.

One reservation should perhaps be registered concerning this granting of primacy to the future, one intended as a qualification not a rejection of such revitalization of the virtue of hope. Hope wills the goodness of God *to ourselves*, but Christian charity, as our reflection of God's *agape* toward us, wills God's goodness *to himself*; we rejoice as it were that God is God. Love of God then which transcends considerations of past, present, and future should not be displaced from its absolute primacy by revivified hope. Simply put, our present love of God is the ground of our hoping for the God of our future.

The Identity of the God Confessed

When questions are altered in being newly proposed the result is a difference in the nature of the answers thereby available. It is hardly surprising then that the identity of the God who is newly emerging is that of historicity. The retreat from metaphysics in favor of a recourse to history refocuses what is meant by divine transcendence: God is now recognized less as the author of nature than as the Lord of history; he is not so much "above" us as "ahead" of us, less a God of the present than of the future. What this derives from is a pronounced anthropological dimension to theology, which is only to say that human experience has become the starting point for theological reflection. The question about God is after all a human question; the subjective component cannot be ignored. Humankind is conceived as historical in its very being; history is essential to human life and not merely accidental, as if we possessed a nature intelligible in itself apart from its involvement in temporality. The starting point then for religious reflection is not human nature in the abstract but concrete humanity as damaged, as bearing the wounds of sin and suffering. Humanity, both individually and socially, constitutes itself to be what it is by the way it actualizes itself in playing out its freedom. Time is not something suffered as an imposed imperfection from which release is sought (as in Neo-Platonic thought) but a valued prerogative enabling humans to mature in a process of self-enactment. This new awareness of how we are immersed in history stresses human freedom and creative praxis in such wise that history is not the mere reiteration of changeless forms but is the genuine succession of new and transient forms, meaning the possibility of growth, of genuine novelty in truth and value.[14]

The upshot of this is that such stress on the historicity of humankind means that God cannot be a God *pro nobis* (and this is after all the God we seek) unless he is involved with us historically. The richest implication of this — and it is not one that should go unquestioned — is not that the deity enters our history from without, but that God himself is historical. Process theology intends this literally: God himself "becomes," actualizing in his consequent nature values made available for his prehension by creatures, values previously lacking to him. This is panentheism pure and simple, by which is meant not that God is simply identified with the world (pantheism) but that he is dependent upon the world for his own beingness. Thus Whitehead can write "it is as true to say the world creates God as that God creates the world."[15] Aquinas strove to preclude such understanding (for him a misunderstanding) by insisting that God's relation to the world — while acknowledged to be actual (God truly creates, knows, loves, redeems, etc.) and intelligible (thus *relationes rationis*) — were not "real" in the Aristotelian sense of bespeaking causal dependence.[16]

A modification of this position appears in the influential work of the Reformed theologian, Jürgen Moltmann.[17] Here too, the thought is pan-entheistic but in the qualified sense that God, who does not need the world by nature, chooses in his transcendent freedom to depend upon and be intrinsically affected by it. The identification of God's being as love demands this, in that love as such opens the lover to being affected by the beloved, to suffering if the latter is afflicted. Theology in the Catholic tradition, granting that this is true in all instances of finite love, is less sure that such is the case with infinite love, which gives altruistically without being enhanced by anything it receives in return (more about this is in a moment).

An alternative position, more accommodated to the Catholic understanding of tradition, prefers to say that while God does change he does so not in his own being but in the world. The genuine import of this is missed if it be interpreted to mean merely that finite realities assumed by God change (the obvious example being the humanity of Jesus). What is explicitly being maintained is that God himself changes, but not in himself but rather in his "other."[18] Undergirding this manner of thinking is a philosophy of identity inspired by Hegel more than anyone else. Here the conception of God as pure being is considered empty and without content until God enacts himself by positing his "other" — non-being in short — so as to constitute himself in the very differentiating of himself from Nothing. What emerges from this is the notion of God as pure becoming rather than being; the very essence of deity is thus "event."

The newness of this concept of God is underscored in what follows logically from it, namely that God is now a God of the future rather than of the past, i.e., not a God who appeared to us once and for all in the past but a God who continues to come to us out of the future — out of the future into the present by way of the past. God is with us not as a presence of eternity within time but as a presence of the future in the present, as the impact of the future upon the present. Thus, divine revelation, while remaining definitive, is at the same time provisional: definitive because it is God's revelation that will not be repudiated and cannot be relativized; provisional in that it is not yet ended and is ever being enriched by new events. Some (Pannenberg, for example) even go so far as to say that the resurrection of Christ remains unfinished and open to future consummation.[19] At any rate, this is certainly taken to be the case with the human enterprise.

This historicizing of God means replacing the attribute of eternity with that of a primal temporality wherein God does not stand outside of time in a motionless *nunc stans*, but embraces all time — past, present, and future — within himself. Yet he does so successively. God accordingly has his own past and his own future granted that due to the infinity of his temporality, his past had no beginning and his future will have no end. So viewed, God's being is in becoming and futurity is the mode of divine being. Such a God is not the ground of the phenomenal world but the source of events which he (as "the power over all that is," in Pannenberg's phrase) determines from within history, but within history understood from its end.

Catholic thought has clearly moved in this direction but once again reservedly so. First, it has insisted that the consummation of history will not be a this-worldly one but something eschatological. Its achievement lies not within the capacities of humanity as such but in the transforming power of God alone when temporal history will have come to an end. Thus the myth of continual progress is resisted — if for no other reason than the paradox of the cross. Second, however, a reservation is expressed on the openness of the future in that a greater claim is made of certainty regarding the direction of human history due to God's promises to which he will be faithful. The kingdom will come, and the Church will remain indefectible and infallible in its mediation of that kingdom. Still and all, that absolute future will not simply come, when history has ceased, as a reward earned in temporal life. It has in fact begun even now and entrance into eternal life will be the maturing of human freedom under grace into the fullness of the kingdom. This will be no mere termination but a true consummation. Genuine history thus constructs in freedom its own definitive stage — granting God's entry into humanity's making of itself. By contrast, for process theology the human project can, in principle at any rate, still end in disaster; and in any case there will be no end to history. For Moltmann, God will be faithful to his promises but in a recreative act which will mean a repudiation of what human beings will have made of history — thus the marked emphasis on the cross as destructive and on the discontinuities rather than the continuities of time. The Catholic nuance mitigates this apocalyptic tone in favor of an eschatological one, i.e., the vector runs from the present into the future rather than from the future into the present. But that future with God lies neither at the end of history as its this-worldly termination, nor simply after history, but is already taking shape in the depths of present history. The heavenly eschaton to come is already transpiring within history.

At the very base of this revised concept of God lies a revitalized doctrine of the Trinity. God is intrinsically processive; divine life is the perichoresis of the Father uttering his Word, and appropriating himself as so uttered in a movement of love that is personified as Spirit. Divine being then is intrinsically self-expressive and self-unitive. But this divine circularity spirals outward, as it were, into the void, culminating in the Incarnate Word as the self-expression of God into the void, and in the Paraclete as God's loving reintegration of that humanity with himself. In this there is found the grounding of human history. It is not that human history is the foundation of the trinitarian processions but the other way around.

At least a caution has to be introduced at this point: incarnation and Pentecost cannot be necessary acts of God, rather they remain instances of his absolute freedom. But contemporary theology tends to view this phenomenon not as a matter of free choice (*liberum arbitrium*) but of freedom in a transcendent sense — something which lies deeper than the opposition between coercion or natural resultancy on the one hand and mere option on the other. One way of expressing this is to say that the Logos eternally engendered within God comes forth as the Logos to become incarnate; one might say as the *Logos Incarnandus*. However, this implies an inevitability, approaching a moral necessity (i.e., that God would not be fully a God of love if he failed to communicate into the world his very self). As such, it can be contested as an excessive assertion. Some qualification seems called for then on the meaning of the verb "is" in the oft-cited proposition: "the economic Trinity is the immanent Trinity, and the immanent Trinity is the economic Trinity."[20] Some such hesitancy seems called for in order to safeguard the gratuity and altruistic character of divine love for the world, of its unique character as New Testament *agape* rather than as Greek *eros*.

Allied to this recouped trinitarianism is the contention that God's relations to the human life of Jesus as it unfolds historically are *intrinsic* ones. That human life, in its finiteness and contingency, in its free decisions of love, is then constitutive of the very being of the Godhead. Otherwise, those events cannot be thought of as the definitive self-revelation and self-communication of God. Wolfhart Pannenberg, for example, contends that God cannot be understood on the basis of the ahistorical immanent Trinity alone. What is required is a "placing in question (*Infragestellung*) of God's deity within history. God is Father precisely in raising Jesus from the dead; he is Son in his self-differentiation from the Father within our history; and he is Spirit in his glorification of the Father and Son. Pannenberg himself goes so far as to write: "God's Godhead itself is at stake in history."[21] The question of God's identity is here inseparable from the question of the meaning and the truth of Jesus' own history.

What is questionable here is why this is not a collapsing of the immanent Trinity into the economic Trinity — a problem even more pronounced in Moltmann[22] — and even an obliteration of the distinction between creator and creature. If intrinsic relation means God is formally constituted as God by his relations to Jesus so that these relationships could not be and apart from them God is not God — then a demurral seems called for. It is rather true to say that these relations are extrinsic to God, in the sense that they are contingent to his being, and willed by him in all freedom. But, once it is granted that God has chosen to create a world, then by a conditional necessity he cannot fail to relate to it and essentially so, since its very beingness both as nature and as history exists only by way of a grounding in God's being. Nonetheless, God does characterize himself as the kind of God he is by the nature of these freely chosen relationships — bearing in mind that in the domain of history God could choose to relate to the world in the mode of silence and of refusal to communicate his very self.

There is another implication of this historicizing of God's being (which is in fact an ontologizing of time, especially when it is understood as universal history as in Pannenberg's *Universalgeschichte*) in the tendency to shy away from the concept "redemption" in preference for the more history-laden concept "liberation." Jesus is less one who overthrows a disorder at the heart of human existence, conveyed in the precise Christian symbol of "sin," than one who inaugurates the freeing of humankind at large from our all-pervasive history of suffering. This is less a repudiation of a more traditional theology of redemption than an insistence that an inner component of that redemption is earthly salvation within this world. Once again an appeal is made to a certain primacy of orthopraxis — without it orthodoxy is something incredible and ideological — and it highlights that Christianity cannot be left as a matter of the heart only, of personal conversion, without a reform of those social structures which oppress humanity. The reason is that God has entered our history precisely as one who (in Schillebeeckx's phrase) "has made the cause of humankind to be his (God's) cause." Salvation, which in the end will be God's eschatological transforming act (and here Christianity distances itself from Marxism pure and simple), is communicated to us within the ambiguities of history and not outside human suffering. The identity of God here emerging out of our inevitable encounter with suffering is that of a living God who enlists himself in opposition to all forms of evil and oppression; and who remains God among us.

If there is a danger here it is that of supposing that the divinity of Jesus consists in his saving significance for us — but that is to misplace the emphasis and is contrary to the intention of most so-called liberation theology. The core theological point being made here is that the divinity of Christ is not something behind or alongside his humanity (this is a common misreading of Chalcedon's two nature theory) but is very God in our midst as human, i.e., in the mode and dimension of our humanity. Thus Schillebeeckx cites approvingly Piet Schoonenberg: "We cannot point to anything divine in Jesus that is not realized in and from what is human," and goes on to observe that failure to acknowledge this tempts us "to slip past this human aspect as quickly as we can in order to admire a 'divine Icon' from which every trait of Jesus as the critical prophet has been smoothed away."[23] One implication of this is that the traditional formula "hypostatic *union*" can perhaps be more richly expressed as "hypostatic *unity*." Every theological position runs the risk of over-stating its basic insights. Two which are at least possible here are: (1) overstressing the humanity of Jesus to the detriment of his divinity, and (2) giving an exaggerated prominence to present experiences (meaning interpreted experiences) as compared to what is available as normative in the New Testament and in tradition. One illustration of both is the coalescence of love of God and love of neighbor. This should not be seen as an uncritical identity of the two. Genuine love of neighbor is in fact an implicit love of God (all three synoptic accounts make this abundantly clear)[24] but this does not compromise the primacy of one's relationship to God.

God's immanence at the heart of our tragic human history has broached another profound and controversial question: Does God's love for us in its kenotic character, and its historical consummation on the cross, mean that suffering is intrinsic to the Godhead? Does God in short absorb our suffering into his own beingness in order to transform and ultimately to overcome it? Once again, this is positively affirmed by process theology of its cosmic God. It is also central in Moltmann's crucified God — not that God suffers by a necessity of his nature, and thus unavoidably so, but rather that his love demands his taking upon himself, freely, the suffering of the beloved, that is, of humanity. Such a perspective enables Moltmann to understand the cross as a transaction, not between God and man but between God and God, i.e., between the Father and the Son.[25]

On the Catholic side, this understanding has been advanced by Hans Urs von Balthasar on the grounds that this is what the biblical symbols lead us to, in a non-metaphysical theology where conceptual clarity in its objectifying of God must give way to the "reduction to mystery."[26] By this, something much more than a *communicatio idiomatum* is intended; it does not intend to say only that the humanity of Jesus suffers, which just happens to be the humanity of the Son of God. Certainly, *finite love* which achieves an identification, on the affective if not the ontic level, of the lover with the beloved (love as such is a unitive force — even in God) but is powerless to overcome the sources responsible for the anguish of the beloved, is a love that renders the lover vulnerable. But divine love is omnipotent (its power is one in the mode of love) and so would seem to require not that God suffer with his creatures but that he enlist himself in the cause of alleviating and ultimately vanquishing that suffering. The way in which God chooses to do this, i.e., the mode of its efficacy, does, it must be granted, remain mysterious. Obviously, he does not will to banish suffering from without, choosing rather to enter into our suffering and overthrow it (we have at this point only his promises and the anticipation of their fulfillment in the resurrection of Jesus) from within. But this is a matter not of God's own being as a history of suffering, his trinitarian history, but of his entering into and taking upon himself *our* history which *we* have marred with sin. The rhetorical and indeed religious power of a God who takes suffering into himself cannot be denied. Theologically, however, a stronger case can be made for precluding all possibility of suffering from the deity on the grounds of divine transcendence.[27] Does it make sense to say that God can will to be something lesser than God? Is it not problematic to conceive of God the Father punishing his Son by delivering him over to the "powers of darkness" rather than allowing such evil, which sin alone brings into the world, to work its destruction upon his assumed humanity out of a loving will to enter into solidarity with suffering humankind? On this view, Christ's cry of dereliction from the cross is not really due to an abandonment of him by the Father. It expresses rather how profound is the alienation from God that results from sin, and its issue which is the experience of death. The more integral truth of the cross is not that God turns aside from his Son on the cross but that he remains with him precisely in the midst of what is, humanly speaking, abysmal failure — as he remains with us in our hour of darkness, inexorably setting his face against everything that kills the human heart. Operative in this concept of a suffering God is the danger of a mystique of death — i.e., the notion that suffering as such is redemptive and salvific, rather than its being such only in virtue of the love wherein it is undergone.

Another clue to the identity of the God we seek presents itself in the revealed name of God, in that name whereby he is invoked by Jesus in the New Testament. There are no parallels in all of religious literature to Jesus' repeated use (170 times in the New Testament) of the name "Father," frequently in its Aramaic form of *Abba*. This is something far different from Plato's idea of Goodness, Aristotle's Unmoved Mover, Plotinus's One, and even from YHWH of the Jewish Scriptures though in this last instance God is being named on the basis of an historical acting in human history. As Claude Geffré has pointed out, this privileged name is not a designation for God but an invocation of him; it corresponds to a proper name.[28] It does not intend then the predication to divinity of male or paternal characteristics as over against feminine or maternal ones, which latter can serve equally as symbols of divine attributes. This revealed name of God is derived from a symbol expressing God's relationship to a unique Son and conveying the notion of obedience — a filial obedience, however, grounded in an unqualified and confident love. What is simply absent from the term is any connotation of dominance or heteronomy. In the Jewish culture of the first century such obedience was highly extolled and was understood in terms of the relationship of the human son to his human father.

God's fatherhood, as experienced for himself and revealed to us by Jesus, bespeaks a predilection for the "poor," meaning sinners, outcasts, the needy, the hungry, the sick, the deprived, the oppressed — a predilection however that is not exclusive of others. God's seeking out of these merely testifies to the universality of his salvific love: if God seeks out even these disadvantaged ones then clearly the kingdom of God is near. But it remains love that is the formal motivation for the liberation which God proffers in Christ. This is a liberation for all peoples from "all the slaveries to which sin subjugates them: ignorance, misery, hunger, and oppression.... In a word, liberation from the injustice and hate which originate in human egoism."[29]

There remains the question of God's responsiveness to the activity of his creatures. Does the God who has made himself the God of and for humanity change in response to the initiatives of men and women? Or does he remain the changeless, apathetic divinity of traditional theism? Seemingly, God's transcendence precludes his determination by any creature in the sense of his acquiring perfections previously lacking to him (or any diminution of perfections already possessed). Still and all, there does remain a possible way of incorporating alteration within God in his dialogic relationship with his rational and free creatures. First of all, this might be understood as mutation, not in the order of God's very being but in the intentional order constituting his knowing and loving. The reason for such a suggestion is simply that God would be a different sort of God than he in fact is if he had chosen not to create a world or to create a world different from the one that does in fact exist. In either case he both knows and loves something that would not otherwise terminate his knowing and loving. This is compounded by the fact that in its human dimension that world changes freely, introducing genuine novelty into the world thereby so that there is obviously something new for God to know and to react to lovingly. This cannot be so without a mutation in the *objects* of divine knowing and loving. It would appear then that one must allow that God does change, not absolutely but relatively; the alteration does occur not in the divine nature but in God's free relating toward his self-determining creatures. The mutation is not one from potency to act (God is already fully actual and so without capacity for further perfecting) but, if we may so speak, from act to act. With Schillebeeckx we can say, "God is new each moment,"[30] but not by way of an enhancement of his being. W. Norris Clarke has expressed this with welcome clarity:

> God's inner being is genuinely affected, not in an ascending or descending way, but in a truly real personal, conscious relational way by His relations with us ... [but without] ... moving to a qualitatively higher level of inner perfection than God had before.[31]

Elsewhere, I have suggested that this insight can be richly exploited in trinitarian terms.[32] Remaining immutable on the level of his one divine nature, God is pure relationality on the distinct level of his threefold personhood. A central defining element in the concept of "person" is relation (the human person is thus a unique and freely posited, self-determining relationality within the commonality of humanity). But why could not this regard not only that subsistent relationality which is the eternal Trinity, but incorporate the relationality of the three divine subjects to human persons as well? If so, then we are enabled to say that

God absorbs into his own experience whatever novelty his free creatures introduce into the world, as these latter mark out their own destiny
within the parameters set by God — that is to say, not apart from certain definitive acts of God such as above all his raising of Jesus from
the dead.

Conclusion

All of this leads to the conclusion that God's radical difference from everything that makes up the empirical world inhabited by men and women
renders our awareness of him provisional and tentative in kind. In his
incomprehensibility, God is known only as (in Rahner's phrase) "holy mystery." Our knowledge is positive, and counts as gain, in that we know
that God is unknown and unknowable. So much so, that there simply are
no proofs for his existence, though it remains possible to verify both the
meaning and the truth of the assertion that "God is." This is verification
in the sense that such an affirmation cannot be shown to be contrary to
either experience or logic, that it is in other words entirely reasonable to
confess God's reality. This is especially true if it be acknowledged that
both experience and reason testify to a dimension in our knowledge of
the world that belongs to mystery and so eludes conceptual grasp and
objectification. The verification in question then is one rooted in concrete human experience, common experience that is always interpreted
experience, and so includes from the beginning a fiduciary element. The
quinque viae then of Aquinas remain valid, not in the sense of proving
God's existence from a state of pure agnosticism, but by way of clarifying the question, pointing in the direction of its resolution, and giving
logical formulations to the answers surmised. Ultimately, however, God
is affirmed on the basis of his own self-revelatory act which is in fact
a self-communication — one that occurs historically and culminates in
the Christ-event. Thus, the question of God is raised today in a non-
metaphysical way, in the sense that the one domain of truth with which
metaphysics does not concern itself is that of historical contingency. It
remains metaphysical in the looser sense that the concern and the language employed is trans-empirical. In the final analysis it is only by way
of the life, the preaching, the death and resurrection of Jesus of Nazareth that God fully discloses himself to humankind, as a hidden God who
wills to be nonetheless a *Deus pro nobis*, proffering salvation to all of
humanity.

On this account, he is the God of humankind's future, vouchsafing to
us his promises, thereby rendering the Christian life one of hope, guaranteeing that he will prevail in the end over against the "deadliness of death"
(Moltmann). Such a God is not dead but present and operative in the midst

of our history, both individual and social. If that presence appears more often than not in the mode of absence, much of the reason is that we look for
him in the wrong places — for example in the structures of power rather
than those of kenotic love — forgetting that divine omnipotence is power
in the mode of love.

FOUR

Does God Know the Future?
Aquinas and Some Moderns

Que será, será — the sentiments of the formerly popular song (and seemingly of much of the popular mind) suggest a future that is already determined and that will be, no matter what. Contemporary serious thought, by contrast, refuses this way of thinking and sees it as illusory. Logicians such as Peter Geach refer to the notion of a determinate future as "a dangerous piece of mythology" and dismiss any seeing of the future by either God or human beings as "a self-contradictory notion."[1] The reasoning is that by definition the future as "that which is not but will be" does not exist: it lacks all actuality and so is in principle unknowable. God can no more know the future than he can know the past as never having been. This is understood as no diminishing of God's omniscience nor of his control over the future: "God is almighty ... God knows in advance all the possibilities and can do whatever he wills; so there is no doubt that he will win and he can even tell us how."[2] Still, he does not know "the way things will definitely turn out, but only because ... there is no such thing to be known."[3]

The principle that undergirds this sort of thinking, viz., that only what exists actually can be the subject of infallibly certain knowledge, of the sort of cognition amounting to intuition or vision, is of ancient and noble parentage. Aristotle approximated it in the fourth century B.C.E. in his rejection of the Platonic forms; Aquinas re-presented it in effect in the thirteenth century in his notion of *esse* as act; and Whitehead offers what amounts to a twentieth-century version in insisting that what is knowable with certainty is a past *occasion*, i.e., a once actual occasion that has "perished," apart from which there is only ideal knowledge as the entertainment of pure possibility. Allowing this principle, however, the question vis-à-vis God's knowing of the future is whether events future to us might not be present and actual to God. The answer to this turns on what it means to speak of God as eternal. Modern thinkers tend to construe eternity as reducible to "timelessness"; God is eternal somewhat as we conceive num-

67

bcrs to be   number in the sense of the abstract mathematical measure as opposed to quantified realities, Aristotle's *numerus numerans* in contrast to what he means by *numerus numeratus*. For Geach, eternity appears to mean not only that God has no future of his own but that he stands outside of time; his relationship to time is accidental in the sense that he has no determining role in the future of human beings other than knowing what transpires after events and acting in a manipulative way upon a humanly determined course of events. In a somewhat similar vein, John Macquarrie views God as a chess player who continually counters the human moves so that the outcome of the game remains in God's hands.[4]

Something very similar occurs with process philosophers and theologians. Whitehead locates eternity on the side of God's primordial nature, which is nonactual. Here God envisages mentally the realm of pure ideal possibility, but not in a way that bespeaks any actual or specific relationality to time. In his consequent nature, God does stand in relationship to a world of time, but this is only by way of (a) prehending values already achieved in the world and (b) supplying initial aims for actual occasions that indicate God's intentions for the future but do not allow for any sure knowledge of what that future is to be.[5] God is obligated to "trust the world for the achievement of that aim."[6] This emphasis upon creative becoming as ultimate category of the real enables Hartshorne to elaborate upon Whitehead by defining the future as "indeterminateness"; only the past is determinate and the present is the process of determination. For Hartshorne, God is not strictly a cause of what will be; he is limited to being a source of "adequate antecedent conditions" for what will eventuate. Thus, he stimulates and guides history, and provides limits to what can occur. But the future remains indeterminate, lacking any specific order to actuality, and so is unknowable in principle even to God. When the future does come about, it will be novel and additive both to finite reality and to God.[7]

Other contemporary thinkers, however, prefer to take the very opposite approach and to think of God's eternity not as "timelessness" but as a sort of "primal temporality" — with nonetheless much the same conclusion regarding divine foreknowledge of the future. Inspiration for this derives to a considerable degree from Heidegger in a well-known footnote to *Sein und Zeit*, where he repudiates "the traditional concept of eternity in the sense of the stationary now (*nunc stans*)" and suggests that it should be construed philosophically "only as a more primordial temporality which is infinite."[8] Proper understanding of this introduces into God the distinction between existence and actuality, corresponding to the human existenzial-existenziell structure, viz., the contrast between existentiality or essential structure on the one hand, and ontic existence or concrete actualization of that structure on the other. Thus God's actual involvement in concrete temporal events by way of his contingent acts traces back to his essential structure as primal temporality, wherein divine being as being-in-the-world (*in-der-Welt-sein*) is in real and necessary internal relatedness with everything else. God's being, then, in its existentiality is (like *Dasein's*) "care" (*Sorge*). Such primal temporality is infinite and absolute in the sense that it is not itself dependent on anything else, whereas everything else is dependent upon and relative to it. Thus it constitutes God's distinctive being, his radical difference from all other historic beings.

Such temporality is existential time, constituted by experiencing itself, in which the future is reduced to a mode of present consciousness engaged in creatively achieving the future in a transcending of present limitations. This allows, even demands, that God act in finite history; moreover, it gives to God a certain transcendence over history; but the future remains indeterminate and open to the cooperative decisions of God and human beings. Indeed, God's own future remains open and yet to be achieved, and stands to the future merely by way of opening up possibilities to it. In the last analysis, it means in Schubert Ogden's phrase that "the final context of our finite decisions is God's own eternal life."[9] Here there can be no future infallibly foreseen by God.

The theologians of hope, notably Moltmann and Pannenberg, continue this emphasis upon creative becoming but in such wise as to give ontological priority to the future over the past and the present. By this they mean the eschatological or transhistorical future, but one already operative within present time. But that future is not yet and remains "an open realm of possibility that lies ahead and so is full of promise."[10] Thus it operates in time only *retroactively*, by coming to appearance within history in an anticipatory way — most forcibly in that event which is the resurrection of Christ. Clearly this is an attempt to understand divinity in terms not of metaphysical ultimacy but of futurity: God is not "above" us but "ahead" of us. Here again, any genuine transcendence of God is collapsed into historical immanence; the most the former can mean is a relative pre-eminence within history.

This can be interpreted — as intended by Ernst Bloch in non-Christian, left-wing Hegelian terms — to mean only that the term "God" signifies some sort of ideal consummation of man's future, that "in a distant future the transcendent will coincide with the immanent.'[11] Pannenberg himself does not preclude this construction when he writes that "God does not yet exist."[12] In such an expression, "God" functions as a code word for humanity's future as one in which something radically new will occur whose force is already proleptically felt in the present, thus giving rise to hope as the basic attitude of men and women as historical beings. Such a future is transcendent only in the sense that it remains the unknown realization of possibilities that will break the confines of present limitations.[13]

Another interpretation, more tractable to Christian tradition, would ground such hope in God's intention to act definitively in the future, an intention signaled by God's *promise* to consummate history in some future eschatological event. But the promise is of an as yet undetermined fulfillment: "Christ did not rise into the Spirit or into the kerygma, but into that as yet undetermined future realm ahead of us which is pointed to by the tendencies of the Spirit and the proclamations of the kerygma."[14] Moreover, what is hoped for here is something that will radically break continuity with and be qualitatively different from that history which is now in the making: "the as yet unrealised future of the promise stands in contradiction to given reality,"[15] it is "to be born of a creative act of YHWH upon his people beyond the bounds of the temporal and the possible,"[16] a creative act *ex nihilo*.

In any event, we are still speaking of a future that is only promised, one lacking all specificity and actuality, one that is understood as operative here and now solely in the sense that it is hoped for. It is without specific content and so beyond all apprehension, human or divine. What God will do lies hidden in the dialectic of history as that sphere in which God will realize himself. The most that can be said (on the basis of Christian hope) is that God will act in the cause of life and in conquest of the deadliness of death. What cannot be entertained is that God is presently implementing within time his freely chosen and eternally envisaged consummation of history.

Thus contemporary serious thought is practically unanimous in denying to God an infallible knowledge of the future, precisely because there is as yet no such thing, either within the existing temporal order (obviously) or within what has traditionally been known as the eternity of God.

Aquinas

All of this is a reversal of the thirteenth-century thought of Thomas Aquinas. For Aquinas, God does know the entire course of the future down to the least detail of every event. As the subsistent act of be-ing, God is the origin and sustaining ground of everything that "is." By definition, this does not admit of exception; thus it extends not only to substances but to activities, conscious as well as infraconscious, free as well as necessary or merely contingent. All free human activity that is yet to eventuate in time, then, first of all originates as predeterminations of the divine will in its transcendent creative freedom. Next, identity of divine intellect with divine will means that God knows all such determinations of his will. Lastly, eternity as an attribute of Being that is uncaused explains that all finite occurrences are present to God not sequentially but actually. Future events are before him in the mode of presentiality, and thus are not known as merely possible but are "seen" in a true *scientia visionis*.[17] Eternity grounds, within divine existence, the simultaneity of all time — past, present, and future — so that events that have not yet occurred historically and which thus lack all *temporal* actuality nonetheless possess eternal actuality within the divine intentionality. The principle from which contemporary thought proceeds remains intact: Aquinas too insists that God "sees," that is, knows intuitively, only what is actual.

Thus we are left dialectically with contrary conclusions: Aquinas and the moderns as position and counterposition. Aquinas saves the transcendence of God; the moderns are obligated by logical necessity to compromise it. Obviously, however, the former creates a problem of its own: Can the Thomistic teaching be reconciled with any genuine notion of human freedom — and, in light of this, is the doctrine of Thomas tenable?

Aquinas's eventual resolution of this aporia is by way of insisting that divine predetermination is not in conflict with human self-determination. It is rather a precondition of the latter, and to fail to perceive this is to pose a false problem at the very beginning of critical reflection.

Thomas's own route to that conclusion, however, is one of gradual development. It is impossible to assign strict chronological stages to that process (they overlap); neither are the doctrinal positions sharply differentiated (later ones are anticipated earlier); but continual rethinking from distinct perspectives does result in a deepened understanding of the problem that is in fact a self-corrective process. In his earliest theological writing he is content to look upon the question of freedom and divine foreknowledge in Augustinian terms as merely a psychological problem of grace and sin. Very soon, however, the ontological problem does urge itself upon him, and here it seems possible to discern three relatively distinct phases in his thinking.[18]

1. In the *Scripta* on Peter Lombard's *Sentences* (begun in 1252) and in the earlier questions of the *De veritate* (begun the year the *Scripta* was completed, 1256) the influence of Avicenna is pronounced,[19] enabling Thomas to maintain that "omnia providentiae subjacent."[20] But at the same time he is concerned to balance this with Aristotle's world of truly contingent realities enjoying their own proper existence and activity. Thus predetermination of th.ngs is general rather than universal; however humans dispose of things in any particular sphere, nothing will escape in the end God's intentions for the whole of history.[21] At this point there is no evidence of an adequate theory of reconciling the two orders. Thus he can write in the *Scriptum super libros Sententiarum:* "multa fiunt quae Deus non operatur,"[22] and in the *De veritate* that the foreknowledge of God is not causal in all cases, and when it is, as in the case of the predestined, this is by way of exhortations and prayers.[23] Historically this antedates any knowledge by Thomas of what came to be known as semipelagianism and its repudiation by the Church at the Second Council of Orange in 529.[24]

2. In the *Contra gentiles* (begun after completion of the *De veritate*, in 1259) and in the *prima pars* (inaugurated in 1266) the divine causality is unambiguously said to be universal. Now Aquinas is writing his Christian

Summae, and the dominant note is a God who transcends necessity and contingency. The contingency of the world is no longer due to secondary causes (as in Aristotle's accidentally contingent cosmos) but is attributed to God himself.[25] God determines not only what happens but how it happens — necessary things necessarily, and contingent things contingently.[26] The universality of such causal determination means its infallibility. This is no violation of the will's liberty, because it is entirely noncoercive in kind. At this point Aristotle's concept of the will as passive potency is uppermost. As rational appetite, the will is indifferent to various courses of action (this is its radical freedom) and determination comes from the intellect. God moves the will freely precisely by moving it by way of the intellect. True enough, the intellect only gives the form of the operation (the *bonum apprehensum*); nonetheless Thomas gives priority to the intellect over the will. "Here there is no infinite regress, for understanding has an absolute primacy. For an act of knowledge must precede every movement of the will, but there does not have to be an act of will prior to every act of knowledge."[27] This explanation of things was earlier anticipated in some of the later questions of the *De veritate.*[28]

3. By the time of the *prima secundae* (1269–72) it is clear that the will retains a radical control over its own act — though this position was even more strongly urged a bit earlier in the *De malo* (1266–67). The occasion may well have been a reaction against the determinism of the Averroists at Paris (as noted by Dom Lottin),[29] but the breakthrough rests upon distinguishing the order of specification from that of exercise. The role of the intellect is now entirely a directive one in the former order, one of supplying content. It is in the order of exercise that the will's freedom properly resides, and this is precisely active dominion over its own act — in short, self-determination. Without this, humanity is not free, but it remains created freedom, and so is unintelligible unless the will's transition from potency to act is explained. But now this is not due to the intellect but to the divine uncreated and creating activity.[30] The finite exists only *in* the Infinite but not *as* the Infinite (though the finite is not a necessary determination of the divine essence, as in the Hegelian dialectic, but a freely willed determination of the divine love). God's causal influx, remaining universal, is no interference with human dispositions because of its transcendentality; it is of an entirely different order. It is not extrinsic to the will (as is the case with all created agents) but entirely from within. A free human decision is not partly divine and partly human, but entirely divine and simultaneously entirely human.

The influence of Being-itself is *toto caelo* different from all instances of finite causality; it remains unknown and in principle unknowable, beyond the pale of all human intuition or conception. Finite instances of causality merely offer a perspective from which it can be affirmed and designated, in what does not go beyond an analogy of attribution. One import of this is that to project causality upon God analogously is to eliminate from it the connotation of overcoming a natural resistancy in the effect (after the fashion in which fire overcomes the resistance of the log to the burning process). The conceptual model is origin, not in the sense of physical efficiency but in the sense of creation. This is to say, the issue is not a matter of becoming which characterizes all finite activity, but of being which *per essentiam* is proper to God alone. Another aspect is that divine activity is not anything temporal but totally outside time; time is itself part of the divine production. This too cannot be properly grasped in a concept, since all concepts deriving from sense intuition necessarily express within a time stream, but it can be named from the notion of time as "eternity." This means that it is somewhat imprecise to speak of God's predetermination or of his *fore*knowledge.

This absolute transcendence of God conveys that by definition he cannot be extrinsic to or in opposition to anything finite; rather he is present within the very occurrence of freedom, necessarily and according to his very substance as the origin and principle of freedom, not its limit or falsification. Our liberty as the free disposal of ourselves, at once our own and rooted in an inexhaustible source, is continually conferred on us as unexacted gift. It is not mere spontaneity in a world of pure (Whitehead), nor on the other hand is it mere self-assertion against *être en soi* as an irrational surd (Sartre).

Second Scholasticism

The revival of Thomism in the late sixteenth century occurred in a cultural ambiance so altered that the questions urged theologically are by no means identical with those entertained by Thomas himself three centuries earlier. The Scholastics of the Counter Reformation faced an entirely new problem — largely created for them by the devaluation of human liberty on the part of the Reformers — and attempted to apply the principles of Aquinas to a problematic alien from the start to that within which the principles were originally devised. The upshot of this was a redefining of human freedom in limiting terms, so that God's predetermination of the human will now opposes the will's free determination of itself. Molina[31] (+ 1600) poses the problem in terms that strive to balance in tension two autonomous causalities, divine and human. The result is the *scientia media:* God knows what the will is to do without any casual determination of it. Báñez[32] (+ 1604), allowing Molina to set the question for him, rescues the universal efficacy of God, but the price is the *praemotio physica:* God knows what the will is to do because he eternally moves it as a "motum, non se movens." Freedom is compromised in the Molinistic schema because God is enabled to foresee in the human will something that is simply not there, viz., that course of events to which the human will has not yet committed itself. The Báñezian scheme, perceiving the inadequacy of Molina's divine concursus, requires a physical premotion in which God alone is active and the will is entirely passive. In its own way, this too compromises the freedom of the human, for the will is able to posit its own self-determinations only in a second moment (an *actus secundus*) under the determining premotion.[33] This should not be interpreted (as Báñez himself insists in his own defense) as if the will's freedom is nothing more than passivity to various divine determinations. Rather he makes clear that freedom is an indifference that is active in kind.[34] Still, the will is initially in potency and has to be first moved by God. So Báñez does posit a pure receptivity, preceding by a priority of nature the will's own activity. Moreover, what is received is motion, physical in kind, and something created.[35] This introduction of a created medium between God and will means that God's reduction of the will from potency to act is no longer conceived transcendentally. The scholars of the Counter Reformation have introduced a new problem, and in the following terms: The finite will is in potency. Thus, it must be moved in every act by God. Therefore, either God moves it indifferently (Molina), leaving it up to the will to specify God's action; or God moves it determinately (Báñez), thereby negating that the will genuinely is self-determining.

Aquinas, by contrast, comes eventually in his developing thought to harmonize both truths: that God's efficacy is universal and infallible on the one hand, and on the other that human persons determine themselves in freedom. He does this by seeing God's actualization of the finite will as causality only in a transcendent sense. Unlike all finite agents that can cause only *ab extrinseco*, God causes *ab intrinseco*, in the sense that his moving of the will is nothing other than his creation of the very freedom exercised.

The Problematic in Contemporary Perspective

Are we in any more privileged a situation today vis-à-vis a resolution of this perduring question? In the sense of anything more than another tentative reach toward what remains a mystery, it would seem not. On the other hand, if the historicity of thought is indeed a real factor, our vantage point in time should be itself a new perspective on the thought of the past that may bring to light intelligibilities only latent and undeveloped there. One general perspective of this sort cannot be gainsaid: that shift in the thinking of being which constitutes metaphysics from the cosmological to the anthropological sphere, from nature to history, from the realm in which human beings exist alongside everything else to a specifically human realm in which persons are coconstitutors (with the given of nature) of their own world of meaning. For better or worse, the contemporary awareness of the positive value of historicity as distinguished from mere history, of time viewed less as Aristotle's *chronos* (a great tyrant to which we cannot but remain submissive) than as the biblical *kairos* (the free inner time of consciousness which leaves us creatively open to the future) must be given its due. At the same time, it must be borne in mind that the latter is situated in the former and is no negation of it on its own level; human freedom, radicated in spirit, does not sever the ontic bond with a world of materiality. Thomas's own thinking of being does not explicitly prolongate itself in this way, though it can be argued that such a move is latent and unthematic in his thought.[36] One pointer in this direction is his clear distinguishing of two orders of being: the entitative and the intentional, that of objective being-there-ness and that of the subjective event of meaning as immanent to consciousness (only in God does there occur a real coincidence of these two orders).[37] Other indices are not lacking: the surmising that existence is act which opens the way to an understanding of historicity;[38] also the doctrine of personhood as neither essence nor existence but as an autonomy (a radical incommunicability) within a common nature reducible to relationality, etc.[39]

But does this throw new light on the question of God's knowing the future? Aquinas himself allows for only two possibilities: foreknowledge of things either in their proximate causes or in their transcendent divine cause. But the first alternative is impossible when the proximate cause is the human will which in its freedom has not yet determined itself, so that there is as yet no future to be known other than a merely possible one, about which there can only be conjecture. Accordingly Thomas opts for the second case[40] and then appeals to the transcendentality of God's causality to safeguard human liberty. The bipartite division, however, would appear to reflect a Greek dichotomy between necessity on the one hand and pure contingency on the other — a dichotomy in which perfection lies on the side of necessity, and the contingent is the domain of the imperfect. But is there not a third, intermediate possibility, one not explicitly adverted to in the above schema, and based upon an understanding of freedom as a self-positing and self-constituting act which in the finite sphere is made possible by, is limited by, and ever controlled by the creativity of God? God would then know the free future of human history (a) not in human wills, which remain open to a future that is merely possible, (b) nor in his own divine will since this would amount to a predetermination of the future (c) but in dialectical encounter, wherein God, from his ontic situation outside history, enters it and interacts with human beings on the level of temporality. Without introducing temporality within his own inner reality, God (kenotically, as it were) opens himself in and through the creature to an order of time and succession. This dialectical relationship is something directly intended by God in giving existence to a creature whose beingness formally participates in that of God himself, viz., a beingness that is personal and free. To say that the human person is the *imago Dei* is to acknowledge, in an anthropology such as that of Karl Rahner at any rate, that humanity is God's *self*-utterance into the void.

If this be taken to imply — as indeed it does — that God is in some sense determined by the creature in its response to the dialogue, then three qualifications must be borne in mind. (1) This is so only because God in His omnipotently creative love has willed to be so determined in the first place. (2) Human determining powers are highly conditioned: (a) by the limitations of nature, within whose parameters alone such freedom is exercised; (b) by God's having finalized (or better, "transfinalized," since we are here in the realm of grace) the goal of human history; and (c) by God's ultimate control over history as it in fact does unfold. (3) The area of determination regards not God's nature but his intentionality, not God in himself but in his chosen relationality toward creatures. It is his knowledge and love which alter, not as subjective activity constituting divinity, but in terms of what objectively terminates and specifies that activity. In this sphere of intentionality, God determines himself to be the sort of God he is by choosing to create this existing universe rather than any of an infinite number of other worlds possible to him. This makes no difference to God's nature nor his activity of knowing and loving, but it obviously makes a difference regarding what he knows and loves. Had God chosen not to create, or to create a different cosmos than the one we have, he would *in this sense* be a different God than he in fact is.

Now if self-determination within the created order necessarily means genuine novelty *in the world*, it would seem reasonable to conclude that while not allowing for novelty *within* God, this does mean that God assumes a novel relationality toward the world. He now knows (in the mode of intuition) and loves what he did not so know and love before. This real alteration is not of God as nature or being but as answering to the concept of "person," of self-constitution, of the root source of subjectivity whence arises creative relationality to the other.[41] Thus the human making of the future does make a difference to God in the sense of objectively determining what God's vision will behold and how his love will continuously transform it.

This view of things safeguards the transcendence of God in the face of its disappearance in much of contemporary thought. In opposition to Whitehead and Hartshorne, God is not here understood as finite and in the process of acquiring his own perfection, but remains pure act eternally possessing within himself the sum total of being and value, and in a fully actual way, that the world can ever reach, and more besides. At the same time it allows that human beings can introduce genuine novelty into the world, i.e., something not determined by God beforehand. What is achieved in history is not a new acquisition *in* God, but does become a new acquisition *for* God in the finite realm. God becomes what he was not — not in himself but in the world and in history. It is not simply the case that what is other than God changes, but rather that God changes — not in himself but in the other and by way of the other.[42] God changes not absolutely but relationally, i.e., in terms of those dispositions of knowing and loving that he chooses to adopt toward a universe of creatures that in a finite and temporal way determine themselves.

In a very real sense, this means saying that God bestows upon the creature a share in his own creative power, which, however, the creature possesses only as "gift," one sustained within its transcendent source. But God cannot choose to assume a history in and through the creature without taking upon himself the real limitations of finitude. His infiniteness of being, wisdom, and love explains that he envisages the future in the full range of pure possibility (a *scientia simplicis intelligentiae*), but only subsequent to human decisions can God intuit (in a *scientia visionis*) what has in fact eventuated thereby. At the same time his providential care ceaselessly urges the course of human history to the maximum fulfillment of his vision. More than this, the promises of God assure us of his intentions to counter the negative moves of heedless humanity in such wise as to guarantee final triumph. Revelation (to persons of faith) conveys that the purposes of God are saving purposes and that they shall prevail. But if this be taken in all seriousness, it means that God's temporal interaction with humankind derives from and will be consummated in a love that is not temporal but eternal. Divine love in its temporal aspect is then an "incarnation" of what God is in an eternal way; it is a particularization in created and human modalities of God as the transcendent ground of both being and becoming. But the concrete form of such particularizations God chooses to leave undetermined.

This need not be viewed as a collapse into Hegelianism, even that Christian version of Hegelianism which underlies much of the thinking of the theologians of hope. It is not the case that the Infinite becomes actual only as the finite. Rather the infinite, eternally actual in itself, becomes actual in a new and finite way with creation. It need not be said with Hegel that at one and the same time "man is not God" — religiously, and "man is God" — philosophically.[43] Rather the infinite qualitative difference remains. Pannenberg's understanding of his own repeated insistence that "God is the future" does not appear to escape this covert "anthropotheism." Taken literally, it means that what is to come as eventual triumph over present limitations is what a believer means by the term "God." It is in this sense that Pannenberg, with Moltmann, speaks of God as not existing, and of the present influx of God on the world as in fact the *retroactive* power of our future.[44] But humanity is not merged with the divine, precisely because the intrinsic infinity of the latter is actual in kind, entirely independent of human beings and world. It is simply that God's transcendent creativity is such that it can bestow upon the finite other a limited participation in its own purely actual freedom as the power of self-determination.

This brings to light another limitation shared by followers of both Whitehead and Hegel. For them, God's relationship to the world is necessary, a matter of intrinsic need. This compromises the divine transcendence, making it entirely relative in kind. What is called God's love for the world thereby loses its altruistic character; ultimately it is self-serving, reducible (in spite of an insistence to the contrary by Whitehead and Hartshorne) to Greek *eros* rather than to biblical *agape*. In such a view human beings are not free to be human because in the final analysis whatever future we are headed for is not a human future at all but God's. True enough — in the vision of things espoused in this essay, God acquires a history and one over which he exercises a lordship. But it is human history that he takes upon himself without despoiling it of its human character. Moreover, this occurs by an initiative of love in which humanity alone is made to be the beneficiary.

Postscript

Undergirding the above thesis is a metaphysics which, without repudiating that adapted by Aquinas from Aristotle, extrapolated from the latter's science of physics concerned with a world of nature in which everything is marked either with necessity or with contingency, does move beyond it.[45] On the basis of the Judeo-Christian world view, it allows that historicity and temporality are essential and not merely accidental to the specificity of being human. Reality ultimately manifests a character that is not only thing-like but also event-like. Humanity's prior lodgement in the domain of matter and oneness with the infraconscious cosmos cannot be ignored, but the Western religious vision focuses rather upon the properly human world, the world of meaning, of freedom, and of personhood. As the ultimate natural entity, human beings transcend the nature of which they are part. In the sphere of historical consciousness human beings, at once individually and socially, "create" themselves with all the attendant risks implied therein. Moreover, this is the world that terminates God's continuing creation and which he assumes to himself in the Christian doctrine of the incarnation. As finite spirituality, humankind exists in virtue of the perduring presence of the divine pure act: (a) as the origin (efficient cause) of being in its properly human mode as free self-constitution, and simultaneously as (b) the destiny and term (final cause) of human historical dynamism. Far from obliterating the radical otherness of divine and creaturely activity, the transcendentality of the former rather grounds one of its effects in so eminent a way as to endow it with genuine creativity of its own. The open-endedness of a history human beings shape by their own decisions does not then gainsay the universality of God's transcendently creative activity. It is rather an index of the perfectness of God's creative act in the production of humanity, a consequence of a creative activity which is nothing less than God's *self*-utterance into the void. Through humankind, God acquires a history open to novelty and creative advance, one not predetermined beforehand in every respect and in all its particulars. It is thus not exhaustibly knowable in a true vision or intuition prior to its temporal eventuation, except in the case of God, due to his eternity. That eternity does not, however, include pre-determination, i.e., neither determination from within time (as one cause alongside the others), nor before time (an illusion). It does, however, involve determination in the manner proper to a transcendent cause, a universal cause of being whose causality is solely a relation of dependence in the effect. God, remaining ahistorical in his intrinsic being, interacts with humankind in a free dialogic partnership. God remains the Lord of history, but by way of his creative adaptations to prior human responses (including negative ones, those of malice and sin) to his own continuing initiatives of love.

FIVE

The Historicity of God

Contemporary theology has had its attention taken by a footnote in Martin Heidegger's *Sein und Zeit* suggesting that God's being might be more richly construed in categories of primal temporality (*ursprüngliche Zeitlichkeit*) which is infinite, rather than in those of a spurious eternity.[1] Among the reasons for this is the influence of Hegel on Heidegger, for whom eternity, like being, was an empty notion devoid of all determination until through the mediation of time it was sublimated into a pure becoming transcendent to both eternity and derived time. Operative too is, seemingly, the biblical view of a God of historical revelation in dialogue with humankind. More proximate, however, is Heidegger's own envisagement of God's being on analogy with that of the human person, wherein the structure of the latter's privileged existence is Care (*Sorge*) that plays out its meaning as temporality. Here, in an avowedly anthropomorphic view, time is essential to the structure of human persons as the sphere wherein we achieve our own being in self-enactment. Like human beings, then, God's being is to be found only in-a-world with others (*In-der-Welt-sein*), manifesting itself as Care.

God as Primal Temporality

Schubert Ogden was one Christian theologian who took up this challenge and attempted to work through its implications.[2] Notably, he began by applying Heidegger's distinction between the ontic or existenziell order on the one hand and the ontological or existenzial on the other. The former represents God's *Existenz*, his concrete involvement in the historical world, a sort of divine derived time, superior to but homogeneous with finite historical events. The latter is properly the concern of the philosophical theologian; it is the formal structure of God's being in which his "within-timeness" is grounded; this is God's primal temporality and represents what Ogden calls the divine "existentiality" in distinction from the divine "existence." Primal temporality is thus a conception closer to "historic"

80

than to "historical," more akin to the biblical *kairos* than to the *chronos* of Greek rational thought. As structuring divine being, it conveys that God is essentially and by inner necessity relative to finite entities. Its immediate implication is that God, existing in the present, is measured by his past as he looks creatively to his future.

More importantly, perhaps, is Ogden's further clarification, namely, that the divine temporality is infinite. This means that God's being, while it cannot be other than relative to a past and a future (and this means a past and a future with others who are in time) bespeaks a past that had no beginning and a future that will have no end (unlike human existence, which is "unto death") and so one of limitless possibilities. It means further that God is not present to some one segment of time (as is true of whatever is finitely temporal) but equally to all moments of time without exception. God exists in dependence upon the others with whom he is essentially in relation, but the character of that relationship is not determined by factors extrinsic to God; thus it transcends the limitations inherent in all finite relationality. In this way Ogden justifies Heidegger's characterization of primal temporality as "infinite."

God as Being in History

The suggestion arising from existential philosophy that God be conceived in terms of "primal temporality" has found fertile ground in theological circles. The neo-orthodox movement gave this (independently) a form of its own in conceiving God not as being but as event. Concretely, this was the event of revelation, which was thus seen as a self-communication indistinguishable from God himself. This has to be understood, however, against the background of the distinction — usually implicit but always operative — between the *Deus in se* and the *Deus pro nobis*. God in himself is not a God for men and women and remains unknown and unknowable. In willing to become a God for us out of love, God make himself identical with the event of revelation. Thus for Karl Barth the doctrine of the Trinity is the immediate awareness in faith of the structure of revelation as divine, the awareness that God is the *agent* of revelation (*God* reveals), the content of revelation (God reveals *himself*), and the very occurrence of revelation (God *reveals* himself).

Neo-orthodoxy succeeded to a degree in its attempt to recoup the weightiness of traditional Christian language that had been put in question since the time of Schleiermacher. But it paid a price that was to prove too dear a one, the jettisoning of a concern for history, a concern indigenous to Christian belief. Historical criticism against Christian claims led Barth to seek safe harbor in a kind of metahistory within God (*Urgeschichte*), the eternal election of Jesus as the Christ. Bultmann, for his part, made faith secure by retreating from the vicissitudes of history into a world of existential decision; here what mattered was not interest in the Jesus of history but rather concern for the kerygmatic Christ, for the Christ proclaimed and confessed, for which confession the life of Jesus provided only the occasion.

In time it became obvious that the ahistorical character of the neo-orthodox movement rendered it inadequate to the demands of Christian belief. An alternative to it was worked out above all with the work of Wolfhart Pannenberg, who, accepting Barth's theology of revelation, viewed that revelation not as a kind of metahistory but as coincident with history itself in its universality (*Universalgeschichte*).[3] History, of course, is universal only in terms of its end, which has not yet arrived — a problem Pannenberg resolved by viewing the resurrection of Christ as an anticipation (for believers) of the consummation of history.

What Pannenberg appears to do is to conceive God as primal temporality (much in line with Ogden's response to Heidegger's footnote) but then to reverse the directionality of time by affording ontological priority to the future. God is not just related equally to all moments of time as they unfold out of the past and into the future by way of the present. Rather, God is the power of the future impinging upon the present, determining it to be what it truly is in virtue of the truth that the true essence of anything is constituted by what it is to become. All reality is then historical, or, differently put, "history is reality in its totality,"[4] which totality lies only in its consummation. In this sense meaning is resident within events themselves, not bestowed upon events by subjects who are obedient to Christ (Bonhoeffer) or who confess the proclaimed Christ (Bultmann). Whatever is historical, then, is revelatory of God.

God is thus the power over all that is (*Macht über alles*), but in the way in which the future (for Pannenberg) is determinative of the present. Such a future, unlike Hegel's, remains open — even for the resurrected Christ.[5] It enables Pannenberg to write "God does not yet exist."[6] When he does come to exist, however, God will reveal himself as always having been. What this does *not* mean, first of all, is that God, fully actual in himself from the beginning, comes to be known by us only gradually with the passage of time. Rather, Pannenberg means "in the eternal God himself a becoming takes place."[7] Since that becoming is historical, it seemingly has to be said that God's being is intrinsically historical. But since that becoming is not the unfolding from the past of virtualities resident there from the beginning, in either an evolutionary or a teleological sense, Pannenberg is able to say (somewhat idiosyncratically) that God will reveal himself at the end as always having been what he has become historically.[8] His becoming is the arrival of the future, understood in the sense that every existent is a mere provisional and proleptic instantiation of that future.

The question this poses is: Has Pannenberg virtually identified God

with the process of history? If this means history in its human immanence
seen as a mere code word for God, the answer is no. But it would seem that
Pannenberg has reduced the being of God to that of a divine historical process vis-à-vis the world. God's being is identified with his reign, which is in
the process of being historically achieved and has been anticipated in the
destiny of the resurrected one. Thus God's being is entirely within history.
Pannenberg has at least collapsed revelation into history (the truth is not
only that revelation is history but even that history is revelation), and revelation is God's self-communication. We cannot conceive or speak of any
other God than the One who is coming into existence historically and who
will exist when history comes to its consummation as the full achievement
of God's lordship. Clearly this envisages a close to history, though Pannenberg qualifies this in speaking of "the possibility of a contortion of time"
after history is completed, meaning an experience of process "different in
some way from the forces of time which we experience at present ... a process into the depths of our present lives concerning the direction of the
relation to God, participation in God's glory."[9] At work here is an ontologizing of history and an identification of God with that history in the totality
of its meaning. God is thus not eternal (in the classical sense of timeless)
but conceived rather as total time, which is time from its consummation.[10]
That consummation yet to come will reveal when it does come as always
having been. And this is not to be understood merely epistemologically
but ontologically.

There is an obvious problem of understanding here — basically that of
the tendency to historicize God. The denial to God of anything suggesting
nontemporal eternity seemingly leads to the virtual identity of deity with
the process of history. This clearly demands a unity to history in the totality of its meaning that suggests the imposition upon the living God of
an abstract, universal, unified *idea* of history in its totality. As something
a priori, it is difficult to see why this does not undermine genuine history
in its event-like character and the truly historical dimension to revelation.
A quite similar reservation is felt by some regarding the ahistorical *Vorgriff*
of transcendental Thomists such as Karl Rahner. But history can be history only if it is not virtually identified with God but remains the result of
a dialogic relationship between God and humankind. Is the Christian vision not rather one of a God remaining transcendent to history in himself,
who only assumes our history, choosing to become in creation the Lord of
history and in incarnation subject to it?

True enough, Pannenberg himself has denied any such identification of
God with the process of history itself, insisting that he only intends denying
that history is "an 'immanence' to which one can and indeed would have
to oppose a 'transcendence.' "[11] But even in this disavowal God remains
transcendent to each particular event by overcoming and surpassing it in
the mode of the newness of event which dawns and negates the previous

event that anticipated it. Futurity, in short, remains the mode of divine being. God is not the ground of the phenomenal world but the source of events which come to pass in a contingent and free way. God thus determines all events, but from within history, that is to say, in the way the future determines the present — in a word, contingently.

Another perspective on the same problem is that such a theology seems content with a finite deity of history whose attributes — granting only the addition of personhood — are strikingly similar to Heidegger's *Sein*. A way around this is to allow that Pannenberg believes that theology can deal explicitly only with the *Deus pro nobis*. Of the *Deus in se* nothing whatsoever can be said. This at least could leave the way open to granting that something like pure act is characteristic of God in himself — of the God who, unknown and unknowable, is not a God of humankind apart from his choosing in unexacted love to become such. Such speculation, however, is not to be found in Pannenberg's explicit thought; it can only be suggested that it seemingly is operative there in a covert and surreptitious way. One oblique indication of this may well lie in his consistent rejection of analogy in favor of doxological language about God.[12]

God as Nontemporal Becoming

Heidegger's distinction between the existenzial and the existenziell order, applied by Ogden to the question about God's being, suggests obvious parallels with Alfred Whitehead's doctrine of a primordial and a consequent nature in God. This very dipolarity, however, raises serious questions of its own centering on the sort of relationship prevailing between the two natures. The prevailing resolution up to the present would seem to be that worked out by Charles Hartshorne and John Cobb.[13] Here the emphasis falls markedly on the consequent nature as alone actual and concrete, with the primordial nature designating an abstract realm of pure possibilities for God that is real only as embodied in the consequent nature. On this view God is eminently temporal — in "his derivative nature ... consequent upon the creative advance of the world," which nature is "fully actual," "everlasting," but "incomplete." What is conveyed by "primordial nature" has receded into the background, namely, that dimension of God's being that, though "actually deficient" and "unconscious," may be called "infinite" and "eternal."[14]

Lewis S. Ford, however, has offered another, more nuanced interpretation of Whitehead that enables us to enter more deeply into the question at hand.[15] This interpretation emphasizes not God's consequent nature characterized by temporality but the primordial nature which enabled Whitehead to refer to God as "a non-temporal actual entity."[16] The primordial nature involves God's conceptual feelings, which as such bespeak no temporal limitation whatsoever (unlike finite conceptual feelings, which originate at some point in time and are dependent upon prior physical prehensions). Divine conceptual feelings transcend temporality altogether then, but are analyzable into an objective aspect and a subjective counterpart to this. The objective dimension consists in God's being confronted with the realm of eternal objects and clearly introduces the notion of eternity into God (though Ford prefers here the designation "atemporal"). The eternity in question, however, is of a negative and abstract sort, like the eternity of numbers or the Platonic forms. It answers to the concept of "timelessness" and designates a realm of values that *in se* lack all actuality; it represents merely an abstract structure of the divine nature taken primordially.

Ford's interpretation of Whitehead, however, stresses the subjective dimension to the primordial nature, namely, the nontemporal decision wherein God renders himself actual as a subject. In so doing, God renders the eternal objects actual by embodying them in the process of becoming. This exemplifies Whitehead's principle that "apart from things that are actual, there is nothing."[17] Here God posits himself, outside time and independently of the world, as the sort of God he chooses to be in transcendent freedom by his ordered envisagement of the eternal objects. What is at work here is Whitehead's later doctrine of actual occasions as self-creating in a process of concrescence. Ford's contention, which takes him beyond other process thinkers, is that the divine self-creating is by way of such a decision — a nontemporal decision, however, in contrast to other entities, whose decisions are temporal.[18] This involves distinguishing between actuality on the one hand, and definiteness or determinateness on the other. It is decision, as the self-expression of a subjectivity, as that whereby an entity posits itself as an existing subject, that accounts for actuality. Definiteness of form or determinateness, by contrast, is rather the immediate consequence of decision and actuality (thus we tend to confuse them with actuality), and in itself bears rather the character of potentiality insofar as it is available for prehension and can contribute to future decisions. In contrast to classical metaphysics, then, determinateness and concreteness are not manifestive of actuality but constitute potentiality for further becoming. By way of bolstering this view, Ford is able to point out the inability of Aristotelianism to surmount the difficulty inherent in a doctrine that derives actuality from form. If the forms bestow actuality on matter, why are they not actual outside of the composite, and so subsistent, as they were for Plato? Whitehead seeks to avoid this problem inherited from Plato by reducing actuality to subjective decision, one which in God's case is nontemporal. Actuality resides ultimately, then, not in substance (Aristotle's *ousia*) but in the successive states of substance, in its becoming or its history. To state this another way: for Aristotle, perfection consists in things being determinate, finished, and limited, whereas imperfection was viewed as the indeterminate, the unfinished, and unlimited, Aquinas found this congenial and gave primacy to act over potency, to existence over essence. Whitehead inversed this order, preferring to look upon the determinate as unfinished and as supplying the potential for further perfecting.

Clearly, all of this issues in a conception of God different from that of process thinkers such as Hartshorne, Cobb, and others, who stress the consequent nature and who view God's actuality and subjectivity in a never-ending series of temporal decisions. Ford's stress upon the nontemporal decision of the primordial nature once again introduces a timelessness within God. But not a timelessness that remains indifferent to all temporal passage — as characterizes the doctrine of the eternal objects taken by itself. Nor a timelessness that includes within itself all moments of time — as is the case with the medieval understanding of eternity. "Nontemporal" here rather means independent of temporal passage as such but capable of being related to any given moment of time.[19] The reason for this is simply that the divine nontemporal decision is an instance not of being but of pure becoming. God is continuously realizing himself by way of one of an infinite number of pure possibilities — precisely in order to make available, through the initial aims he supplies, real possibilities for temporal concrescence in the world. Thus in his very reality God is a God of constantly emerging novelty, of eternal becoming. What Ford has done in effect, in a convincing interpretation of Whitehead, is ground the God of a temporal becoming in dependence upon the finite world (the consequent nature) in an ontologically prior nontemporal becoming that is the source of the never-ending creative advance into novelty."[20]

The Eternal God of Being

The foregoing attempts at reconceiving God in categories of primal temporality, historicity, or eternal becoming are all indebted to the discovery in contemporary thought of human historicity. Implicit in this is the understanding that all statements about God are at the same time unavoidably statements about humankind. Temporality is viewed, in the modern experience, not as defect but as boon — as holding out to men and women the possibilities of self-enactment. This gives a certain priority to the future on which basic humanity can rescue the past and enrich the present; it means life in hope through transcending the limitations of present existence. Metaphysically, this has meant a swing of the pendulum from being as absolute value to that of becoming. Theologically, this thinking has been extrapolated from anthropological considerations and introduced into notions of God. Classical thought (Stoic, Platonic, Aristotelian, and medieval) showed by contrast a preference for permanence over change. The Greek discovery of *logos*, and the equation of intelligibility with being, meant that temporality was understood as a diminution of being, its admixture with potency for change, and so an approach to nonbeing. Time was thus rooted not in being, which as such bespoke no limitation, but in being as finite, i.e., as subject to motion and so to measure; the truly existent, the really real — e.g., Plato's forms — represented a storm-free area, one isolated from such deficiency.

In such a thought system God is presented as pure being with the attribute of eternity, utterly transcendent to all diminution of being arising from temporality or becoming. The most critical version of this mode of thinking appears in Aquinas's transformation of theology into something analogous, in the domain of faith, to Aristotle's *epistēmē*. Here created things are not the explanation of their own existing; they exist contingently, exercising an act of being bestowed on them by that being that is alone its own existence, namely, God. As such, all creatures are finite and intrinsically mutable — such mutation being a consequence of their drive toward fuller actualization. Time is precisely the measure (one and uniform in the mind, then) according to before and after of this process. God's reality was surmised, on analogy with that of creatures, as consisting of pure being, fully actual in itself, and thus ontologically incapable of alteration or change — simply because there was nothing lacking to God which he could acquire by changing. The pure actuality of God thus grounded his immutability, which was in turn the proximate foundation of his eternity as the negation of any way of measuring succession or passage.[21]

Eternity is, etymologically, a negative term bespeaking the denial to God of temporality, just as immutability is in virtue of the *via negativa* a denial to God of all imaginable modes of created mutation. But what is designated by this negative use of analogy is a positive attribute of God that remains unknown in itself. Thus eternity means timelessness, but only insofar as it is interchangeable with the dynamism expressed in the pure act of "to be." God, who is "unmoved," is misconstrued unless it be understood that he is by the same token the *primum movens* of everything else. Thus the medieval preference for stability over change is not an option for a static notion of being; rather the opposite. This led to conceiving eternity imaginatively as the *nunc stans*, on analogy with the *nunc fluens* of time; here time is, in Plato's phrase from the *Timaeus*, "the moving image of eternity." Eternity, then, is not procession without beginning or end, which would be rather everlastingness (nor is it what the medievals termed "aeviternity"),[22] but a mode of being beyond all measure and duration, characterized by the total absence of all succession. Most commonly, this was appropriated by way of Boethius's classic definition "the perfect, total, and simultaneous possession of interminable life."[23] This answers to timelessness, but a timelessness that (granting the existence of time) includes all time within itself. God in his eternity is

by necessity related to every moment of time — not just as each temporal moment unfolds, for that would subject God to time in its succession,
but as overarching all of time in its entirety. Divine eternity, in Aquinas's
view, is not God's one universal history with us (Pannenberg); nor is it everlastingness (Whitehead's consequent nature); nor atemporality, which
abstracts from all temporality; nor nontemporality, which bespeaks internal succession and relates only to particular moments of time (Whitehead's
primordial nature).

All of this, of course, represents the received doctrine of the Christian
tradition up until the time of the Enlightenment. Contemporary theology,
facing the phenomenon of pluralism, is by and large agreed that, whatever
other methodological path it pursue, theology today must proceed her-
meneutically. By this is meant that the believer, far from entering upon
presuppositionless thinking, must think from within a tradition that is mediated historically. This sets the theological task as one of appropriating a
tradition critically, that is to say, interpretatively. The intent is to grasp the
living *traditio*, not just to repeat the *tradita;* this can be done by entering into
dialogue with the subject matter as presented in the texts of the tradition,
but in light of present experiences. It is only present experience as interpreting and as being interpreted by past experience that allows meaning to
happen and, in the case at hand, God's revelation to come to pass.

If this be so, then the conceptions of God as eternal on the one hand
and as primal temporality on the other confront one another. The question that needs exploring is whether these remain irreconcilable or whether
the two conceptualities might not condition each other in some mutually
illuminating way. Primal temporality is argued for in two distinct versions:
(1) as a divine historical process that will come to consummation (Pannenberg), and (2) as a divine ahistorical process that is in principle without
end (Whitehead).

For the first of these, an insistence upon God as eternal *in himself*
serves to indicate that divinity is not self-identical with historical process.
The latter is rather God's chosen means of communicating and mediating himself to a temporal world. This means qualifying Pannenberg's own
statement that God is identified with his coming reign; it demands, rather,
explicit acknowledgment that God transcends his willing of himself as the
goal to history. Thus it makes clear the gratuitousness of God's choosing
to render himself a God for humanity in and through history. It is difficult to see how this is safeguarded if — as maintained by Eberhard Jüngel,
who offers a more Barthian version of Pannenberg's vision — it is godless
to speak of a God without men and women.[24] At the same time Pannenberg's approach has the advantage of emphasizing that humanity's relation
to God is basically historical, in such wise that priority is given to the future,
and moreover a future that remains an open one. In short, the two aspects
need to be seen together; the God-world relationship must be grasped in

the two dimensions of history on the one hand, with all the risks attendant upon the exercise of freedom, both divine and human, and of being on the other (grounding a metaphysics) wherein historical process is tethered down so as to escape being merely arbitrary, contingent, or voluntaristic.

If this primal temporality be reduced back to where it signifies a never-ending process of becoming intrinsic to God himself (as in Ford's interpretation of Whitehead), then the traditional notion of eternity calls this into question by contesting the legitimacy of introducing potency into the deity. The divine nontemporal decision, after all, is God's actualization of himself by way of one of the infinite possibilities objectively available to him from the realm of eternal objects. Such infinitude of possibilities is seemingly not extrinsic to God; this, were it the case, would subordinate God to something nondivine.[25] Whitehead's principle that nothing is real which is not actual in some subject demands rather that such infinity be an intrinsic structure of God's primordial nature. But for process thought this can be at best a potential infinity; possibly it can explain Whitehead's ultimate category of creativity, which is itself nonactual. God's nontemporal decision, which does constitute him as actual, is only an ongoing instantiation of creativity. This is simply to say that God, in his actuality and reality, is finite.

The contribution of Ford's interpretation of Whitehead, on the other hand, is that the notion of a nontemporal self-actualizing decision on God's part suggests a deepening of the concept of eternity. It is not too farfetched to see Whitehead's thought here as articulating in different conceptual categories what Aquinas means by eternity as the measure of subsistent being — as long as due emphasis be given to being as act. Existence or actuality for Aquinas is not mere facticity nor givenness but the exercise of existential act;[26] the existent "is," somewhat as analogously the runner runs or the singer sings. The ultimate source of such exercise can only be what Aquinas calls, borrowing a Greek term, the *hypostasis*, that is, the subject-person (or, granting the Christian doctrine of the Trinity, the three persons). This seems an approximation of Whitehead's principle of reformed subjectivity, and suggests that a God of nontemporal becoming is somewhat akin to a God whose being is surmised as that of pure actuality. In either view divine reality is a dynamism: the former that of a potency to act process, the latter that of a process that can only be represented as that of act to act (as in the eternal relating that constitutes Father, Son, and Spirit). The enormous difference, of course, is that Whitehead's God continuously attains to a newness of perfection that is intrinsic to his own developing divine being; the eternal God of Thomism can be seen as acquiring new relationships to the novelties introduced into the world by his creatures but without undergoing enrichment in his own inner beingness.

Two Corollaries

Two corollaries deserve mention by way of conclusion. The first is that conceiving God as eternal, and so as immutable, does not preclude allowing that he is really related to the world. Such real relations are, it is true, denied verbally by Aquinas, who understands all relations of God to world as rational relations. But that rests upon a precise understanding of real as implying causal dependence. In this understanding, whose roots go back to Aristotle, God is not enriched by these relationships to the world; the creature's activity does not contribute anything to God's already totally perfect being. Such relationships of God to world nonetheless remain *actual* ones founded on God's own causality toward the world. God does truly know, love, create, act upon, redeem, etc. this universe of creatures. In this sense there is no problem in designating such relations as real. Aquinas prefers to avoid the term in order to make clear that the proximate foundation for the relation is the creature's dependence upon God, while the remote foundation is God's pure causality as unaffected by the effect upon which it operates. This is simply a way of saying that the motive of the divine causal acting cannot be any self-enrichment of God, who is already fully actual, but only an altruistic gifting of the creature, who is thereby "really" related to God in this sense of the term "real." What Aquinas wishes to avoid is any suggestion of ontic relations accidentally accruing to God's being. Modern usage, however, would sanction using the term "real" to cover God's effective altering of the creature vis-à-vis himself.

Second, predicating eternity of God rather than primal temporality does mean denying, at least without qualification, that God suffers intrinsically in his own godhead. That God does so suffer is taught in all forms of process theology (finding inspiration in Whitehead's designation of God as a "fellow sufferer") and is echoed in many theologians who tend to historicize God's being — notably Jürgen Moltmann and Eberhard Jüngel. The doctrine of an eternal God that claims to be Christian must obviously make room for a God who suffers. This is usually explained as suffering not in his divinity but in the humanity he had made his own in Jesus the Christ. But that humanity is confessed as the humanity of God, which means that in some mysterious sense God suffers. Further explanation was forthcoming in the tradition with the doctrine of *communicatio idiomatum*. But that seems inadequate to the mystery. Somehow a way must be found to say that God is beyond all suffering in his own inner being (a notion which process thinkers explicitly deny and which Moltmann leaves ambiguous),[27] and yet in his love opens himself freely to "experience" human suffering in a way that does not diminish his beingness.

In short, if God really relates to a world of creatures, and if those creatures creatively introduce genuine novelty into the world (as they do), and if they truly suffer (as they do), then this cannot remain alien to God's experience. Thus in some sense, without jettisoning the divine immutability (which would dedivinize God), God responds knowingly and lovingly to such suffering. One suggestion may be made here as an alternative to the dipolar nature introduced into God by process thought. The suggestion is to acknowledge as irreducible the distinction between nature and person (or, in a trinitarian context, persons) in God. It might then be possible to maintain that *in his nature* God is eternally the infinite act of being and as such is incapable of any enrichment or impoverishment of his being; here the divine being is considered in its absoluteness and remains immutable. *In his personhood*, however, we are dealing with God's being in its freely-chosen self-relating to others, in that intersubjective disposing of the self that is self-enactment and self-positing. Here we are concerned not with *what* God is in his being as transcendent to world, but with *who* he chooses to be vis-à-vis a world which he creates and redeems in love. Seemingly this allows for a never-ceasing newness of personal relationship without implying any qualitative aggrandizement or diminution of divine being absolutely taken.

But even here — if one can grant that God does will freely to undergo change, not absolutely, but relationally — this is not to introduce temporality into God. For he does not change successively, as if waiting on our decisions; rather, he chooses to be affected by, and responsive to, our temporally achieved transformations in a mode consonate with his eternity. He knows all alterations, including those that are not determined by him but truly rise from our freedom, in the mode of simultaneity.

In the end, this is only to say that none of our finite categories of thought are adequate to the utter transcendence of God. Eternity as mere timelessness is an empty concept. Primal temporality secures God's relevance to the temporal order, but at too great a price. Dialectical recourse to both measures of duration is unsatisfying in that this leaves unexplained why introducing temporality, and so potentiality, into the deity does not compromise divine simplicity and thereby render God finite. Eternity in its medieval sense as encompassing all time within itself comes closest to designating (in its negative form as *e-ternitas*) a positive attribute of God that remains resistant to conceptual grasp.

SIX

The Implicate World: God's Oneness with Humankind as a Mediated Immediacy

Whereas the natural and empirical sciences can and indeed must resist any improper incursion of theological conclusions into their own spheres, it has become more and more acknowledged that these disciplines presuppose some sort of world view (*Weltanschauung*) that ultimately implies not only a philosophical but a religious option as well. But it is equally apparent that theology cannot ignore the discoveries and postulates of the natural and social sciences and the humanities such as history. This is true, at any rate, if theology is conceived not solely as a confessional activity addressed to believers but also as a reflection upon a word addressed to the world at large concerning the ultimate meaning of human existence, for which purpose it must strive to be adequate to all the data available from the empirical world. Obviously, it must do this in a critical way, applying its own criteria of meaning and truth, and not simply accepting all the claims of science in a unexamined fashion. Frederick Ferré has put this succinctly in stating, "theologians must not only find ways of incorporating current scientific explanations in their wider conceptual schemes but must also have a way of distancing themselves from the theories and models of science at any given time."[1]

The Implicate World of Modern Science: David Bohm

This being so, David Bohm's theory of an implicate world behind the explicate world of daily exchange, or more accurately stated, of an implicate world that lies within the explicate world which is the unfolding of that implicate world, cannot for the theologian fall upon deaf ears.[2] Indeed, theology finds here an ally in its own cause of surmounting a world so fragmented (Bohm's explicate world) that it appears devoid of ultimate intelligibility and loses all semblance of being truly a cosmos. It is commonplace to locate the origins of this fragmentation in the Cartesian shift of focus from reality to the concept as a surrogate of the real, providing consciousness with the certitude sought by critical philosophy. This fascination with our knowing of things rather than with realities themselves has to a degree resulted in the multiple and varied distinctions of reason being superimposed upon reality. This ratifies our preoccupation with the explicate order, with the consequence that we tend to overlook an order of existence, ontologically prior, which is one of wholeness and unity. Such a realm, called by Bohm the implicate world, accounts for the origin of forms which are "enfolded" in the implicate order and "unfolded" into the explicate order. The forms do not, in Platonic fashion, preexist in the implicate domain as changeless eternal archetypes; they rather develop creatively out of that domain by a process in which the totality projects and injects itself into the explicate world. In short, the implicate realm is envisaged as a realm of creativity whence there occurs, not simply a replication of forms in new individual instantiations, but the origin of species themselves. Rupert Sheldrake (confirming Bohm's theory from the disciplines of bio-chemistry and physiology rather than from Bohm's own discipline of theoretical physics) refers to this as "formative causation" and as "morphogenesis" which he further describes as a process transcendent to time and space.[3] This causation is exercised by the totality projecting itself into its sub-wholes of the explicate order, somewhat as the sea is causative of its waves. Significantly, for the theologian at any rate, is Bohm's added observation that in such causation, which is in fact the phenomenon of creativity, the implicate order manifests a deep purpose and intentionality that does not always manifest itself in its explicate forms.[4]

The Metaphysical Realm as Implicate World

Clearly, at this point, a world view (*Weltanschauung*) enters the picture, at which juncture theological concerns arise. The limited interpretative framework of science is such that it cannot address directly the deepest dimensions of human reality. The question which urges itself on us is whether there is anything congenial to Bohm's implicate world in Christian thought, especially in the tradition of the Church Catholic. To approach this question in very broad terms first of all: both Bohm and Sheldrake view their theories as compatible with any one of four world views — materialism, idealism, immanentism, and transcendentalism. These views ground creativity in, respectively: matter, consciousness, the universe itself, and transcendent reality. Bohm indicates his preference for the latter two, and indeed would seem to ultimately opt for the fourth possibility when he speaks eventually of three realms of existence: The explicate, the implicate, and the ground source.[5]

The Judaeo-Christian commitment, of course, is congruent only with an over-all vision of reality as the creation of a God who transcends it in an absolute sense as its creator. For those who stand in the tradition of the Christian West, the closest approximation to Bohm's implicate world is the world of finite being in its unity and wholeness as sought after and thought out in the discipline of metaphysics. By this is meant not the complex *concept* of being which comes at the end of the metaphysician's labor and is the product of it, but the domain of real being itself encountered at the origin of the metaphysical task. Here all things are one in the sense of that similitude-within-difference known as the analogy of being. The doctrine is well known, was rehabilitated during the neo-Scholastic revival, and can be rehearsed here rather briefly. It still retains some illuminative power as undergirding a thought system in spite of Heidegger's claim to have overcome metaphysics, as well as the tendency in contemporary theology to replace analogical unity with a dialectically achieved identity. Analogical unity establishes itself neither in virtue of form or essence which differentiates the species and accounts for variety, nor in virtue of matter which individuates and accounts for plurality, but in virtue of being itself. The formal note vis-à-vis being is *esse* or existence (at least in Aquinas's account of things which critically speaking is perhaps the most defensible form of analogy), not as mere facticity or givenness but as ultimate actuality.[6] Outside of being then is only non-being which cannot be, but only can not be; there simply is no "beyond" to being. This exercise of existential actuality is grasped by us on the model of our intentional acts of knowing and loving (at least, these are the paradigm cases as David Burrell has indicated)[7] wherein the act of knowing precedes ontologically the positing of the known formally as known and the act of loving precedes the positing of the loved one precisely as the beloved. In other words, *esse* enjoys ontological priority over the essences it makes to be actual, as act retains priority over potency. Thus, being is to the essences that surge within it, thereby determining and delimiting it, as *cognoscere* is to the *cognitum*. As *esse* or existence, it is exercised act which cannot be thought of apart from that which it actualizes, namely essence — yet the two are really distinct so that *esse* constitutes a distinct order of intelligibility. Existing is then an act exercised by existents, which corresponds to knowing as an act exercised by knowers. This is to say that, in knowing, the intellect lives in its own intentional order, the being which the known has in its own order outside consciousness.

As to how the intellect becomes aware of this analogical character to being, i.e., this relative or proportional unity of all realities at the heart of a more obvious plurality, there is a spectrum of opinions. Most influential among these at the present moment perhaps is that of the transcendental Thomists who, viewing the knowing subject as embodied spirit, endow it *a priori* with the capacity of "performing being," in virtue of a nonobjective, preconceptual pre-grasp (*Vorgriff*) of being itself as the infinite horizon of its knowing.[8] The knowing of categorical objects (a realm not unlike Bohm's explicate world) is thus a thematization of this nonthematic oneness with being as such. However, the *a priori* element here seems a gratuitous assumption (one made by way of a transcendental method which is seeking the ontological pre-conditions for the phenomenon of knowing and loving). Without sacrificing the dynamism of intellect on which this theory rests, a more objective and *a posteriori* explanation offers itself as an alternative.

In this second theory, the human intellect grasps, at the very dawning of consciousness, the analogical character of being, i.e., the relative or proportional unity of all realities at the heart of a more obvious plurality, in an intuitional act that is at once conceptual and judgmental. The conceptual element is a laying hold of the intelligibilities offered by the various natures known; that action vis-à-vis the real order is spontaneously consummated by the judgmental element that lives out the quite distinct mode of intelligibility which is the existential actuality of those natures. In this manner, judgment attains to *esse* or existence as act, on which basis it surmises the relational oneness of what is existentially plural.

What is *explicitly* grasped in this judgmental intuition is being in one or another of its various finite modes, that is, as constricted to essences which limit it to being the actualization of some particular potentiality. Underlying that, however, is an *implicit* intuition of all beings as constituting a whole, a totality. This is due to a dynamism on the part of the intellect's act, one that is not subjective and *a priori*, as in transcendental Thomism, but objective and *a posteriori*. It is constituted by what Aquinas refers to as the *"excessus ad esse,"* meaning thereby the mind's elan beyond essences to the mysterious and analogical intelligibility of existence. It is thus a nonconceptual aspect to intellection which latter is always at the same time conceptual.

The grounds for this awareness of wholeness are that act does not of itself bespeak limitation. This latter is rather a determination on the side of the essence which is rendered actual. Thus, implicit in the intuition of being is a nonconceptual and unthematic awareness of the unity of all finite reality in a common relation of dependence upon a source which is *purely* actual, i.e., unconstricted by any essence distinct from act that would delimit it to its own potencies for existence. Thus, the pure act of being (*Ipsum Esse Subsistens*) does not participate in anything beyond itself because beyond it lies nothing in which to participate. At the same time, it itself is the source and ground of all finite entities upon which it bestows a limited share of its actuality. All realities are one, then, in virtue of differing proportions to this one creative ground upon which they are dependent for their very being.

This notion of an intuition of being can appeal to the authority of Aquinas on three counts. First is his contention that the first note of intelligibility of which the mind is aware is that of being. He means by this that whatever is known is known first and foremost under the formality of being, i.e., we know that something is before knowing what sort of thing it is. The import of this is that apprehension and judgment coexist, each enjoying a priority over the other in distinct orders, in such wise as to issue in an implicit intuition of being. The judgment by intellect that "this thing exists" (which thing is already encountered in sensation and represented in the phantasm of sense) spontaneously gives rise to the primordial concept of being, to a grasp of finite being in all its analogicity as "that which is." This amounts to an implicit intuition of the act of being in all its analogates, not as a mere empirical given, but as the impact of the beingness of things bestowing itself upon us in that "super-intelligibility" which is something more than the intelligibility proper to the whole order of essences.[9]

Further support is provided in recalling with Aquinas and others that the faculty of intellection is itself spiritual. But intuition is the co-natural mode of knowing for spirit. This represents the express teaching of Aquinas on the manner of knowing proper to separate substances known as angels.[10] The human intellect is, of course, a faculty of embodied spirit proportioned to know the single material entity. But even as embodied it does not cease to be spirit, and conceivably this intuition at the origin of consciousness is a vestige of that spirituality. Thus, it might fittingly be called "abstractive intuition."

A third distinct argument derives from Thomas's noting explicitly that first principles are known "simpliciter" and "naturaliter," prior to all rational exploration.[11]

This encounter with being as at once plural and yet one in virtue of its participation in the absolute, is something spontaneous and lived by the intellect; only later, reflexively, is it articulated into the concepts of metaphysical science. What it amounts to, then, is a pregrasp (or *Vorgriff*) but one that arises *a posteriori* rather than *a priori*, bespeaking a dynamism of intellect that is objective and fully cognitive rather than subjective and volitional.

The creative ground in virtue of which all reality is one, is eventually recognized in metaphysical reflection as the prime analogue in a causal analogy of intrinsic proportion. Such analogy excludes any common *logos* between God and creature. It excludes, in short, what Aquinas calls "analogy of many to one," allowing only for a "analogy of one to one."[12] The latter means that the concept involved embraces only created perfections (running a spectrum of modes in which the finite perfection is realized) which are not themselves projected onto God, but only serve as points of departure from which God can be designated but never represented. Nonetheless, it is the very substance of God that is designated in this use of analogy, and positively so, even if always in a merely relational and inadequate way. One relevant factor to be drawn from all this is that it can serve as a safeguard against "conceptualism." Thus, the importation of models from science such as physics (which are understood to be provisional and heuristic in kind) into theology, functions there in aid of *conceptual* clarification. The theologian, however, must eventually surmount the conceptual level (with all of its differences) by way of an openness to the act of existence; it is existence with all of its objectivity that lays fast hold upon us in our act of judgment, and ultimately the existence of God.

All of this amounts to a philosophical account of creation, a doctrine open in principle to rational discourse but seemingly a discourse that is only entered upon *de facto* by believers. "People do not think themselves into belief in God"; thus natural theology is not an enquiry that seeks to reach faith but one which "investigates it once it is there, seeing whether it is coherent and true."[13] It is in this sense that the ways (*viae*) of the rational mind to God, however legitimate and indispensable, are not "proofs" properly speaking, nor demonstrations in the strict Aristotelian sense, but objectifications of a prior lived dynamism toward the source of being.

At any rate, Christian thought has always viewed creation as a causality *ex nihilo*. It is not *ab Deo* as some sort of emanation from divinity with corresponding undertones of pantheism; nor is it *in Deo* in the sense that what comes into being is consubstantial with divinity as is the case in the trinitarian processions. There is, however, another sense in which the created world can be said to be "in God" in that the omnipresence of God means less that he is in all things and places than that they are all contained in him. To speak in this way is to understand "outside of God" as the realm of pure nothingness, the void which lacks all semblance of reality and can be thought of only in a negating act. Rather, God, as it were, makes room within himself in a self-emptying act, in a divine *kenosis*, wherein the creature can come to be. What creation *ex nihilo* is meant to convey is that the origin of the creature is not by way of an act of self-realization on God's part whereby he arrives at the fullness of his divinity, but an occurrence in which God, in uncreated freedom and in an act of altruistic love (New Testament *agape*), gives existence to the creature as its (the creature's) own autonomous existence.

What follows from this is that the divine does not enter into the definition of, for example, the human formally as human, but it does enter necessarily into the definition of the human as creaturely — which is not to deny that the *humanum* is not fully known apart from an awareness of its creatureliness. In fact creatureliness is nothing more than this relation of dependence of the creature upon the creator for both its coming into being and its continuance in being. The creative act consists in something of the actuality of God coming to be in the created effect. The creature participates in (from *partem capere;* to take some formality in a partial and so diminished way) the pure actuality of the Transcendent. Thus, creation, taken actively, does not imply any alteration or change in the divine cause; it suffices that there be a transition from potency to act in the effect.

The Problem of Created Freedom

Preeminent among the challenges to theistic thought is the objection that to postulate the existence of God is to compromise human autonomy and freedom. Christian thought, almost without exception, however, has maintained that God acts in every act of each creature, including the free act of the creature made in the image of God and so endowed with freedom. God acts in the free acts of men and women and not, as it were, alongside of them. At the same time, as possessing its own act of being and freedom, the human creature truly moves itself and determines itself to become the sort of person it does become — since, in Rahner's phrase, freedom radically is not simply the choice of one good in preference to another but ultimately the decision about self.[14] The divine causation in and through finite liberties — something not unlike Bohm's unfolding of the implicate order into the explicate order — is not, however, a determination or pre-determination or finite wills. On the contrary, through its self-determination, the human creature posits itself. It is this that constitutes the historicity of humankind — possibly the major philosophical and theological emphasis of this century — a historicity that is not to be confused with historicism. The apparent contradiction in these two assertions — namely, that God acts in each and every act of our freedom, and that we freely determine ourselves — is reconciled with the recognition that the divine and human agents are not partial causes of one free action but each is a total cause on a different level of causation. The sixteenth-century dispute on grace, with the Jesuit Molina insisting on the primacy of human freedom and the Dominican Báñez on the primacy of the divine motion, were thus the consequence of posing a pseudo-problem. The common mistake in the very beginning was in conceiving the divine and human causalities as in opposition to each other, each competing with the other. A truer starting point would recognize that the more extensive and intensive the divine causality, the closer to God in perfection will the effect be, i.e., the profounder with be its autonomy and freedom. This is confirmed by the trinitarian principle — the more perfectly something proceeds the more it is one with that from which it proceeds[15] — wherein the Son and the Spirit remain one in an identity of nature with the Father from whom they proceed eternally.

All of this then avoids the suggestion that men and women posit themselves in an act of absolute freedom. Human freedom is situated freedom — situated, first, by the parameters of human nature which is a given, and second, by history, i.e., by the weight of the past and the opportunities of the present. These limit obviously the degree to which humankind can anticipate and so determine its open future. In short, human freedom is not rooted in sheer indetermination, even as it remains true that the human person possesses a capacity for determining the course it shall take in pursuing its destiny. As Emil Fackenheim has contended, the issue is not that of a total self-positing as in Fichte's notion of finite freedom, but that of an existential self-choice of a destiny already offered by a saving God; that is to say, what is at issue is the free appropriation for oneself of one's destiny and the means thereto.[16] To put this in more explicitly Christian terms: human history unfolds in dialogue with God, but the ultimate horizon to that history has already been set by what God had done once and for all in Jesus as the Christ, especially in the resurrection wherein the "deadliness of death is overcome" (*Moltmann*). But when and how and under what circumstances that destiny will be achieved remains to be determined in the continuing dialogue with God. In more general terms: because human being is anchored in a prior metaphysics of being, it issues in a genuine history as opposed to mere contingency and meaningless arbitrariness. It is a case of a necessary order of being tethering down a genuinely non-necessary order of history, setting the parameters within which history is made possible and given creative meaning.

In effect, this is to allow for a genuine panentheism wherein the divine is immanent to and active within each and every activity of the world. It is not a panentheism, however, in Hegel's sense of that term wherein the infinite is empty and meaningless apart from realizing itself in and through the finite, so that the dependence between the two is mutual. For Hegel, the possibility of the finite limiting the infinite is overcome by including the former in the latter — with the consequence that Hegel finally locates the true being of things within God. On the contrary, the pure actuality of God means a similar pureness of causality, so that in causing creatively the divine being retains its autonomy, its transcendence of that which it calls into being. Creation, as the coming to be of some share of the divine actuality in the effect, does not necessitate any change or alteration in the divine being itself. Such alteration characterizes, not causality as such, but only finite causality wherein the cause undergoes a transition from being able to cause to actually exercising such causality, a transition alien to a cause that is already and always the fullness of act. In short, God is operative at the heart of all creaturely activity but without being acted upon by creatures in return in such wise as to gain something previously lacking to him.

This is the basis of Aquinas's generally misunderstood teaching that the creature is really related to God, whereas God's relation to the creature is a relation of reason only.[17] This is only intended to preclude any relation accruing to God accidentally as an increment (or diminution) of his being which would then have to be conceived of as lacking something of the perfection of being to begin with. It is not meant to imply that God does *not actually* create, know, love, redeem the world, and the like. The resulting relationship is not a mere extrinsic denomination on the part of human knowers. It is designated a relation of reason to convey that the fundament for it is something intrinsically intelligible within God, namely an actual exercise of causality on God's part vis-à-vis the creature. Indeed, in the instance of creation, the divine causality precedes any possession of existence by the creature, and so creaturely causality of any sort.[18] Failure to note this, however, lends substance to W. Norris Clarke's suggestion that ambiguity as to the meaning of "real" in contemporary thought warrants jettisoning the phrase "relation of reason" in this discussion.[19]

Neither is the panentheism suggested here to be confused with that advocated by process theology, in which system God's consequent nature, which alone in God is actual, is constituted by his prehending the data provided by the world. So, with Whitehead, it is equally true to say that the world creates God as to say that God creates the world (in supplying initial aims for actual entities).[20] Here, God's transcendence is merely relative in kind, consisting of his envisagement of an infinite number of possibilities. Indeed, God and actual entities of the world are seemly coagents subordinate to the pure process transpiring between them called creativity. For Whitehead and many of his followers, it is creativity, not God, that is the ultimate category, a creativity which is not itself conceived as in any sense actual. It should be noted, however, that some commentators on Whitehead — notably Lewis S. Ford and Langdon Gilkey — have attempted to overcome this impasse by locating creativity within God rather than as something impersonal that enjoys ontological priority over God.[21]

In a genuinely Christian panentheism, the very transcendence of God — on which grounds our awareness of him is more an unknowing than a knowing, but a positive gain for us in that we know him to be unknowable — is itself the ground of the divine immanence in everything that partakes of being. The total otherness of God explains that he is not present and operative in any one place but simultaneously in all places giving them their very powers of location; he is not present to any one order of being but to everything whatsoever that participates in being; his active presence is not an impediment to finite freedom in contestation with it but is the root, the very creative ground of created freedom and its exercise. Contrary to Sartre then the existence of God, far from being an impediment to freedom, is its indispensable condition.

Theological Wholeness:
Unity with a Self-Communicating God

Bohm's theory of the implicate world, however, invites us to a more explicitly theological reflection. This occasions a shift in focus from nature to history, from being in its necessary structures to events in their historical contingency, and (as regards method), from science to narration. Nonetheless, this is not meant to imply the misleading dichotomy that history is the proper domain of the theologian while the exploration of the scientist and the philosopher are restricted to the ahistorical domain of nature and being. But it is meant to suggest that history, not nature, offers the most comprehensive manner of conceiving the totality of what is real — and that revelation from God, in the full sense of the term, occurs within history, and even as history. Thus justice cannot be done to the level of intelligibility and meaning proper to the "event" by treating it simply as another kind of thing, as reducible to the entities of nature in their metaphysical oneness of being. It does imply that historical events, as the products of human freedom, do possess a meaning specifically their own, that they are realities of people as those who freely determine their own future.

The problem now, however, is that history is still continuing; it remains in its very contingency, still unfinished and open to the future. Of itself, then, history lacks totality and cannot be grasped as one and whole. The Christian believer supplies this on the basis of promises concretized in what God has already done in Jesus the Christ, above all in raising him from the dead. But even here, the total meaning of history is not something we already participate in but something we *anticipate* to come. The anticipation, however, is based upon what God has already done historically in Christ — thus, we believe trustingly in the kingdom of God already begun yet still to be consummated. What this can mean then is that "historical particularity does not do away with universality but manifests it."[22]

At any rate, here too, in history, the unity and coherence of all events is granted ontological priority over diversification and fragmentation. But this is not surmised by way of an implicit intuition of finite being as one in its differing relations to a purely actual source. Rather it occurs in virtue of sharing the life of a self-communicating God, something achieved by way of a faith-response to those disclosure experiences in which God is encountered — whether explicitly or implicitly, whether knowingly or unknowingly, in terms of reflexive awareness. What explicit faith can discern here is a unity of all humankind (and, through humanity, of the rest of the universe) in the offer of salvation coming from God. It is a unity that does not precede the creative constitution of things in their derived but autonomous existence, but consummates that natural unfolding of an implicate world into an explicate world. It enjoys ontological priority in that God would not have gifted creatures with intelligence and freedom as natural endowments apart from this intention to consummate the world of nature with a world of grace mediated humanly and so historically. It is this insight which led Tertullian to write, *"anima naturaliter Christiana est."* It offers ground for the claim that Christianity is not one religion among the religions but rather the inbreak of God's kingdom into the world, transcending all religions. It extends to all men and women in that it is a universal summons to all without exception to participate, not in being as such, but in that uncreated being which is proper to God alone. This participation in divine life can never be exercised by the creature as its own autonomous being derived from God, but only as a gratuitous sharing in the innermost divine life which never becomes connatural to the creature. Emphasis upon the universality of this offer of salvation from God draws attention to the fact that the distinction between the natural and supernatural order, however necessary and real a distinction, is nonetheless only an abstract distinction of formalities. In the concrete, no human exists in the natural order solely; everyone is in a state of at least implicitly either accepting or rejecting God's offer of salvation.

This approach of God to the human obviously involves his activity in the world and in history. It is important to note, however, that God remains God even in such activity; his activity remains a transcendent one and so is not to be conceived as "intervention" that is in conflict with the normal course of events. Neither is it is the case that we are simply affected by the divine power acting through these realities of nature and history. Rather, in them, God communicates to us his very self. Various theologians have referred to this as a "mediated immediacy."[23] By this is meant that God relates to us only mediately; his grace (or at least its offer) comes to us, we might say, not vertically but horizontally. But in doing so, he gives us nothing less than his own divine absolute closeness. What he mediates to us is his very immediacy. On our part, we can never encounter the divine directly but only in its mediation by creatures. But in that mediation, God himself can really come near to us. God makes himself immediately present, but only in various forms of mediacy. The immediacy at issue here is one that not only does not exclude mediation but actually constitutes it. The relationship of the creator to the creature, then, does not suffer the restrictions that characterize relationships of creatures to one another. This notion of "mediated immediacy" avoids on the one hand a supernaturalism in which God intervenes in the world, acting in a way that is alien to, if not contrary to, the normal course of events, and on the other hand, a naturalism that misplaces God's immanence in such wise as to divest him of his transcendence and view that immanence anthropomorphically. All of this is only to say that God's grace does not come to us solely within some isolated private sphere of interiority, but from within the whole of reality, including the social and the political, of which we form part.

Also, it is obvious that the unity in question here is a unity formed by a community of persons — in imitation of that unity indigenous to the three divine hypostases: Father, Son and Spirit, who form in consubstantiality the one Godhead. This clues in the Christian, at any rate, to the truth that there is a dynamic interrelational, intersubjective, interpersonal plurality at the very core of the deepest form of unity, and one that is not destructive of that unity. All of this, of course, is acknowledged only in an act of faith. Still and all, it is grounded in human experience. The only alternative to this is a Barthian positivism of revelation which, viewing humankind as basically corrupt, dispenses with all human mediation of God's Word. The experience in question, moreover, is an interpreted experience since it is the experience of a subject existing in history and bringing the whole of his or her pre-understanding to the matter at hand. By this is meant not so much the undergoing of an experience and then the subsequent interpretation of it (though that indeed does happen too) but rather that the interpretation is ingredient in the very experience itself. The pre-understanding peculiar to the Christian, which the latter brings to present experiences, is living tradition; here, the norm above all others, the norm not itself normed (*norma non normata*) is that articulation of God's Word that is the New Testament. Thus, there takes place what Gadamer calls a "fusing of the horizons"[24] in which the horizon of understanding out of which the text originally emerged fuses with the horizon of understanding that arises from present experiences in the existing world which also in their own way are revelatory. This introduces the hermeneutical element into theology whereby its task becomes that of reinterpreting living tradition in the light of present revelatory experiences. Thus is the *ipsa traditio* more important than the *tradita* which mediate it. Accordingly, the theologian is one who, through what the text does say, dialogues with the subject matter in order to hear, in light of present questions and concerns, what the text does not say explicitly. From a world of presently lived encounter a bridge is thrown back to the world behind the text in order to open up the way to a world in front of the text, So to speak, a world of new possibilities for humankind with God in an open future. Each generation of believers, then, must appropriate God's revelation for itself. The Christological concern, for example, is always "Who do *you* say that I am?" (Mark 8:29).

This experiencing, which lies at the heart of our enrichment through God's self-revelatory act, and which comes to us as grace not only in a vertical way (from heaven as it were) but horizontally too (since it is always mediated by creatures), is not (as previously noted) an intuition of the oneness and wholeness of things in the plenitude of being. Indeed, the question can be raised as to whether justice can be done to what occurs by describing it in strictly causal terms, wherein God is conceived as agent and humankind as patient. Even if it be granted that the "laws" of causality operative within the universe do also hold between the universe as a whole and the transcendent (which is not a certitude beyond all questioning), and allowing therefore that divine causality is involved in the production of created grace within the souls of the justified, there remains the mysterious union with God himself brought about by way of such grace. This is a union with the Holy Spirit bestowed upon us as uncreated grace.[25] Here, beyond the explanatory categories of causality, lies the experience of a presence, i.e., of God presencing himself in the order of the intersubjective and the interpersonal — a process suggestive of Heidegger's *aletheia*, i.e., of Being (*Sein*) unconcealing itself through the beings (*die Seienden*) to consciousness structured receptively as *Dasein*. The parallelism is merely a suggestive one since Heidegger's *Sein* is finite and grounded in nothingness (*das Nichts*).

The point is, however, that presence is always presence to another, thus bespeaking a basic relationality between conscious subjects, but not necessarily a causal relation involving dependence in being. A prime example of this (from theology) is the inner trinitarian relations which are real and intrinsic to divinity but not causal in kind. Human agents act causally on one another — for example, in addressing another in speech — but within that causal relationship occurs another phenomenon that is the self-communication of one person to another. This strictly personal self-donation transpires in the intentional sphere of knowing and loving.

The significance of all this is that on this intersubjective level, on the level of personhood as opposed to that of nature, it would appear quite legitimate to speak of relations between God and human persons as reciprocal, to allow that God alters in his freely chosen relationships to a world of free creatures. When the creature in its self-positing freedom changes, as indeed it must for either better or worse, God knows this and so his knowledge changes as regards its content, with the consequence that his love alters too in a tactical way in response to creatures. Since this is not a change in God's subjective acts of knowing and loving, acts identical with God's nature, he undergoes no increment or diminution in that nature, i.e., in the natural or entitative order as distinguished from the intentional. But there is a sense in which God is different, in virtue of having created a world of free beings, than he would be had he chosen not to create at all; he is different for having created this kind of world rather than a radically different kind of world. In short, he is different not absolutely but relationally.

To express this somewhat differently: the existence and freedom of finite beings does not compromise the infinity of God because he is already, in his eminent mode of being, everything that the creature is or can become. He is not acted upon by creatures in the sense of being passively determined by them for he is already the fullness of all determinations in the mode of simplicity. Thus, God is not in the process of becoming something that he was not previously; he does not undergo a transition from potentially having a perfection to actually acquiring it, simply because he is already omniperfect, and "outside" himself are only finite beings whose very beingness is only a deficient sharing in that fullness which he is.

Still, finite creatures endowed with freedom, and so self-determining, do introduce genuine novelty into the world. Vis-à-vis such determinations there do occur alterations in the content of divine knowing and loving. God gathers these into his own experience (if we may so speak) without incorporating them into his nature as new perfections (or imperfections). If this be so, then there is no obstacle to speaking of God as rejoicing in the values achieved by his creatures, and lamenting the disvalues — as long as "rejoicing" and "lamenting" be understood as metaphors. This line of thinking about divinity has been argued for in detail, and cogently so, by W. Norris Clarke who sums up his understanding in these succinct but lucid words:

> God's inner being is *genuinely affected*, not in an ascending or descending way, but in a truly real, personal, conscious, relational way by His relations with us ... (but without) ... moving to a *qualitatively* higher level of inner perfection than God had before.[26]

Clarke's focal distinction is that between the intentional aspect of the divine consciousness and the realm of intrinsic real perfection in God himself. This chapter (more explicitly theological in character) relies rather on the contrast between nature in God conceived as absolute and the Trinity of persons conceived as intrinsic relations. These subsisting relations within the Godhead constitute really distinct hypostases or persons, but are not conceived as divine perfections, i.e., they are not understood as pertaining to the order of essence at all but to the quite distinct order of personhood. The term "person" is here taken not only in its structural or foundational meaning as that which is distinct in a relational way (with the implication that the personal always implies the interpersonal) but also in its conjunctural or specific meaning as a distinct focus or center of consciousness, which in the divine instance means three distinct centers of a numerically single consciousness. The real distinctness at issue here rests solely upon an exercise of relationality (which Aquinas calls notional act as opposed to essential act)[27] which relationality is an eternal dynamism of becoming within the Godhead. But such divine self-communicating is not causal in kind; trinitarian language, in short, transcends the categories of causality. It is possible that the mystery can be further explored in terms of that presencing of Being which Heidegger calls *aletheia* or *Anwesen* (as earlier noted), and in which he sees the overcoming of metaphysics. What is suggested here is rather the indispensability of the metaphysical order, but as grounding and making possible an order of genuine historicity, wherein persons posit themselves in the exercise of radical freedom (i.e., a freedom that is not merely free choice, *liberum arbitrium*, but an ultimate deciding about the self). If this be plausible, then, just as we attribute nature to God on analogy with finite nature, and existence on analogy, with the finite act of "to be," (granting the real identity of the two within God), then why can we not predicate historicity of God on analogy with human historicity? If so, then what would be understood by this latter are the trinitarian processions as an infinite, eternal becoming that cannot not be, and at the same time is what it is in uncreated freedom. Perhaps, in the end, this is only to say that the divine reality exceeds our limited conceptions of necessity and freedom. If the suggestion be a bold one, the motive in offering it lies in the fact that it enables us to allow for a dialectical relationship between the divine persons and finite persons who truly determine themselves and so forge their destiny — yet not apart from God.

All of this need not call God's eternity into question; it need not imply succession within deity but is reconcilable with the simultaneity of all time — past, present, and future — in God. Predetermination by God is something entirely different, and does compromise the genuineness of created freedom, reducing it to the mere lack of coercion or to mere spontaneity. The creature's being is its own even to the extent that it is the co-creator of its own future. God's awareness of this is not strictly a *fore*-knowledge, as if it lay in some mode of duration antecedent to time, or in an infinite, primal temporality embracing all time as one, but in eternity as a standpoint outside of time.

Conclusion

By way of conclusion, it remains to be asked what all this has to do with the theories of Bohm concerning the unity and wholeness of an implicate world. At least this: the Christian philosopher or theologian has no way of integrating such a theory into a world-view that grounds creativity ultimately in matter itself, or in consciousness, or in the universe as a whole. But no such incompatibility appears in a fourth world view which locates creativity in a transcendent source or *arche*. How God mediates being to his cosmos in his continuing creative act remains an open question still to be pursued. The history of initial resistance to theories of evolution on the part of theologians should caution us against closing off possibilities too precipitously. This may well be by way of an intermediate world (Bohm's implicate world) which if not open to empirical investigation can at least be thought of in terms of a theory and model such as Bohm's. Apart from not excluding a Transcendent, any natural, implicate world, whether giving evidence of teleology or not, should not be construed as an obstacle to humankind's shaping of the human historical world, in freedom, yet in dialogue with the living God. Beyond this, the theory of an implicate world represents a challenge to theology to enter into a self-critical conversation with a contemporary horizon of understanding not its own.

For another, it would seem to offer an antidote to the radical decon-struction of metaphysics — in favor of an emphasis upon the givenness of reality as recalcitrant to the manipulation by human knowing of the real.

Again, there may well be merit in its affording to Christianity the chal-lenge of moving beyond a *participation model* (where one appropriates for oneself truth already in possession) to an *anticipation model* (where one looks forward to truth that lies ahead of us), on the basis of what is yet to unfold out of the implicate world.

Most of all, perhaps (in an age wherein belief in God is considered ir-relevant for both thought and life) the theory of an implicate world can justify — or at least contribute to — the postulate that God as an an-tecedently existing ground of discourse can indeed be the foundation of theology, and that theological language about God can indeed be based upon access to the real referent of such language.[28]

SEVEN

Does the World
Make a Difference to God?

If God is indeed the Lord of history so that the human enterprise is somehow his project, and if that project in its genuine historicity and precariousness is contingent and can fail, then what the world is and becomes must of necessity affect God. If such be the case, human beings are no marionettes merely acting out in a kind of "shadow-screen" world what has been predetermined from the very beginning. On the contrary, *in some sense* our choices then seemingly determine God, making him to be the kind of God he now is and will be. But then is God any longer God? Or have we not simply (as Engels sees Hegel doing):

> onto the throne self-consciousness prodded hoping to see the old
> time God ungodded?[1]

Seemingly, the above envisagement means the concept of God must embrace contingency and temporality, qualities heretofore understood as precisely non-divine, as constitutive of the creature in its very creatureliness. Why, then, is this not to call into jeopardy the principle of the infinite qualitative difference?

Theologians in the Catholic tradition have, until recent date, remained largely immune from the urgency of the question. Such is no longer the case; the problematic can no longer be avoided due to the speculations of a large array of thinkers with a common commitment to the categories of process philosophy — thinkers representing philosophically a neo-classical metaphysics and theologically a post-liberal Protestantism.[2] Nonetheless, the essays which have thus far appeared are clearly programmatic in kind, tentative probings toward solutions rather than definitive statements, leaving the question an open one and warranting still another sifting of the problem.[3]

The Solution of Dipolarity

At the very forefront of all contemporary efforts to come to grips with the problem stands Whitehead's principle of a dipolar God. A real duality is introduced within God who is viewed as immutable in a primordial nature and ever-changing in a consequent nature. In the permanency of the former God seeks fluency, in the fluency of the latter he seeks permanence. The primordial nature is conceived as a "mental" pole wherein God "prehends" all values, thereby making such values available to the "living occasions" which constitute this world — here, God is eternal, infinite, but not actual. The consequent nature is conceived as a "physical" pole wherein such values are rendered actual, but dependent upon their prior actualization in the world — here, God is temporal (everlasting), finite, but fully actual. What Whitehead has done, quite simply, is to extrapolate the potency-act principle characteristic of all finite being and project it upon the concept of God, whereby "God is not to be treated as an exception to all metaphysical principles, invoked to save their collapse (but rather as) their chief exemplification."[4] Indeed, God is a "derivative" notion, in the sense that he is demanded to explain genuine novelty in the world. Every actual occasion in the world is a new mode of feeling (physical prehension) for values provided by the past, by its ancestors — but only God's prehension for it of values unavailable out of the past allows for creative advance rather than merely some new transformation of old values. But in the process God is necessarily affected thereby, achieving a higher mode of actualization of those same values in his consequent nature. God is thus that dimension to total reality wherein all achieved values are preserved, values which in the world are mere moments of a pure flux and so constantly perishing.[5] All perfections are rescued from ever perishing and are guaranteed endless advance in God's harmonious synthesizing of the actual perfections of his consequent nature with his prehension of the infinite forms in the primordial nature. Whitehead carries the process one step further; God pours back into the world (in an act Whitehead calls superjective) the actual values now harmoniously synthesized within himself. As an act of his consequent nature such values are not ideal but physical, not mere "lures for feeling" (which the primordial nature offers) but content for actual entities. This, put into a religious context, is God's love for the world, his saving of what he did not create.[6] Still, in the final analysis: "Both [God and World] are in the grip of the ultimate metaphysical ground, the creative advance into novelty. Either of them, God and the World, is the instrument of novelty for the other."[7]

Apart from obvious difficulties in reconciling Whitehead's God both with the creator God of the Judaeo-Christian tradition and with the incarnate God of salvation-history, three brief but critical observations should be made by way of indicating how radical is the departure from classical theism in this suggested alternative to it.

(1) First, the infinity ascribed to God in his primordial nature is reduced to nothing more than pure possibility; it is not an actual infinity at all. Distinguishing mental and physical poles, as Whitehead does, means that the former is unbounded only at the cost of being unreal; its ideal values disappear into a Platonic world and can be realized only as physical and thereby as limited. To declare that God is eternal (primordially) is then no more than to negate of him the limits of temporality; it is to take the concept of time, despoil it of all actuality, then project the remainder upon God. But this is only a spurious infinity; it is non-actual timelessness and not the purely actual embracing in eminent simultaneity of past, present, and future. In Whitehead's world every actual entity includes in itself potency, not as delimiting its actuality but as a perfection — as a referent beyond itself driving the world on to constant novelty. In God this potency is simply inexhaustible; only in this negative sense is he infinite. Divine infinity, then, is not that of pure form but like that of the formal cause of the composite *outside of its matter*, i.e., the form as ideal and so lacking all actuality.[8]

(2) Second, God's love for the world, conceived either ideally as offering lures to feeling or physically as superjecting content for actual entities, is *eros* and not *agape*. The motive for the love in the final analysis is the self-fulfillment of the divine lover. God is at least morally obligated to bring the world forward in that process whereby he of necessity interacts with it. God acts upon the world precisely to derive values from it, values which perdure only in himself. The initiatives of God cannot, in this account, be seen as purely altruistic, benefiting the beloved for the latter's own sake.[9] This is not the understanding of God's love that is grounded in viewing him as creative act.

(3) Third (mentioned here because it will serve to highlight a counterpoint to be made later in this chapter), is the difficulty of giving any genuine meaning to the notion of personhood, either divine or human. Allowing unity of self-identity only to individual occasions which are constantly perishing, Whitehead construes persons as special kinds of societies of such occasions, no more than the continuity in a succession of ordered moments of experience. In their actual existence God and human beings are actual entities rather than persons.[10] The latter notion obviously cannot express any sort of perduring substantial self-identity. But neither, on the other hand, does it allow for any genuine existential self-constituting. While each actual entity does subjectively determine itself (including, in Whitehead's panpsychism, infra-human ones), it does so only to become instantly a mere objective datum for succeeding occasions. Thus self-constitution dissolves in a flux of continual surrender to succeeding occasions in which the original self disappears; the person is lost in a sea of pure process.

At bottom, this would appear to be a result of Whitehead's reduction of love to mere relationality and of the freedom radicated in love to mere contingency. Failing to distinguish between the entitative and intentional orders of being, he sees love as little more than a relation to mere data selected from past perished occasions. True enough, Whitehead does distinguish between physical and mental poles of an actual entity, but even the latter allows only for feeling the attraction of ideals that are totally non-actual; there is no "intending" of the actually real, no commitment to an actual other on which basis the person can constitute itself in perduring self-identity. The relationality here is contingent (in the sense that it need not be as it in fact is) but not genuinely free (in the sense of a perduring self-determination that is entirely from within). Decision, in Whitehead's system, determines what data is to be handed on; it does not determine who the person is to be. An assumption, in what is to follow in this study, will be that personhood is achieved by a self-positing in acts of love arising out of freedom.

Alternate Explanation: A Presupposition

I would like to theorize here that latent in the thought of Thomas Aquinas, but entirely undeveloped there, is the discernment of a radical distinction within the concept and the reality of being. The explicit basis for this is Aquinas's clear distinction between the entitative and the intentional orders, which mirrors the difference between viewing reality in cosmological terms or in anthropocentric ones.[11] In the human being who is part of the cosmos and yet gifted with the capacity of transcending it, these two orders coalesce, remaining inseparable but distinct; in God the two merge into real identity, distinguishable only conceptually. To entertain this is to suggest that there is some faint premonition within the *theological* corpus of Aquinas of what surely has been the major development in the history of Western thought, the so-called Copernican Revolution, namely, the turn to subjectivity inaugurated with Descartes' "Cogito," transformed into both epistemological and metaphysical theory by Kant, and carried into Idealism by Fichte, Hegel, and more contemporaneously, Hüsserl. This, of course, is discernible only in the light of what has in fact happened in the realm of speculative thought subsequent to Aquinas, but if one is willing to grant at least some unity in Western man's continuing endeavor to think being, then it becomes more plausible that some clue as to what was to come appears in the thought of a metaphysician as original as Aquinas. Perhaps the richest and most explicit exploitation of the distinction at issue here is to be found in Heidegger's "ontological difference," namely, his distinguishing within *Dasein* of the existenziell and the existenzial dimensions, or of the ontic and ontological orders.[12] Here, the human person as finite transcendence is first of all a being among beings, albeit a privileged one. Yet within that ontic structure, and inseparable from it, is a distinct *a priori* structure whereby human consciousness is open to the Being (*Sein*) structure within the beings (*die Seienden*), is itself the place (*Da*) of that "lighting-up" process which is the coming to pass of the event of Being (*Sein*), and so becomes the locus of meaning.

Aquinas remotely parallels this in his understanding that meaning is a phenomenon that occurs only within the domain of intentionality, wherein human persons transcend the beingness that they share with infra-human realities. The theological uses of this distinction were occasioned for him by the felt tensions between the intelligibility inherent within Aristotelian metaphysics and a quite distinct intelligibility experienced in the faith-response to Christian revelation, which latter did not entirely yield to the expressive power within the conceptual categories of the former. There came a point at which their "carrying power" was not quite adequate to the mystery, to what was in the end a personal encounter with a living tri-personal God. More specifically, the distinction is at work within the context of his theology of God, most fully developed in the *prima pars* of the *Summa Theologiae*. Noteworthy here is the transition from reflecting upon the unity of God's *nature* (qq. 3–26) to reflection upon his *threeness of personality*. (qq. 27–43) In working out his doctrine of the Trinity he in fact moves to a new level of reality where the notion of personhood is allowed to come center stage, a notion distinct from essence-existence and bespeaking pure relationality (*"esse ad"*) to the personally other as its correlate. True enough, when a divine person is conceived as a (subsisting) relation, both aspects of the concept "relation" have to be preserved, namely, *esse in* and *esse ad*, but the former designates identity with the divine essence whereas the specific character of relation resides in the *esse ad*, the sheer reference to the other. On this assumption a person existing in isolation, i.e., without other persons, becomes, both within divinity and humanity, meaningless.

God as One Immutable Nature

Any comparison of divine nature (conceived with Aquinas as the sheer unreceived act of being) to *natures* of the world issues in the necessary conclusion that the relation of the former to the latter cannot be real in God and so is achieved only as a consideration of the mind.[13] There are two distinct kinds of relation possible here, and Aquinas is clear that neither may be affirmed as real on God's part. The ultimate reason in both cases is simply that the ontological fundament of such relationality is the potency-act structure indigenous to finite reality and totally excluded from divinity.

Transcendental Relation

The first instance of such relation derives from a certain radical relativity on which basis the be-ingness of some entities is *essentially* incomplete and cannot be fully grasped save in reference to something else toward which they stand in necessary and dependent relationship, e.g., matter to form, body to soul, faculty to formal object, etc. Here the ground of the relationship is not any mutual interacting of realities upon one another but is the very reality itself as essentially relative to some other. Since this ranges over all the categories, such relations are called "transcendental."[14] The inappropriateness of incorporating them within God is that this would allow: that God is inconceivable apart from the world; that he is ontically dependent upon something other than himself; that the creative act is not free; that the creature no longer is fully contingent in existing. In short, it would be to subordinate God to a "whole" prior to and more ultimate than himself. This, seemingly, is exactly what the thought of Whitehead leads to — a subordination of God to pure creativity as a larger process involving himself and lesser beings of the world.

Predicamental Relation

More exactly to the point here, however, is an entirely distinct category of relations — those grounded in God's causing, knowing, and loving, of the world, granting that such a world is not a necessary correlate to God but something really summoned into existence by pure creative act.[15] On such an assumption God could not fail to be related to the world, nor could the relationship be reduced to an accidental self-relating by God; rather it must be essential to God (as creator), resulting in a presence to the creature of his very substance and not merely of his activities. But the concepts of causality, knowledge, and love here (in Aquinas's Christian adaptation of Aristotelian metaphysics) are entirely *analogical*, expressing that such activity in God is pure actuality. It stands transcendent to a finite universe wherein activity is a transition from potency to actuality; God's acting is not mutation or change. The ensuing relations then, grounded upon such activity, cannot be *real*, for "real" in this sense would bespeak some alteration intrinsic to God's being, some increment (or diminution) of his own reality. If God is the pure act of being, he is already all that can be. For him to become in his nature something that he already is not, is to render him patient of an alien causality, thus homogeneous with the finite and the creaturely; no longer creator and thus no longer God. Denying the reality of the relations in question is then indispensable to preserving God's genuine transcendence, to understanding him as answering to what the Greek Fathers called *"agenetos."* Relation, as here used, is one of Aristotle's categories of *finite*, being, i.e., predicamental relation, and

St. Thomas means no more than that such a categorical concept must be denied of God. Essentially taken, in its own specific character, relation expresses only "reference to" some other; to be real, however, that essence requires an act of existing, and this is its accidental inherence in the entity so related.[16] The *"esse ad,"* if abstracted from the *"esse in,"* bespeaks no imperfection and so can be said of God (as happens in the trinitarian relations), but then one is no longer speaking of predicamental relation, and the realness of the relations has to be sought elsewhere.

None of this, however, implies that God does not *really* cause, know, and love the world. It is only to say that causing (as something of the ontic or entitative order) and knowing and loving (as something of the intentional order) can be conceived of as in a pure state wherein the agent acquires no newness of being thereby. It affords some clarity, nonetheless, to recognize that the case is somewhat different in the two orders.

Pure Causality

For God to become a cause is quite simply for an effect to begin to be; the latter alone is the beneficiary in the altruistic bestowal upon it of being. The realness of the transaction lies entirely on the side of the effect, serving as the basis for extrinsically denominating God as really causing. Thus for God to really cause is for the effect to really come to be. But this implies no transformation *intrinsic* to God; *extrinsically*, however, he can be designated differently than before, namely, as cause.

Knowing and Loving

Still, somehow or other God with a creation and God without it are not entirely the same thing, and it appears overly facile to dismiss this as exclusively on the side of the creature. There remains the possibility of intrinsic difference in God's knowing and loving; difference which need not bespeak any transmutation of his being. No entitative transition from not-knowing to knowing or from not-loving to loving is implied. But God does freely determine himself to know and love this actual world rather than any of the other infinite number of possible worlds. Out of the multitude of divine ideas known by a *scientia simplicis intelligentiae* as possible, one is in fact known by a *scientia visionis* as actual;[17] moreover, this latter involves the "specifying" of an act of divine love which is not the case in God's knowledge of possibles. Ultimately, God is choosing, in unqualified freedom, to so specify himself. But the point is that there occurs a determination within God as knowing and loving, on which basis he is other, relatively speaking, than he would be had he determined himself in some other way.

True enough, the divine knowing and loving constitute in real identity the divine nature and as such do not found real *predicamental* relations to the world. But considering the intentional order formally as such, wherein God constitutes or posits himself as the kind of knower and lover he is fact is, an entirely different concept of relation comes into view — one whose basis is not extrinsic to God but intrinsic.

God as Three Subsisting Inter-Relations

In the tract on the Trinity, thinking upon natures is surmounted by thinking upon persons which latter within God are related one to another really and mutually, without any causal dependency whatsoever, so that in fact a divine person is formally that very relationality itself as subsisting. This involves no illogical compromise of the divine simplicity whatsoever because the relationships are nowise those of *natures*. There is no abandonment of the basic understanding of being (as *ens*) when Thomas moves into the discussion of the Trinity — there remains in God but one nature which is itself one act of existing, really identical with each and with all three of the persons of the Trinity. But there is the conceptual rise to another realm of reality, to that of pure "relation" as mere subsisting *"esse ad"* — which is not then Aristotle's category of relation as either an accident of a nature or a nature itself considered relationally. Reality here, if compared to the divine essence, *is* that essence in total identity, but of itself it is pure reference to its correlates and in its own formal concept simply does not bespeak any comparison to essence at all. The Father in God is not a relation to his own divinity but a relation to the one who is his Son and to the one who is their Spirit. This explains the difficulty experienced by the Scholastics in allowing that the subsistent relations in God and all that pertains to the Trinity could be considered, in a strict and formal sense of the word, as *perfections* of God.[18]

Within God it is the intentional order of knowing and loving that grounds the real distinctions constituting the Trinity of persons. Such real distinction is entirely relational, and the question under exploration here is whether or not such relation might not be extended analogously to explain the rapport of a divine persons to human persons. The implication of this will be the possibility of allowing God as tri-personal to be really and intrinsically related to human beings as forming a community of persons, without involving any immutation of his nature.

Knowing and loving in God are eruptions within being whereby it is self-manifestive and self-unitive. But the Trinity cannot be adequately understood as the mere inner-relatedness within a nature or of a nature. This is a way of thinking with which Augustine struggles in his *De trinitate*; it led Pseudo-Dionysius in an inverse approach to overstress the distinctions of the Persons, making them more than relational, in his *De divinis nominibus*.[19] What enables Thomas to avoid such an impasse is his key

concept of "notional act." Unlike Durandus and Suarez who view the trinitarian processions as emanations of nature, Thomas looks upon them as
genuine *"actiones."*[20] As such, they are acts: (1) *of persons* (as *principia
quod*), (2) which are intentional in kind, i.e., tending beyond themselves,
(3) and tending to what is other than the intending principle, but (4) not
other in essence, only in pure relationality. As "notional," such activity
both constitutes and makes known the "principles" (originating and orig-
inated) which are revealed as pure relations (mere *esse ad*), which while
subsistent (*esse in*) are yet distinctly subsistent, thus answering to the concept of "person." The underlying explanation is that knowing and loving
constitute *personal* dynamisms that ontologically demand the personally
"other." This is clearer in the case of love bespeaking as it does a drive
toward *union:* less clear in the case of knowledge which terminates rather
in intentional *unity.* But if one averts here to the necessary order between
them, to the character of knowledge (as only one dimension to spirit) as
grounding and making possible love, then knowledge itself demands the
really other, not as known (where the distinction could be merely logical)
but as utterance or as word.[21]

At this point, it becomes possible to speak of the three subsistent relations in God as three distinct inter-subjectivities. This, seemingly, offers
richer possibilities than Rahner's view of the persons in God as "three
distinct modes of divine existing."[22] Obviously however, it cannot be understood ontically, in terms of the divine essence-existence but only, ontologically in terms of the self-determination radicated in divine knowing and
loving. This transition in thought categories must be made since one cannot mean here distinct *psychological* subjects, as if the Trinity implied three
distinct centers of consciousness in God.[23] All that can be said here is that,
for example, the Son is another one (not another entity) distinct from the
Father only in terms of pure relationality; he is everything the Father is in
exact identity except Fatherhood, and that is the Father's pure relationality
to his Son. The person then lies outside of the area of definability (thus the
use of proper names for human persons) and is identifiable in terms of his
or her determining relationship to others and their determining relationship to him or her. Clearly, this is to take personhood in its most formal
sense and so to abstract from the consideration that human personality
also renders the common nature to exist in an individualized way (due to
that nature's materiality).

The category of subjectivity is appealed to here on the grounds that
selfhood is self-positing and self-creative precisely in its free relating of
self to others. Ultimately this rests upon certain creative spontaneity of
freedom; differently, however, in God and in human persons. In God, the
categories of necessity and freedom are only analogous to their incidence
on the finite world. In the former each divine person knows and loves
the other two by a knowing and loving that is infinite, completely neces-

sary, and identical for all of them. Thus the personal distinctness, while grounded on knowing and loving, must be grasped formally in terms of a self-communication within those immanent activities whereby, for example, the Father "makes himself" to be Father by the giving of all that he is to the Son, save his very fatherhood, which is what he constitutes himself to be personally in virtue of his generative act. The "eruptions" within Being as pure act whereby it is self-manifestive (as *Logos*) and self-unitive (as *Pneuma*) are then on this showing: (1) *necessary*, both in the sense that they could not not be, and in the sense that the terms can only be respectively *Logos* and *Pneuma;* and yet at the same time, (2) *free,* without thereby being contingent, in the sense that nature in God, while never under impulsion from without, is not mere spontaneity either but is always conscious and willed activity. The Father wills to generate the Son whom he could not not generate. Such generation is within God a real self-relating, and as radicated in divine love it is, in its, unexactedness, self-gift. Each divine person "posits" the others as over and against himself and thereby posits himself in his hypostatic identity. What all of this bases itself upon is the understanding that the Christian revelation of the value of freedom as radically constituting personhood enables it to function as a category that surmounts the Greek dichotomizing of reality into contingency and necessity.

The Relationality of Divine and Human Persons

If one grants that the creature is necessarily a similitude of God, though only analogically so (at the same time denying the inverse of this), then seemingly personhood in the finite realm is also definable in relational terms. The human "persona" is then a distinct and unique relationality within the commonness of human nature. Obviously, such a relation is not itself subsistent but rather renders an individualized nature to subsist. The actual exercise of personality is thus always causal, i.e., operative only in and through the nature. But such psychological activity is in fact the embodiment of a prior metaphysical uniqueness reducible to pure relationality. To exist humanly then is to be outside nothing and outside one's causes as a particular kind of reality (namely, nature), and at the same time (if the nature be capable of intentionality and thus of personhood) to be a relationally distinct instance of that nature. This relational distinctness is first of all ontic but over and above this is ontological. That is to say, it is radically the uniqueness of an individual existent human nature, capable of knowledge and love, but beyond this it is a uniqueness constituted by the actual exercise of consciousness consummating itself in free decision on which basis the self makes itself to be,the inimitable self it is. On this ontological level, rooted in the order of intentionality formally considered, persons are self-positing and self-creative. They make themselves to be who (not "what") they are *relationally to others*.

When God creates, then, he ultimately brings into existence some*one* capable of dialogic relationship to himself, namely, finite persons who, gifted with transcendence whereby they do in fact surmount their involvement in the world as cosmos, are called to inter-subjective, inter-personal relationships with the divine persons. Such relationships however, radicated in freedom, are self-determining and self-defining. This allows one to say that *in this sense* God is determined by the community of human persons. That is, his willing to enter into relationships with human beings, who as persons determine themselves to be the kind of persons they are vis-à-vis God, is on his part a willingness to be determined *on this ontological level of freedom and personhood*, without any corresponding mutation or determination *on the level of nature*. The relationality here is *real* in a mutual sense, though clearly the reality in question is of another order than that founded upon Aristotle's category of relation as the accidental alteration of a substance.

The import of all this is that creation is a prolongation to the realm of matter, to the domain of space and time, of the inner-trinitarian processions. God's creative act is ultimately the calling into being of finite "others" who are further called (though only in a gratuitous consummation of nature by grace) to inter-subjectivity with the uncreated persons of the Godhead. He causes to exist a universe at whose apex stand human persons summoned to appropriate their nature in such fashion as to constitute themselves in freedom as "who" they are, both before other human beings and before God. All the activities of human nature, including the free activities, originate with God as pre-determining, first cause. But, at the core of this, is a self-positing that is not activity but the precondition to activity as free. What is involved here is saying that the human person is not of itself active but always through the mediacy of its nature; the person is thus the "term" of its nature, but it is *in its pure relationality* something else besides. This means that God enters into *real* relationship with human persons as so self-constituting, without any causal dependency on the part of the divine nature being thereby asserted. Still, these relationships do "determine" God (though only because he has so willed to be determined by creating finite persons in the first place) in the sense that such relationality is in part defined by the "other" to which it relates.

This is most clear in the incarnation where God is now not merely the Lord of history (as was YHWH in the Old Testament) but enters himself (not as nature but as person) into history. There he unveils himself and offers himself to humankind as the kind of God he chooses to be toward us, i.e., as one who waits upon our free return gift of self. Thus God's free entrance into history means in a genuine sense his submission to that history (without any abandonment of the prerogatives of his uncreated nature). What human beings do then, their history, does make a difference to God as dialogic partner with them. In terms of God's total otherness to the world this demands allowing that his omnipotence and sovereign freedom are such that he can will to subject himself to conditions of finiteness and temporality without any sacrifice of his transcendence in the domain of nature and causality.

EIGHT

In What Sense Is God Infinite?
A Thomistic Perspective

Process theology shares with Thomism the endeavor to use the full resources of reason in seeking to clarify the being of God, a project that brings both into the domain of metaphysics. But there is a quite distinct metaphysics pursued in one and in the other, with the consequence that the one God who is sought has differing identities in each. The twentieth-century work of Whitehead and the thirteenth-century work of Aquinas represent massive refinements of, respectively, Plato's many gods subordinate to the forms and Aristotle's one god as "thought thinking thought," but the two continue to represent distinct lines of historical development. Whiteheadians, having secured God's involvement with the world on the basis of his dipolar nature, continue to address the problem of how such a God can be infinite in other than a relative sense. Contemporary Thomists, preferring to safeguard the "infinite qualitative difference," affirm God's infinity in absolute terms which preclude all finitude, but are still striving to make intelligible how there can be any genuine concern on God's part for a finite order toward which he bears no ontic receptivity.

Lewis S. Ford addresses the problem seriously in reading Whitehead's descriptive definition of God as "the nontemporal entity"[1] to mean that God is actually infinite in the sense that his "nontemporal completeness must include an actual infinity of possibilities." God is infinite, and actually so, in his envisagement of the entire range of *pure* possibilities that excludes only "the self-contradictory notion of infinite determinateness." The envisagement of *real* possibilities, by contrast, would allow to God only a potential infinity. Yet what is here denied appears to be precisely what the thought of Aquinas ascribes to God as the pure act of "to be." The categories of explanation, at any rate, are mutually exclusive; seemingly we are left with a genuine *aporia*. Is Ford's explanation a radical alternative to that of Aquinas? Or is it an attempt to address something left unsaid in the thought of the latter? Are there any prospects here for something like

120

Heidegger's *Kehre*, i.e., a development within thought itself that represents a change in direction, yet one latent in the movement of earlier thought? The question remains — and it can best be served at this point by a continued exploration of the virtualities inherent in each thought system. What follows, then, is less a rebuttal or repudiation of Ford's illuminating endeavor than an engagement in the dialectic which the question itself urges upon intelligence.

The Denial of "Concrete" Infinity

The dipolar God of process theism is at once finite and infinite, the supreme instance of both categories. He is finite insofar as his actuality is always such in some determinate way — in fidelity to Whitehead's principle: "all actuation is finite, as the exclusion of alternative possibility."[2] But is it logically impossible to ascribe to God an infinity that is at once actual and determinate? This is surely so, as long as one remains in the realm of *essential* determination (whether the essence be viewed specifically or individually does not matter at this point). To be an oak tree is precisely not to be an elm tree; to be this oak tree is exactly not to be that other oak tree. But this is precisely the kind of determinateness that Aquinas refuses to God in calling him the pure actuality of be-ing (the hyphenated form serving to draw attention to the participial character of the term). God is not an essence having being (existence) and so trimming the latter to the modal determination and limitation of itself, thereby excluding all other essential determinations. Rather, what answers to essence in his case is in fact the sheer act of "to be" (*esse*).[3] The Godhead then, in Thomas's thought, is not a being (*ens*), nor the sum total of what all the beings are or could possibly be (*esse commune*); God is rather *"supra ens"* and located "beyond substance."[4] Neither is divinity "being itself" (as in Tillich's phrase) which is the abstract contentless ground of the beings, a symbolizing of the unknown that lies beyond being; God is rather being in the sense of subsisting actuality (*Ipsum Esse Subsistens*). "To be" (*esse*), as such, is not essence but act. It is the mysterious dynamism at the heart of things that explains why there are beings rather than no beings at all. As "act" it bespeaks of itself only perfection, but act which can submit to limitation when, in the case of creatures, it functions as the act of essence. What comes to be in the latter instance is obviously not subsistent but sustained in the exercise of its "to be" by God as subsistent being. Clearly at issue here is the real distinction of essence (as form or content) and *esse* (as actuality or existence) in the finite realm. The affirmation of God as transcending all such distinction — as precisely an exception to the metaphysical principle rather than (as Whitehead prefers) its prime instantiation — is not an admission that God's being is contentless, however, but, on the contrary, the ascription to him of the very plenitude of all content.[5]

He is this actual plenitude nonetheless in a way that remains unknown and unknowable, i.e., though *affirmed* by way of concepts and from a perspective provided by human concepts, he is not properly *represented* in any concept.[6] To admit there could be a concept of God is to admit that his essence is something other than the act of being (esse). Precisely because our judgments necessarily manifest a subject-predicate structure they cannot properly grasp a God whose being transcends what is isomorphic to that structure, namely the essence-existence distinction. Thus, God is what he is in a way that cannot be properly grasped in a concept because the latter expresses only a mode of being. This is not to deny, however, that after the affirmation of God in judgment the mind can present God to itself in an act of eidetic visualization. David Burrell is correct in noting that "we must say — without knowing what we say — that 'God's very nature is to exist.' "[7] God's being lies beyond essence, and indeed beyond existence in the sense of mere givenness or facticity (which is being as the most abstract rather than the most concrete of concepts). *Esse* is rather that actuality immanent within things whereby they are anything at all. Moreover, it is act in a unique and ultimate sense as that which gives actuality to all other acts, so that it is the perfection of all perfections[8] — a notion that Cornelio Fabro tries to convey in his phrase "intensive act." The determinateness of God, far from being exclusive of other determinations, is all-embracing in a unity transcendent to the rich diversity of the finite. All that is excluded is what pertains not to beings as such, but to their diminished or defective states, to being as it suffers privation in its finite instances with such *sequelae* to finitude as, e.g., evil. This is but to say: God is wholly infinite and nowise finite.

By contrast with this there is a marked tendency in thought of Whiteheadian inspiration to conceive being exclusively after the fashion of essence, as expressing specificity, rather than to conceive it as self-identical with existential act. At bottom, this is a refusal of the real distinction that lies at the core of Thomistic insight into finite reality. Whitehead is preserving the potency-act relationship as basic but this he understands concretely more as a form-matter structure than an essence-existence one. Thus, he affirms the dipolar structure of everything, including God: a mental pole that is abstract (in God, the prehending of eternal objects) and a physical pole that is concrete (in God, his partial realization, as an actual entity, of such pure form).[9] On these grounds it is consistent for Whitehead to say that God creates himself[10] something unthinkable in the Thomistic schema, which views existence as the mystery *that* something is at all rather than the distinct phenomenon that it is in this or that determined way. As hopefully will be suggested below, Thomism can at least entertain the logical possibility of saying that God creates himself in this latter sense — the sense, that is, of God's decision determining the kind of God he chooses to be vis-à-vis humankind, but not in the sense of divine decision determining that there be a God rather than only the void.

Here, perhaps, the irreducible difference between Aquinas and Whitehead comes most clearly to the fore, a difference that grounds the opposed conclusions concerning the sense in which God is said to be infinite. For Aquinas, God is the ultimately real to which nothing is prior ontologically or logically. For Whitehead, God and world are correlates; each is an actual entity subordinate to what lies beyond them both, namely creativity as the category of the ultimate.[11] Only actual entities are fully real, but they are such as instantiations of a creativity that is itself devoid of all actuality. In Aquinas's system, entities of the finite world are grounded in something at once fully actual and unlimited (with the consequence that God alone is the source of creation). In Whitehead's differing vision, actual entities are grounded in something that is nowise actual even if unlimited. The former is subsistent *esse;* the latter is pure process called creativity Whitehead's eternal objects explain content but not actuality. The novel concrescence of such content (in the actual occasion's self-creation) explains *essential* actuality, that is, the concretion or individuation of some formal perfection. But *existential* actuality remains unexplained and ungrounded, and this occasions Whitehead's recourse to the category of creativity.[12]

But all of this brings us to the question that process theists cannot easily dispose of: How can anything that lacks all actuality function as the explanatory principle of the fact that there *are* finite instances of actuality (that there are beings rather than nothing)? At this point differences appear logically irreconcilable. The Gods of Thomas and Whitehead are, respectively, infinite determination and finite determination because the former is an inference from the finite beingness of the world while the latter is an extrapolation of the dipolarity that characterizes human conscious activity.

The Affirmation of "Abstract" Infinity

Rejecting a physical infinity, one that is actual in a determinately existential way, Lewis Ford believes the divine infinity can still be saved by viewing God as actually infinite in his envisagement of an infinity of pure possibilities. The possibilities themselves constitute only a potential infinitude. Any actualization of them by way of divine decision remains always finite. The real question then concerns God's actual relationship to such a realm of possibility. Ford suggests that this relationship is one of an envisagement that is at once actual and itself infinite. But how is this position distinguishable from Aquinas's own?

The answer lies in attending to the dipolar structure of the God of process thought. For Aquinas, the existential being and the conscious being of God are one and the same, indistinguishable save mentally. For Whitehead they must be kept in a state of real distinction, for otherwise dipolarity loses all significance. Whereas Hartshorne's clarification of Whitehead makes clear that the mental pole of God's being, his primordial nature, is entirely non-actual, Ford's thought departs markedly from that of Hartshorne in conceiving the primordial nature as fully actual and so infinite.[13] But the actuality and infinity are non-temporal in kind and so unlike the finite actuality of actual occasions that are temporal. This means that God's infinity, far from excluding finitude, in fact demands it. The infinity as restricted to an envisagement of an infinitude of pure possibilities itself needs completion by way of further actuality which is temporal and determinate in a physical sense. But then the actuality of the primordial nature is no longer *pure* act.

If God's envisagement of creative possibilities is unlimited — and here Thomists and process thinkers are in agreement — there can be only two possible explanations of this. Either it is itself grounded in a vision of pure actuality (Aquinas), or it remains groundless and self-explanatory (Ford). But in the latter case what is ultimate is the pure possibility that God envisages, not his envisagement thereof; the former seemingly represents a realm that is abstract and ideal, reducible in the final analysis to mere indefiniteness. What is at issue here is the way in which the metaphysical principle of potency and act is viewed. For the Thomist, all possibility is ultimately grounded in and derived from actuality: what is determines what can be. For the followers of Whitehead metaphysical priority is given to the realm of the possible: the eternal objects offer limitless promise of the world that can be. Thus a universe of process has no terminus other, than an inexhaustible becoming. But because the eternal objects are themselves devoid of all actuality, the limitlessness they found is an ideal and logical one. Transition to actual existence by way of self-positing decision is always finitizing.

It is at this point that Ford's thought has recourse to God's envisaging act, prior to all decision. Such envisagement means that the open realm of possibility becomes ordered and meaningful, yet remaining *pure* possibility — that is, not yet constituting *real* possibility, which Ford maintains can be only potentially infinite. What constitutes the move to real possibility is availability for some actual occasion, on which basis the latter can actualize the possibility in a way proper to itself, without yet having done so. Before making one or several possibilities truly available, by supplying the initial aims for actual occasions, God grasps an infinity of possibilities in the mental pole of his being.

A reservation on this divine envisagement of pure possibility, however, is that it appears to be subjectively finite and only objectively infinite. The vision, as something actual and constitutive of God's mental being, remains the finite vision of a non-actual infinitude. Infinity is petitioned in terms of content, in terms of what God knows rather than his very knowing. The infiniteness of God's primordial knowing, then, is not the contemplation of his own unlimited actuality as this is realizable in an infinite variety of possible worlds. It is rather the intending of an infinitude not grounded in God himself, but constituting a realm unto itself that is (1) non-divine, (2) non-actual, and (3) an eternal, uncreated correlate to God. What is truly possible then may be viewed in two ways: either it is grounded in God's own actuality (Aquinas), or else pure possibility itself must be allotted the status of ultimacy (Ford). It is at this point that the concepts of God as dipolar and as pure act appear mutually exclusive.

Postscript: The Further Question

But this Thomistic alternative to Ford's development of Whitehead leaves a problem of its own unresolved. A God infinite in the Thomistic sense is by necessity immutable, and thereby can relate to history only in a fully determining way, seemingly evacuating the temporal process of all intrinsic meaning and value. Does this not fly in the face of contemporary persons' deepest convictions about and commitment to their own authentic being as temporal? Such convictions seek to rescue the value of an ever fleeing present precisely by viewing human consciousness as ever moving out of history toward the realization of its projects. But an infinitely actual God makes that a mere illusion; whatever emerges in history has at best only a relative novelty with respect to its antecedents, and so finally "there is nothing genuinely new under the sun." A God not susceptible of further determination seemingly means a history determined beforehand in its terminus and its course.

If Thomism is not to be a closed system it must be capable of absorbing, within the perspective of its own wisdom, insights into truth originating elsewhere, but without violating its own inner coherence and character. In this spirit, I should like to draw attention to three possible ways out of the above dilemma. (1) One is to take the path of Karl Rahner and introduce into being as pure act the dialectical dimension borrowed from Hegel. The beingness of God is then processive in kind; it is a dynamism that ever comes to itself by continually going out into the other. This occurs *within* God without any addition or alteration to his own intrinsic being (the inner trinitarian processions), but it is prolongated outside of God who thereby does change, yet not in himself but in the other (the Logos become flesh). But in this latter instance it is God himself who changes in the other and not simply the other in its autonomous being.[14] This ingenious explanation does allow us to take seriously the phenomenon of becoming and so not to dismiss history as the mere reading off of a script

written beforehand. It does, however, carry with it difficulties of its own.
Apart from the fact that being for Aquinas is not dialectical but analogical (something quite different), and is this in its ontic and not merely in
its logical structure, such a theory appears to compromise God's freedom
in choosing to extend himself into a world. The "infinite qualitative difference" is called into question, if not in fact replaced by the dialectic between
the two poles of being. Rahner's grasp of being in these latter categories
appears to have the peculiar consequence of ascribing a quasi infinity to
finite spiritual being.[15] At any rate, the suspicion remains that, in the logic
of Rahner's thought, God's being is affected *in itself*, and his denial of this
is only a verbal one.

(2) W. Norris Clarke has addressed the problem differently, yet still
from within an ambience that is Thomistic. He allows "genuine novelty
... both in the real being God communicates to creatures, *and in the intentional content of His consciousness* determinately knowing and willing them
[which is] not change in His own intrinsic being or perfection"[16] (emphasis
supplied). Here, in effect, the creature does add a determination to God,
rendering him thereby receptive toward humankind, but one limited to the
content of what God knows about the world, and so to the values toward
which his love responds. This is intelligible because such determination
is "only a delimitation (i.e., partial negation) or channeling of the way in
which I allow His active cooperating power to flow through my will."[17]

(3) This, however, suggests a third way of dealing with the question,
one that seeks a more radical ground for the sort of distinction suggested
by Clarke. Heidegger's discovery and exploration of the ontological difference, of the distinction between Being (*Sein*) and beings (*die Seienden*), has
served to draw attention to another realm entirely, one prior to that of essence and existence. If, for Heidegger, this domain is reduced to that of the
pure process whereby things come into being, nothing prohibits its being
reconstrued as the domain proper to freedom — so as to overcome Heidegger's characterization of it as Fate. So recast, it becomes that sphere in
which persons, in a self-determining and self-creative act, posit themselves
as *who* they are and will be. What is posited in such a self-creative process
is not nature but a pure relationality within nature, i.e., between the sub-
jectivities of a nature that allows for freedom. The personal is that which
precisely "lets be" the other in its very otherness, and in this way defines
itself by the other. Its prime instance is that subsisting relationality within
the Godhead which is constitutive of a divine life of inter-communication,
of the divine *koinonia* of Father, Son, and Spirit.

These latter two explanations face a common objection, namely the
real identity in God of existential and intentional being (Clarke), and of
nature and person (an alternative explanation). There is of course such a
real identity (thus, these distinctions stop short of introducing the sort of
dipolarity within the divine nature of which process theists speak) but there

is a formal distinction that enables us to say of one what cannot be said of the other. Knowing and loving represent modes of becoming that do not preclude a permanency or changelessness on another level entirely. Compassion at the suffering of a friend means in one sense that I suffer what he or she does, yet in another sense that I do not; I may die a thousand deaths with him or her without undergoing his or her biological death. In a remotely analogous way Father, Son, and Spirit are one identical God but not thereby identified with each other. The basis for making such a formal distinction is that the reference in one case is made to what is intrinsic to God, and in the other to his extrinsic relationality *ad extra*. This is somewhat different from speaking, as process theists, of a dipolarity within the divine nature itself which seemingly means two intrinsic components to divinity. In their case, the conceptual contrariety between infinity and finitude precludes treating the distinction as merely formal, such as that between attributes not mutually exclusive, e.g., mercy and justice.

The key to such conceptual and linguistic differentiation, in the case of nature and person, lies in the mystery of freedom. Abstractly, freedom is a property of nature, but its exercise is the prerogative of person as the existential instantiation of nature. The person viewed ontologically (as subject of the act of existing) thus determines itself through its nature to be the sort of person it is, viewed psychologically and historically. In the instance of finite natures with limited freedom, this self-determination is by way of personal choice among the various causal influences unavoidably exerted upon its nature. An infinite nature whose freedom is transcendent suffers no such passive influx; here the personal decision occurs in uncreated freedom. And, in the mystery of a love that allows the other to be in its very otherness, that choice is one of willing to be constituted, personally and so relationally, and in this sense to be determined, by other free beings.

So envisaged, what results from this is a creature with a given unalterable nature who yet remains the maker of history, the one who determines who he or she is within the limits prescribed, singly and collectively, by that nature. God then determines what such a creature is summoned to by nature (and by that transfinalization of nature that is grace), but actual attainment thereto is left as something to be won out of history, to be appropriated in modes that remain open to the dialogue between God and human persons.[18] Something of this is exhibited by the cosmos itself on the infra-human level; there evolutionary change occurs within a system that guarantees identity and continuity, and thereby forestalls intelligibility collapsing into mere randomness.[19]

Thus God, remaining transcendent in his immutable nature, chooses in the freedom of personhood to undergo history, and to wait upon humanity's gift of self (or its refusal). When God comes into the world (in the incarnation) it is as person, not as nature; it is humanity that supplies the nature to the Logos.

NINE

Two Gods of Love: Aquinas and Whitehead

The thought systems inaugurated by Aquinas and Whitehead, while differing vastly both philosophically and theologically, intersect at one point at least, where dialogue between them is a definite possibility. This is the intellectual crossroads at which it is possible to discourse about God himself, and not simply human aspirations toward the divine, and to do so on some sort of analogy between God and the world. Other theological systems prefer to take refuge in Jonathan Edwards's warning about the "Western licence of affirmation," and reduce the language of theology to poetic and mythic discourse. Theology cannot dispense with these latter modes of discourse; their evocative and disclosive power renders them religiously indispensable. But neither can it rest content with such language alone, and dispense with all recourse to the conceptual and analogical — not if to believe is spontaneously to seek to understand, and if one allows that religious experience extenuates itself into thought. The attempt to do so rests upon a confusion of conceptual contents, which supply a perspective of limited intelligibility in which one can refer to God, with the uncreated and unknown being of God as he is in himself — as if the *Deus Absconditus* is somehow represented in the concept rather than merely discoursed about *from* it. Obviously, divinity cannot be discoursed about as can the entities of the empirically given world, but neither can theology be faithful to its task if it fails to strive to speak of God in every way available.

This shared assumption, at any rate, delivers to Thomism and to process thought at least three common conclusions: (1) there is a God, apart from whom reality would cease to be intelligible; (2) human action or agency is the analogue for our conception of the deity, who is thus conceived as interacting with the world; and (3) such divine agency is in the final analysis that of love, in which lies our identification of God. However the character of this divine loving agency toward the world differs radically for the followers of Aquinas and those of Whitehead. Seemingly, two op-

128

posed views of the nature of that agency suggest two different senses in which God is said to be a God of love. It is this difference that the present chapter will seek to explore.

A First Presupposition: Some Metaphysical Considerations

The original thought of both Aquinas and Whitehead agree in affording ontological priority to act over potency. This metaphysical point of departure, nonetheless, is differently conceived. For Aquinas, actuality or existence is the exercise of the act of to-be (*esse*) by the metaphysical subject (*suppositum, hypostasis, subsistentia,* or *persona*), an act specified by the essence or nature in and through which it is exercised. Whitehead speaks, in categories quite alien to these, of entities as "occasions" which exist on the basis of their own self-actualization consisting in the act of selectively prehending data made available by previous, now perished, occasions. Succinctly put, the difference is that between a philosophy of being as act and one of essence as concrete.[1] For Aquinas: essence is the source of formal determination or structure, while existence — which is not of the order or intelligibility of essence at all, but really distinct from it as its ultimate act — explains actuality. For Whitehead: an occasion is actual insofar as it is the concrescence of some formal perfection or value; it is actual precisely as a definite concretion of the realm of ideal possibilities that Whitehead calls "eternal objects."

The difference is thrown into sharp relief with the concept of God that emerges within the respective thought systems. For both God is the fully actual entity, but the Thomist God is purely actual without any admixture of potentiality, while the Whiteheadian God is a process of ever advancing self-actualization. For the former, God's essence is his very act of to-be, and so admits of no distinctions other than those imposed upon it by the finite mind which seeks to know it in accord with its own limitations.[2] The only real distinctions are the trinitarian ones confessed by faith and understood as lying beyond essence on the level of personhood. For the latter, the divine essence is a process which, in order that it not lack all structure and intelligibility, demands a certain real dipolarity. One pole represents pure formal perfection that is infinite and eternal but lacks actuality; the other pole expresses actual perfection that is determined and so finite and temporal, admitting of further development. In God these are known, respectively, as his primordial and his consequent nature.[3]

In neither view is the deity a being in the sense of an individual substance; rather, primacy belongs to the concept of being itself (*Ipsum Esse Subsistens*) in Thomism, and to everlasting becoming in process thought. These differences are well known and it will suffice here to rehearse the contrast by way of the following five points of comparison. The Thomist vision means that: (1) the world becomes, God does not; (2) the world in its becoming is dependent upon God; (3) he is thereby a creator God summoning the world out of nothingness; (4) whose loving agency is universal and unilateral; so that (5) God is the ultimate source bestowing all value upon the world and receiving none intrinsic to himself in return. For theists who follow the inspiration of Whitehead: (1) God and world both become in a common creative advance into novelty; (2) the mutual becoming is one of inter-dependency in which the world's progress is necessary to God's and vice versa; so that (3) God is not strictly a creator but rather a unique partner with human beings in the march into the historical future; in which (4) God is less the ground of all worldly becoming then a special and privileged agent in the universe; who (5) not only pours values into the world but is also the recipient of values the world makes available to him.

Underlying these specific divergences are two basic ones that deserve mention. First, Thomism works from within a strict notion of analogy as a way of speaking about the unknown with concepts that directly represent what is known; it does this in virtue of the creator-creature relationship that is itself understood only on analogy with finite causality. Process thought, by contrast, employs what is not strictly analogy in this sense at all, but rather paradigm or model. There is, it is true, an "analogical" power to these latter but only in the sense of Cajetan's so-called analogy of proper proportionality, which contemporary Thomists have by and large jettisoned in favor of the analogy of attribution alone — where knowledge of the transcendent is sought. The epistemological implications of this are that process theologians seem content to speak of what Gordon Kaufman calls the "available God," while Thomists defend the possibility of referring through ideas, in a limited and approximate way, to what Kaufman rather means by the "real God."[4]

Second, what is metaphysically ultimate in the thought of Aquinas is God himself, whereas in the thought of Whitehead such ultimacy is rather assigned to a category of the non-divine that he calls "creativity," to which is subordinated both God and world.[5] The import of the difference lies in this, that *Ipsum Esse* (God) which is the source of all finite actuality is itself fully actual, while creativity is not itself actual at all and yet is appealed to as the explanation of the actuality of the God-world process. Both thinkers extol actuality over form, but Whitehead's actual entities, including God himself, merely instantiate creative process, whereas Aquinas's substances are creatures that participate in the full actuality of the creator God. Whitehead's God is the cause of the definiteness of what exists; Aquinas's God is the cause also of the very existence.

A Second Presupposition: Love as *Eros* and as *Agape*

These differences, of course, are philosophical in kind, but they form the infrastructure of a divergence that is more markedly religious and Christian — namely, the sense in which God is a God of love. The paradigm (for process theology) or analogy (for Thomism) for God's loving agency toward the world is provided by that phenomenon of human love. But at the very core of the latter lies a certain ambiguity, an ambivalence regarding who is of ultimate concern in such love: the other or the self. (What is at issue here is human love in its highest reaches as consciously personal and social; love in its secondary and derived senses, in which it serves exclusively utilitarian and pleasurable ends, need not engage us at the moment.) The paradoxical element in this becomes a problem when the two motives conflict; both cannot be ultimate but one must be subordinate to, and formally determined by, the other. Simply put: ultimately, one loves one's friends either for one's own sake or for the sake of the friend.

The mystery of love in its all pervading depth and complexity can be explored only with multiple terms and concepts. The most general term of all, from the Latin *amor* — whose equivalents are to be found in all European languages: "love," *amour, amare, Liebe*, etc. — runs the ambit all the way from a perverted penchant for the vile and debasing to the "God is love" of the First Epistle of John (4:8). The spectrum of meaning conveyed by *amor* appears in such varied Latin terms as *delectio* ("predilection" in contemporary English), *electio, affectio, pietas, caritas, compassio, misericordia*, etc. Plato's reflections, however, in the *Symposium* and the *Phaedrus* uncovered a basic distinction that has remained a constant in all subsequent thought. This was the discovery of a foundational love that was the origin and term of all forms of love; this was *eros* as self-fulfilling love, distinguished from love for others conveyed by such Greek terms as *storge* (family affection), and *philia* (friendship) with its derivatives *philanthropia* (love of humankind) and *philadelphia* (love between brothers and sisters). *Eros*, unlike *amor*, tends to exclude what in fact debases rather than enriches the subject: for this the Greek term *epithemia* (desire or lust) tended to do service while *eros* was reserved to mean love of the true, the good, and the beautiful. Joseph Pieper suggests the sweep of the concept:

> Affection kindled by physical beauty; intoxicated Godsent madness (*theia mania*); the impulse to philosophic contemplation of the world and existence; the exaltation which went with the contemplation of divine beauty — Plato calls all these things *eros*.[6]

Eros is self-love, not in the pejorative sense of selfish love, or of love with an eye to its own reward after the fashion of what Leibniz calls "mercenary love," but in the sense that even in its noblest instances self-fulfillment is the irreducible motive of the love. The formality calling forth the loving response of the agent is the being intrinsic to the object loved, perceived as a "good" precisely because it corresponds to the agent's nature in a perfective way. Love lies at the base of that dynamism which is life itself; a dynamism unleashed by the deep-down goodness of things. Aristotle characterizes this ontological relation of the good to appetite as that of act to potency, and thus gives to the good a telic character.[7] The ontological basis of *eros* is then both need or perfectibility on the part of the existent and the abundant richness of being in which existents can participate. Plato's connotation of passionate intensity (explaining the contemporary shading to "erotic" love) arises from awareness of the self-transcending power of *eros*, of how the goodness in the beloved enraptures the lover, drawing the lover irresistibly out of self (ecstasy) and beyond self.

But this is Hellenic love that owes nothing to Christian religious experience. If it is imported later into Christian thought to clarify the human capacity for love, including love for God, it is never used as descriptive of God's own love for himself and for humankind. The former is due to an appropriation by the early Fathers of Stoic and Middle Platonic thought; the avoidance of *eros* in the latter instance is explained by a sense of God as transcendent to all need, as rather the unoriginate source of all being, beyond whom lies no higher realm of possible value in which he can participate. Christian appropriation of Hellenic thought forms was invariably selective, and always a transformation of them to its own religious purposes. Plato, for example, gave ultimacy to the forms, which while subsisting do so precisely as forms; Plato's gods, by contrast, are subjects who act for their own enrichment quite as do other particular existents, even if on a heroic scale. Neither the Old nor the New Testament pay homage to this; there God is a loving agent of creation and salvation. The New Testament stresses and specifies the love character of that agency by recourse to a term not to be found in classical Greek literature: *agape*.[8] The term, in its substantive form, is devised from a neutral and colorless Greek verb meaning simply "to like"; as used in the New Testament it gains the note of estimating as of great worth, with the connotation of committing oneself to action in behalf of what is so valued. It conveys a love that is appreciative rather than appetitive, a matter more of will than emotion; the passion and intensity of *eros* is lacking, and so is the sympathy and intimacy of *philia*. *Agape* is divine love which, in marked contrast to *eros*, is altruistic in that nothing accrues thereby to the lover. It is a love unknown to men and women in any exploration of their own innate impulses to love, and becomes manifest only in the words and conduct of Jesus as God's self-revelation. It is what Paul has in mind when he writes that "God was in Christ reconciling the world to himself' (2 Cor. 5:19), and what John carries beyond its appearance in Christ to where it constitutes God's very being, in writing that "God is love" (1 John 4:8–16).

The Gospels also employ *agape* to characterize both human love for

God (even Paul uses *agapao* in this context: Rom. 8:28; Eph. 6:24; 1 Cor. 2:9, 8:3) and love between Christians. But it does so in a derived and extended sense of the term, in which the intention is to emphasize that Christian love is not at all religious *eros*, but rather response to God's prior love of humankind. The impression remains that in its full sense the term designates a love that is the prerogative of divinity. Behind this may lie the awareness that human love for God falls short of an unqualified *agape* on several counts: it is not spontaneous but caused by God's love; it cannot bestow upon God anything that would enhance his own being; and it cannot escape the dimension of always being self-enriching for human persons. Paul's use of the word to mean human love for God is rare; usually he means it to convey love of Christians for one another. But here he appears to say that *agape* can be an ingredient (for the Christian) in human love, insofar as it is dependent upon, conditioned by, and an imitation of God's love for us.

Luther, however, undertook a spirited defense of the position that Christian love was no wise self-enriching, but entirely "an overflowing love" (*eine quellende Liebe*).[9] Love among Christians is thus, pure and simple, *agape* — and radically opposes every dimension of *eros* (though Luther himself does not use these two terms). But for this to be so, it had to remain in fact God's own love poured out into the Christian and spilling over, as it were, onto others. This notion of Christian love has been championed by Karl Barth in his *Kirchliche Dogmatik*[10] (with however a softening of the opposition to *eros*); its most brilliant defense lies with Anders Nygren's influential *Eros und Agape*.[11] One reservation has to be registered on this project: it makes the loving to be something divine and not anything human at all; human beings become mere channels or instruments of God's own love. But then we are deprived of our personhood and our subjectivity precisely at the moment of turning in Christian love to others. The same objection can be urged in psychological terms: do we really want to be regarded with a disinterested love, one indifferent to our own intrinsic worth? Even God's love for us (if it is to be real in the sense of making an ontic difference) creatively calls forth in us real intrinsic values that the love regards. Love between Christians seemingly should be in response to values which, even if made possible only by God's prevenient love, nonetheless cannot leave unchanged the one graced by them.

Aquinas: Beyond *Agape* to *Amicitia*

Medieval exploration of love tended to view New Testament *agape* as the prerogative of God and to consider innate human love in terms of classical Hellenic *eros*. But the real discussion focused on a third kind of love, namely, God's agapic love for human beings insofar as it sedimented itself in them as a real intrinsic component of their own existence. Such love was acknowledged as entirely the unexacted gift of God; it was "grace," bringing about "justification" and "righteousness" and constituting what the apostle Paul named "the new creation," which was life according to the Spirit (*Pneuma*) in opposition to unredeemed life according to the flesh (*sarx*); its effects upon human persons were described as "rebirth," "regeneration," "adoption," "sonship," etc. Such love was given the name "caritas" and was conceived as an ingenious blend of *eros* and *agape*. It was love for the other (simultaneously God and neighbor) that was unavoidably self-fulfilling because it answered to the deepest aspirations of the finite lover. Augustine had earlier touched upon it, in his typical paradoxical way, in noting that the Christians who love themselves are in danger of losing their souls, yet in not wishing their souls to perish, they are in the deepest way loving them.[12]

Aquinas's technical handling of this subtlety relied upon distinguishing acquisitive love (*amor concupiscentiae*) from personal love (*amor benevolentiae*), and on this basis the *finis qui* of the love (some impersonal good desired) from *finis cui* (as the one to whom and for whom it was desired — either one's self or one's friend).[13] Selfless love was willing good to one's friend rather than to one's self. But the ontological intentionality of the act itself, its intrinsic motive and finality below the level of consciousness, could not fail to be an enrichment of the lover's own subjectivity. This was the *finis cuius gratia* of the loving as a reality of the lover's own being. Indeed, the more selfless the love, the more does it enrich the one who loves precisely as a human person, as a free subject existing in community and called to self-transcendence. The Christian is for Nygren, a pure conduit of God's own act of love; for Aquinas, one who incarnates that love in human form.

But why is not divine love itself, as pure *agape*, also self-fulfilling in this same sense? Aquinas's reply is simply that such love is subsistent. Uncreated and unoriginate, it is the source of all the value in the universe and does not come into existence by way of a response to values originating elsewhere — a point on which Luther is in explicit agreement with Aquinas.[14] Divine loving cannot be conceived as an accidental or contingent accretion; it is rather constitutive of God's very being in its pure actuality and so cannot be thought of as enhancing his own being intrinsically. The sole beneficiaries of such love are creatures loved for their own sakes. God wills existence and salvation (*finis qui*), to humanity (*finis cui*), for its own sake (*finis cuius gratia*) — even though the divine goodness (and so God's love of himself) is the irreducible explanation (but not the cause) of why he wills good to the creature. God's love of creatures is not a way of his loving himself; it is rather the outpouring of self-subsistent love upon others that has no cause and no motive other than love itself. The goodness achieved in the world does not contribute to the goodness intrinsically constitutive of deity. It does contribute to what is called God's glory, but that is ontically extrinsic to God and the reflection of his being within the domain of creaturehood. True enough, God's love for the creature is at the same time a love for himself, but in the sense that he wills himself as end and the creature as to that end.[15] The meaning here is not that creatures are means to some achievement within God himself, but only that creaturely existence is a self-transcending dynamism toward inexhaustible divine goodness. It can be said, of course, that God desires our love in return, as answer to his self-giving love. But even here the reason is not need on his part, but the will to give himself to human persons as their highest happiness. What most accords with infinite goodness is its self-effacing (kenotic) communication to others.

There is, however, yet another dimension to Aquinas's analysis of love that illumines love in its divine form. Christian love seeks the good of one's neighbor, and so what predominates in it is the element of *agape*. It is thus "benevolent love" rather than "concupiscible love," "gift-love" rather than "need-love" in C. S. Lewis's succinct phrase.[16] But this *caritas* is more than mere benevolence in that it adds to the latter the two elements of mutuality and of communication in a shared life.[17] It thus moves in the direction of what Aristotle calls "friendship," and is in fact a genuine *amicitia* between God and human beings. The shared life can only be God's communication to the human person of some finite participation in his own uncreated life of love. Our *caritas* toward God thus rests upon his *self*-communication to us, his *agape* or gift-love that graces us with the state of adoption. Here, the deepest element in love between God and humankind (and so in love between Christians) appears not precisely as the wishing well to the other, but as what issues from this when it is the mutual and efficacious giving of self to the other, namely that *unio affectiva* that constitutes the lovers in a perduring state of love. Aquinas develops this from an insight of Pseudo-Dionysius, expressed in the latter's characterization of love as *vis unitiva et concretiva*.[18]

Love is then, most formally, union which precisely as union (rather than unity in the strict sense) demands two or more autonomous and free subjects. It is a union proper to love, that is, something affective in kind rather than entitative, in which others are "let be" in personal otherness, and so loved for their own sake. The import of this — where divine love in itself is concerned — is that God's love for humankind is, in origin, *agape*, love that gives and does not receive; but on its own initiative it extends itself beyond this to where it establishes the human person as a dialogic partner to the love.

Whitehead: Return to *Eros*

Whitehead's metaphysical system means a differing concept of God and so a differing concept of divine love; something other than what is conveyed by *agape*, understood as God's self-communication issuing in that effective union which is true friendship between God and humankind. Whitehead's thought is commonly and aptly called a philosophy of organism, in which entities are not substances, but rather immanent principles of process called occasions. Such organic development, as the universal law of the universe, is the realization, in the form of actual occasions, of abstract and infinite ideal possibilities, called "eternal objects." But this demands positing an originating principle of such continuing realization of value. In this way, Whitehead introduces God into his world view as a "derivative notion," by which he means an explanatory principle, along with eternal objects and actual occasions, of process as ultimate. God's function is that of a limiting principle adapting limitless possibilities in a realistic and efficacious way to occasions of the world in their process of self-becoming. God accounts for this by envisaging what is concretely the ideal possibility for each ever-emerging occasion, and offering it to that occasion as its "initial aim," thereby luring it into the "creative advance into novelty."[19]

Because he is "not an exception to metaphysical principles ... but their prime exemplification," God is himself an actual occasion, differing from others only on the basis of his non-temporality, which renders him exempt from transformation into something that is not God.[20] This means that he not only envisages ideal possibilities for the world (in his primordial nature) but also prehends values for himself in his own becoming in the physical pole of his being (his consequent nature). Thus, the supplying of initial aims to the world not only lures it into advancement but also enables the world, on the basis of how it chooses to actualize the possibilities available to it, to provide the raw material out of which alone God can further actualize himself. Whitehead gives expression to this in one of his antinomies: "It is as true to say that God creates the world, as that the world creates God."[21] God's basic relationship to the world then, by way of both the primordial and the consequent nature, is one of love. But the love in question reveals itself as akin to Platonic *eros* rather than to New Testament *agape* and its medieval development into *amicitia*. This seems clear at any rate in *Adventures in Ideas* which presents God, less as seeking his own unique satisfactions, than as the source of the universal surge toward fulfillment in which he himself is caught up.

There are at least three structural points in Whitehead's thought that implicitly determine this view of divine love. First, God's relation to the world, though benign, is neither strictly free nor creative. The world is necessary to God, and so thereby is his relationship to it. Moreover, in itself the world is just as necessary as is God, and exists quite apart from any act of love on his part summoning it into existence. Worldly existence as a mere "given" loses its gift-like character; at the very heart of the mystery of being there is no act of transcendent freedom that has no motive other than love for what it calls into existence. God is no longer the creator, but only the ideal companion to humankind, since "both are in the grip of the ultimate metaphysical ground" which is the impersonal "creative advance into novelty."[22] Second, the motive of God's love for the world is God's own advancement. He makes values available for emerging entities, not ultimately for their sakes but for his own; his luring forward of the world is, in the end, only a means to his own continuing actualization. Third, a confirmation of this is that whatever values are realized in the world immediately perish. They cease to be actual in themselves and become only data to be prehended by succeeding occasions. Only in God is the world's achievement preserved and so rescued from oblivion.[23] Divinity is thus the final depository for whatever good human beings may win out of nature and history. Moreover, God's reception of such values is a transformation of them into something more in accord with his own creative becoming. Metaphysically, this rests on the assumption that the cell units of reality are perishing occasions, not substances which have their own proper, autonomous existences, their *ipseitas*, and which when conscious possess thereby a perduring identity as subject-persons.

There is, however, one strength that cannot be easily dismissed in this conception of divine love as *eros*, one that has been fully exploited in the process theology that has developed subsequent to Whitehead. It does enable one to envisage God as lovingly involved with suffering humankind. Indeed, it is taken in all seriousness as meaning that God himself suffers;[24] a truth that finds its strongest warrant in the cross of Christ. By this account, there is no suffering in human history that is not at the same time God's suffering — an understanding with vast implications for a doctrine of redemption. Moreover, it is precisely love that opens God to the genuine risks involved in the encountering of evil. This principle is more strongly urged, it is true, in certain other contemporary theologies that look more to Hegel than to Whitehead.[25] These latter view divine love as a pure *agape* that kenotically empties itself into the world in such wise as to become vulnerable to all the negativities of that world. In process theology, by contrast, God has no choice but to experience in his consequent nature the waywardness of history. Still, his love determines the concrete ways in which he exposes his loving initiatives to the world's distortion of them, as he seeks to counter them in his own experience.

The point being made in all this is that passivity and receptivity, an openness of the self to being affected both favorably and adversely by what befalls the beloved, is indigenous to love as such. Apart from this there may be benevolence, but not genuine love which is an identification of the self with the beloved in the latter's struggle to win values out of a processive

universe. This is undoubtedly true of finite love which in seeking to enrich
itself runs the risk of frustration, and is unavoidably exposed to forces of
resistance and negation. But is it ingredient in love as such, and so of love
conceived as infinite? Love is an identification with the beloved, and if
the latter is in a state of wretchedness, seemingly the lover lays himself
or herself open to the same anguish. Differently put, love is a matter of
giving, and ultimately the giving of oneself, to the beloved; any evil that
may afflict the latter would seem to afflict one who is one in heart and
mind with the beloved. Words of Augustine come readily to mind here,
"Well did one say to his friend: 'thou half of my soul.'" But — to speak
formally — the identity and the self-communication proper to love as such
is not ontic in kind but intentional. It is a union in heart and affection that
seeks not to suffer with the friend but to alleviate his or her suffering; if I do
suffer with my friend, that is motivated by a desire to lessen the anguish by
bearing it with him or her and not by a craving for suffering as such. The
precise formality of love lies not in the *compassio* but in the efficacious
intending of the welfare of the friend. To merely feel piety or experience
compassion without striving to alleviate the anguish of one's friend would
hardly qualify as genuine love. Compassion is always an accompaniment of
love between humans, but that is due to the fact that such love cannot be
entirely transcendent to the causes of suffering at work upon the beloved.
The mark of divine love is not its sharing in suffering but its saving and
rescuing from such evil. True enough, process theology explains that the
evils of the world, as experienced by God, are overcome within himself.
But even this is less a saving of the world than a harmonizing of its discords
within divine experience.

   Is the process doctrine of a compassionate God entirely alien, then, to
Christian thought? Hardly — if one takes seriously that it is God himself
who suffers on the cross, and not merely the humanity. But a Christian
reservation may well be felt on making that suffering something that divine love *must* undergo rather than something that such love embraces
in its transcendent freedom. In the latter view, God who cannot suffer in
his very deity, can lovingly choose to do so by becoming human. With the
cross of Jesus, the cause of human suffering lies revealed not as love but
as human malice, whose Christian symbol is sin. Suffering is something
that sin, precisely as the human refusal to love, carries *ontologically* in its
wake. God's love is such as to wish that such sin be overthrown from within
human love, from a love that loves enough to enter into the depths of suffering. Thus, even now, divine love intends efficaciously the vanquishment
of the power of evil — but it wills to achieve this historically, and in the domain of human freedom, through God's assuming as his own the human
history that bears the wounds of sin. God's love is mysteriously such as to
will to involve human liberty (whence came sin and suffering in the first
place) in the overthrow of evil from within. It is God who casts down the

reign of sin, but not in and as God; rather in and as the human beloved, and so not in power but in lowliness and humiliation.

To attempt to say more than this would take one into questions concerning the mystery of iniquity and a theology of redemption — questions which, while cognate, fall beyond the scope of this modest study.

The Christian Option

God Appears, and God is Light
To those poor Souls who dwell in Night,
But does a Human Form Display
To those who dwell in Realms of day.[26]

If, in the final analysis, these two concepts of God as love — owing inspiration respectively to Aquinas and Whitehead — are conflicting and irreconcilable, an option has to be made. For the Christian, dwelling in the light of revelation, the sole norm for such a choice is the human form that divine love has assumed in Jesus the Christ. The following three observations are simply among the more obvious of the many reflections that follow upon that acknowledgement. First, Jesus calls God his Father. He is uniquely the Father of Jesus, and only derivatively of other human persons who are open to the encounter with God he mediates. But the root meaning of that fatherhood derives from the Old Testament awareness of the Lord as the creator God who summons the world into existence out of the void, and takes sovereign initiatives toward it. This is as alien from Whitehead's notion that God is not God without the world as it is from the Greek understanding of the eternity of matter. Process thinkers are unanimous in viewing God as a special and privileged agent in the world process. But the radical obedience of Christ to his Father speaks rather of One who is the transcendent ground of every instance of agency. The God of Jesus is hardly recognizable as a particular efficient agent appealed to at moments of indeterminacy in the natural and human world. Closer to the mark is a God of transcendence who calls finite freedom into existence in the first place, sustains it without violating it, and indeed makes the creature to make itself. In Whitehead's thought, the actual occasion retains an autonomy over and against God, in virtue of which it is self-creating. Its freedom, and so its capacity to love, are not rooted in a love that is itself uncreated and creative but are merely postulated as a given. If this self-creative process be in selective response to lures coming from God, still, God is at most a persuasive companion in the transaction.

Christianity has consistently confessed Christ as himself the bearer of God's salvation, not as an intermediary who offers to human beings the means of saving themselves. Christ, as the human face of God, enfleshes a reconciling and saving love that is self-effacing, and that raises humankind to friendship with God; the Christian does not encounter Christ merely as an enticement toward present enriched experience that will perdure only in God, and so is finally an aspect of God's love of self. Another indirect way of saying this is at hand in the Christian understanding of the human person as *imago Dei*. On such grounds, our love in its Christian depths seeks to imitate divine love in its creative power. It intends, not any absorption or manipulation of the beloved to the lover's own purposes, but an affirmation of the loved one in his or her own being and goodness. Love, in this sense, is a finite continuation of God's own act of creation. Joseph Pieper calls attention to the gratitude that attends the very first stirrings of love, betraying that the lover responds less to appealing *qualities* in the beloved, than to the phenomenon that the beloved simply *is*.[27] This is only a faint and finite reflection of love in its divine mode.

Second, Jesus summons his followers to *koinonia*, to a fellowship of love. That fellowship is the effect in human beings of God's transforming love mediated by Christ. And it reveals itself as constituted by the intersubjectivity of a genuine community. Hans Urs von Balthasar has noted that "the essentially communitarian character [of Christianity] can only be achieved by genuine personalization of all its members."[28] If the love mediated in Christ forms us in this fellowship with God and other men and women, it is far more than divine *eros* it is *agape*, and even more, *amicitia*. It is love that regards persons in the full sense of those who exist in their own right, as free subjects, and so as capable of intersubjectivity. Indeed, its fullest realization appeals to the doctrine of the Trinity as the *koinonia* of God's own inner life. Here, the richest analogy of all between God and us becomes an analogy of relational love. And here it becomes clearest of all that divine love is gift-love, not need-love. By contrast, the God of process theology in loving the world is not a person at all but only a principle. An actual entity is a person (in Whitehead's sense) only as it constitutes a society of occasions, expressing thereby continuity with its ancestor occasions — but on this level God does not influence or love the world at all, much less love it as a person bringing human beings to their full personhood.[29]

Last, the love and reconciliation mediated by Christ is known in the New Testament as "rebirth," "adoption," "sonship," etc. The import of these terms is not just fulfillment of humankind's deepest capacities but a genuine elevation, something beyond the human drive to temporal transcendence, not only quantitatively but qualitatively. Process theologies, too, allow for the introduction of novel values into the world by God's love, but these are homogeneous to God and humanity. Other actual entities contemplate in the conceptual pole of their being, though on a lower scale of appreciation, the same eternal objects as does divinity. If God aids the world in its organic growth, this is because he himself is in pursuit, on a higher level, of the same objectives. Once again, such divine love is *eros* because its carrying forth of the world is the way to its own self-achievement. This is different indeed from divine love as *agape*, from love that can incarnate itself as human and surrender itself upon the cross for humankind, from love that can make human beings friends of God.

TEN

Christian Panentheism: Orthopraxis and God's Action in History

"The heavens belong to the Lord, but the earth God has given to human beings" (Psalm 115:16). The contemporary mood in theology is one of strong and seemingly irreversible emphasis upon orthopraxis, one that may well bode a sea change in the future. What emerges from an exploration of this theme is that Christian orthopraxis is indeed the well-spring whence there emerges new meaning in theology. If theory (to which faith belongs as *fides quae*) precedes faith in the sense that the word of God precedes our acting in creative conformity to it, and if praxis as such can never be the grounds for the truth of a theory,[1] still Christian faith is always ordered intrinsically to action and the latter safeguards orthodoxy from collapsing into mere ideology.

This puts the focus sharply upon the acting human subject, and raises a problem concerning the trans-subjective dimension to orthopraxis. The problem can be stated this way: Does God act in our history in such wise that orthopraxis is the living out of God's initiatives in history, and so in an historical way? Religion affects the direction things take, but is God himself a factor? Christians believe he is — both in Jesus and in the Spirit — but it can be said that Jesus has disappeared from the horizon of present life and the activity of the Spirit is anonymous and ambiguous. Again, is God active only in these specific events, or does he show his hand in the unfolding of universal history? Is it possible any longer, after several holocausts, to discern the presence of God in universal human progress? Can such progress truly be growth toward the kingdom?

Put differently, are the strivings after genuine value of historical men and women (and historicity surely gives Christianity identity among the religions) autonomous achievements? Or do they derive from God, receiving from him their impetus and identity? If the former be true, then our free

142

decisions seemingly contribute to the self-creation of God (as long as one avoids thinking atheistically). If it is rather the latter that is true, then is not the contemporary meaning of human freedom compromised? Modern historical consciousness views freedom in terms of genuinely creative initiatives which cannot be reduced to the mere implementation of what has been foreordained. Freedom as the matrix of history cannot mean only that what eventuates does so in a spontaneous and non-coercive way. Rather it allows that men and women are originating sources of novelty, responsible for the making of themselves and of their world.

Is it possible to walk the razor's edge of this dilemma and suggest both (1) that our Christian acting springs from a freedom that is without divine antecedent determinations and so is a genuine self-positing in which human persons living in society determine their own futures both in this life and in the eschaton to come; and (2) that God himself, remaining the ground of that freedom and its exercise, does not become thereby a God *of* history but remains transcendent to and intrinsically unaltered by what human beings make of themselves and of history? This is only to ask if the sole motive for God's acting in the world, creatively and redemptively, is to be sought in the divine reality itself, or if the creature makes determining contributions to such divine activity.

Precisely from within what we experience as the free historicality of our existence there appears a dimension of ultimacy that cries out for religious symbolization. Such spontaneous symbols, at least negatively and covertly, implicate God.[2] And in so doing they echo the constant language of both the Old and the New Testament concerning a God ever active in human affairs. To recognize that language as mythological is only to set the further theological task of seeking to discover whether such myth and symbol can be translated into ontological categories.

A first appeal for help can be made to Langdon Gilkey who writes that "we experience ultimacy not as the all-powerful, extrinsic and necessitating ordainer of what we are and do [indeed this runs counter to almost every facet of the modern consciousness of history] but precisely as the condition and possibility, the ground of our contingent existence, our creativity, our *eros* and meaning, our intellectual judgments, our free moral decisions and our intentional actions."[3] Here the category of "cause" (from Aristotelian realism) has given way to the less precise but more flexible category of "ground" (from German idealism). Still, it functions to explain that God both preserves the structures of the past and establishes new forms of life that break continuity with the old. More to the point, the term "ground" does this by presenting God as acting, not as an autonomous agent alongside other agents but "in and through the ordinary creative and destructive actions of men in history."[4]

But does not this run the risk of dismissing God as a superfluous hypothesis, useful only as an explanatory device? God seems suddenly

deprived of his deity. All talk of divine providence, election, and predestination, for instance, either disappears from theology entirely or is watered
down to a very thin gruel — when, as in process theology, God is conceived
as a metaphysical structural principle of the universe, as in Whitehead's
phrase "the great companion, the fellow sufferer who understands."[5] Is
there not in all this the collapse of theology into religious anthropology,
with the suggestion that the phrase "God is love" really means "love is
God"? Or, in terms of Wittgenstein's language games, that the expression
"God loves us" does not describe some objective state of affairs but creates
the very reality to which the utterance gives expression, and means when
deciphered that our humanness calls us to love one another"? Surely our
Christian symbols seek to say more than this. Namely, that God is at the
very origin of our freedom in such wise that he is not only love but power
as well, alpha *and* omega, not only the ground of being but himself *the*
transcendent being.

Pannenberg's thought moves in this direction by defining God as "the
power over all that is" (*Macht über alles*). But to avoid any return to notions
of a fore-ordaining sovereign, he identifies divine power with futurity — futurity is the mode of divine being. This enables God to determine all events
not from outside history, not from "above" it as it were, but from within
history itself, yet after the fashion in which the future as it occurs determines what preceded it, altering the meaning of the past without violence
to the historical process itself. "God is revealed then not as the unchangeable ultimate ground of the phenomenal order, but as the free origin of
the contingent events of the world."[6] But this maneuver does seem in the
final analysis to historicize God in the sense of relating him intrinsically to
history. Or perhaps, viewed the other way around, it ontologizes history.
What Pannenberg calls God's eternity is closer in fact to what Heidegger and Schubert Ogden call "primal temporality." Pannenberg interprets
Rahner's phrase that God changes "in the other" to mean logically that he
changes in himself. At the same time he appears to distance himself from
the Whiteheadians in speaking not of the *Deus in se* but of the God whose
deity is identical with his coming rule.

Apart from the peculiarity of equating the past with darkness and sin,
and the future with light, hope and salvation, the further question can be
raised as to whether this does not functionalize the idea of God. God
is defined in function of human beings and their history; he is humanity's absolute future. Like all functional ideas of God, this lends itself to
replacement by equivalents.

Still and all, it is untoward to view the being of God as contesting
genuine human freedom. Are we left then only with the alternative of
Fichte who contends that seeking to ground finite freedom, to conceive
it as other than autonomous, is quite simply contradictory?[7] It is possible to focus the question more sharply by reflecting on two contemporary

and viable explanations that make the most impressive claims to challenge Fichte's conclusions. One is more variant upon the panentheism of Hegel. For Hegel, all history is the self-manifestation of God to humanity. Even for so orthodox a Catholic thinker as Rahner, this man Jesus is the auto-expression of God. Things and events are for Hegel the finite appearances of Spirit; thus (without denying their genuine reality as other than God) their true being is to be found in God.[8] Accordingly, the infinite and the finite are necessary to one another, otherwise the infinitude of God is merely a rational extrapolation from finite spirit's transcending of its own limitations — thus, the finite "re-presents" that of which the infinite is creative. Pure being (*Esse Subsistens*, e.g.,) is a meaningless concept because without finite mediation it lacks all content. If religion "represents" humanity and God as distinct, philosophy surmounts this disjunction and "thinks" rather of "a single activity which can be described as 'human-divine.'"[9] What follows from this is that God's knowing is at once his revealing and his being known by men and women in the act of faith, as it not only seeks but attains understanding.[10]

The immediate objection to this is that it appears to do away with the autonomy of creatures; finite freedom appears as a mere epiphenomenon. What eventuates is not an historical transaction between God and humanity, something rooted in the contingencies of love that offers itself to faith, but rather a process that unfolds with logical necessity, that structures not faith but speculative thought.

At the same time it would be short-sighted to fail to note the positive contribution in the thought of Hegel, who thought through, more profoundly perhaps than anyone else, the paradoxical relationship between the infinite and the finite. What is illuminating is the intentionality of his thought over and above its strictly logical implications. His panentheism — if we interpret him benignly as circumventing the pantheism he himself wished to avoid — refuses to set the infinite and finite over against one another. His mistake was that of making their relationship one of mutual need. The Christian tradition on the contrary has always insisted that the sole motive for God's othering of himself in the creature lies in divinity itself, in the divine goodness as self-communicative by way of a love that is not Greek *eros* but New Testament *agape*. Classical theism, in its denial of what Aristotle meant by *real* relations on the part of God toward creatures, has been caricatured as if this were a denial of *actual* relations, of the truth that God creates knows, loves and saves the world. Whereas what the Aristotelian-Thomist teaching sought to preclude were only relations that were "real" in the sense of bespeaking ontological dependence. The way remains open then for relations on God's part that may be called "real" as long as they are understood as arising not out of divine need (*ex indigentia*) but out of divine super-abundance (*ex abundantia*).[11] Hegel understood that the infinite is not limited by the finite if it includes the latter; his error was in the kind of inclusion. All this need not be taken as a denial that God is affected by the triumphs and failures of his creatures only that the affecting is not one to which he must submit by nature but rather one to which he opens himself in the mystery of love.

This brings us to the second challenge to Fichte's autonomous freedom — one worked out in Langdon Gilkey's attempt to translate the Christian symbols of election, providence, and predestination into the categories of Whitehead's thought. He does this, however, by taking one major liberty with Whitehead's system at the very beginning. He eschews the notion that God is in the grip of process as something transcendent to himself. The divine agency is not subordinated to creativity as the category of the ultimate that is non-actual in itself and instantiated somewhat differently in God and in creature. Rather, for Gilkey, divinity is itself ultimate and absolute, and all process is rooted in it. Genuine process does, nevertheless, mean the self-creating of the entities which constitute it, bespeaking genuine novelty in the world not derivable from God. Thus it means allowing (unlike Hegel) that the finite limits the divine, and indeed contributes in a determining way to the self-constitution of God in what process theologians call his "consequent" nature. For followers of Whitehead, God does not create our freedom but is rather a privileged participant in creative interactions between entities whose freedom is self-posited. God only shapes and molds that freedom as he lures it forward by providing relevant possibilities out of which it achieves its own actuality.

Gilkey radically alters this to where, conversely, God is the ground of all process, necessary to it yet not contingent within it. He is not a creature of process, arising out of a process of which he is not the ground. Nonetheless, he does participate in this process in his intrinsic beingness.[12] This is only to say that God, who is not limited by any absolute, transcendent to himself, chooses to limit himself by becoming the creative ground of entities that freely set the course of their own destinies. But this renders his being (for Gilkey) both subject to change in itself, and temporal rather than eternal.[13] God so conceived is able, for example, to know the free future, but only as possible, not as actual.

In Hegel's solution creaturely freedom loses that autonomy essential to it and history (including Christian history that grows out of orthopraxis) is characterized by the kind of inevitability that marks the logical process proper to reason and concept. Human freedom is the mere appearance of true freedom which is divine. In Gilkey's alternative, it is God's freedom that is compromised in the sense that its transcendence is relativized by the determination that comes from finite freedom — granting that this is only because God's loving omnipotence wills such self-limitation. If Hegel minimizes the distinction between God and humanity, Gilkey over-emphasizes the same distinction. For the former, the true being of the finite is really only a moment in the being of the infinite. For the latter, the finitude of human freedom cannot be real and taken seriously unless it is set over against the freedom of God in a way that limits it — even if making this to be ultimately a self-limitation is a way of rooting finite liberty in God.

Is there any way out of this dilemma, any other way in which the relationship between absolute freedom and finite freedom can be thought through? In suggesting that there is, I should like to begin by pointing out two characteristics shared in common by Hegelians and reformed process thinkers such as Gilkey. (1) First, both think upon God and world dialectically, that is to say in a way that is reductively univocal because essentialistic.[14] When God and creature are thought of as akin in essence, the consequence is a tendency to collapse one into the other — whether with the conceptual language of Hegel one unmasks human freedom as the moments of divine freedom, or with the symbolic language of Gilkey one anthropomorphizes and views divine freedom on the model of finite freedom. (2) Second, behind such thinking is the all-pervasive contemporary phenomenon of giving ontological priority to possibility over actuality. Here freedom is instinctively grasped as an unfulfilled capacity that faces out on limitless horizons of possibility, while actuality is a stricturing of such possibility to present achievement as a temporary stage of development. When such ontological priority is given to potentiality over actuality, to the future over the present, then God is not yet fully actual in his own being and process can no longer be movement toward a *telos* already actual in divine intentions. Pannenberg suggests as much in allowing that "in a restricted but important sense God does not yet exist."[15] If he means something more than this, then he is covertly giving actuality to God and qualifying what he means in speaking of futurity as the mode of divine being.

The Hegelian denial of the principle of identity means understanding God's creative act as a divine "othering" of self in the creature — with therefore a certain inevitability attending both creation and incarnation.[16] God cannot be *thought* of apart from the latter two events, even if he can be so *represented* religiously. But there is a different way of mediating between the infinite and the finite, or in the present context, between uncreated freedom and creaturely freedom and praxis. This is by way of conceiving of them as constituting not a dialectical relationship but a community of analogy, wherein creatures participate in divine be-ing conceived as existential act.

Here human being and freedom are neither collapsed into God (Hegel) nor set over against God (Gilkey). Rather, the divine causality moves on a different level than ours entirely, a level creative of being in the strict sense (*ex nihilo*), so that God is not only the cause (in an ultimate and transcendent sense) of what eventuates but even of the very mode of its eventuation as free. The divine causality does not then withdraw from the scene (as it were) to let us be free, but explains ultimately that our freedom

is genuine self-determination. In this sense, the greater the divine causality involved, the more autonomous is the effect produced. The closer God
draws to the creature, the more it is set free for an open future — not,
however, a future without God. From this it follows that we can only speak
of God's action in our history analogically — that is, by using the contents
of creaturely concepts from which we can at best designate God's action
shrouded in mystery.

The plotting of human history and destiny then, which does involve the
introduction of genuine novelty into the world, is not really a question of a
synergistic cooperation between God and human beings — indeed, that is
to put the question falsely. A more illuminative approach to the problem is
to understand with J. B. Metz that human freedom is not at bottom a matter of choice (*liberum arbitrium*) but more radically is the very structure
of human beingness.[17] To view our freedom in this transcendental sense
is to obviate at the very beginning vexing questions concerning interrela-
tionships between intellect and will. More to the point, it would appear to
be a basis on which orthopraxis can have its full significance. For freedom,
so conceived as humankind's mode of being in the world, is revelatory of
what it means to be human and what men and women are summoned to
make of themselves. Such finite freedom can exist only "in" God (outside
God there is only the void); at the same time, it is in itself a creaturely
self-positing which can come about only through a divine *kenosis*. God (so
to speak) makes room "within himself" wherein the creature can constitute itself.[18] But this finite occurrence of freedom need not be seen as a
moment of infinite freedom. It can be seen as a creation of divine love,
whose being is rather given to it as its own. The love in question is not
eros as divine self-enactment, but *agape* as divine self-giving. Then history
is not a mirror image of what occurs eternally in the depths of the Godhead, even by way of the trinitarian processions. It becomes something
specifically human into which God can enter only by becoming himself fully
human, and so subjecting himself humanly to the historical process. Without being a God *of* history, he becomes a God in history. The history that
issues creatively from our praxis is not able then to be subsumed under the
aegis of rational thinking (as in Hegelianism). Rather, at least insofar as
it is praxis measured by God's acting in history, it represents "the travails
of an incarnate human spirit endeavoring to redeem the time."[19] This is a
far cry from Descartes' attempt to disincarnate human being, or Hume's
alternative of fleeing historical knowledge on the grounds that all genuine
knowledge arises from within subjectivity.

But such history is not mere human endeavor that transpires without God. First, because finite liberty is God's creation and thus a limited
participation in the infinitely actual freedom of God as the power of self-
determination. The latter, far from contesting human self-determination,
actually makes it possible by endowing it with a creativity of its own. Pre-

cisely because finite freedom is anchored by inner necessity in the divine goodness as its origin and *telos*, it is set free to determine itself vis-à-vis all lesser goods. But second, every enactment of freedom is in fact a dialogue between God and humankind. Surely, when we read that God made human creatures *ad imaginem Dei*, this means that he intended a dialogue to ensue. But this can be only if God enters history. Not that the interior workings of grace are thereby voided but rather that such grace requires concrete content which is supplied by the events of history. These events center on Jesus who is the Christ of God and whose resurrection, as the earnest of ours to come, becomes the horizon of human history with God. These events perdure in the mode of proclamation and sacrament within the Church, gaining a new form of historical visibility thereby. Moreover, the resurrection is simultaneously the sending of the Spirit upon the Church to inaugurate our history — which need not be looked upon merely as a prolongation of the Christ-event and so unchanging except in accidental ways, but can be seen as a movement set in motion by the Christ-event. It can add to the Christ-event in the sense of constituting unique historical appropriations of and responses to it. God's exchanges with men and women then occur not only through revelatory events of the past but through present responses to our on-going history, at once creative and destructive. Here John Macquarrie's image comes to mind of God as a divine chess player whose wisdom and love controls the outcome of the game by countering, in the end, the ill-chosen moves of human beings.[20]

Nevertheless, if the deity of God is to remain intact, it seems necessary to say that in all this God remains unaltered in his own beingness. In his infinite actuality he is not subordinated to the historical process itself (history and time are rather the creations of God) — not even (as Gilkey would have it) in a divine act of freely willing to be constituted in his consequent nature by the world. We do not contribute to the self-creation of God for the achievements of history are determinations not of God but of human beings themselves. The import of this refusal to compromise and relativize God's transcendence is that it safeguards the utter gratuity of grace. This precludes only that kind of panentheism which views God as in need of a world wherein he enacts himself: it insists that God's love for the world is truly altruistic — *agape* and not *eros*.

But how is this reconcilable with God's involvement with a world in travail? Only because — apart from having created finite freedom and set his own infinite goodness as its horizon — God has chosen to enter the temporal order as a human being subject to history in his humanity: he who is ahistorical, who has no history of his own, has assumed a history — but *our* history. The theological explanation of this is ultimately trinitarian. Catholic theology has always understood that when God enters history at the incarnation, it is as person (in the Greek sense of hypostasis) not as nature; it is humanity that supplies the nature. This at least raises the question as to whether what is divine in Jesus is to be sought precisely in that dimension of his being wherein he is human. Edward Schillebeeckx circumvents the problem with the daring suggestion that all human persons as such are in and of the divine in the sense of being enhypostatic in God.[21] What is true is that, in the Christ-event, God does not manifest himself otherwise than in human form. This by no means need deny that many biblical expressions (those referring to Jesus' pre-existence, for example) may well be symbolic, and bear as their primary meaning God's immanence. It is only to suggest that, integrally taken, such symbols refer to the immanent Trinity even if they do so only through our participation in the immanence they represent. But this allows us to say that the divine nature as such, as the subsisting act of be-ing, remains unaltered both in the ahistorical communication which is creation and in the historical self-communication that is salvation. This saving self-communication is the advent of God not in his deity, but in and through the concrete humanity of Jesus. In the thought of Aquinas, person or hypostasis in God is a pure subsisting relation, reducible to true immanent action which, however, is not causal in kind.[22] Persons, of course, do act causally but only through the natures which they personify in a process of ontological termination. This suggests that person belongs to an entirely different level of intelligibility than does a constituted essence; it conveys rather a continuing process of becoming, of creative self-positing, rooted in the pure relationality of self-revelation (knowledge) and self-donation (love). Thus, in willing to enter history in the mission of the Son, and then to animate the Church in its subsequent history in the mission of the Spirit, God chooses to interact with men and women in free dialogic partnership on the level of personhood as Father, Son and Spirit. He remains the Lord of history but by way of his creative adaptations to human responses (including the negative ones of malice and sin) to his own continuing initiatives of love.

Still, our future is dependent upon what possibilities we actualize now. Even the precise character of our eschatological future may depend radically upon present human choices. That that future will be with God and consist of a beatific vision is merely a formal designation that says nothing of the concrete shape that such beatitude will assume. Johann Baptist Metz suggests the full implications of this when he writes that "even the dead, those already vanquished and forgotten, have a meaning which is as yet unrealized."[23] In our praxis then, as the deployment of our liberty under God, we are engaged in the process of transforming time into eternity (not escaping time into eternity). The phrase "life *after* death," then, may well be misleading because the word "after" suggests some kind of duration subsequent to cosmic time rather than the sublimation of our present time into eternity.[24] Karl Rahner is closer to the mark in writing that "true human history constitutes its own definitive stage and is not merely rewarded with it."[25]

If all this be true then it is a precarious thing to be human; to be a man or a woman is a delicate undertaking. The human person truly is, as Aquinas observes, a *minor mundus*, existing at the point where the temporal and the eternal intersect and converge.[26] The spiritual and the corporeal are so unified that human beings cannot (as Neo-Platonists wish) repudiate the lower in order to attain the higher. Aquinas claims this in insisting, for example, that the goodness of a virtuous action is intensified when it is executed with passion.[27] The human person thus leads a dangerous existence as he or she "continuously moves on the frontier between truth and untruth, between freedom and constraint, between good and evil."[28]

Are there any practical consequences to all of this for us? Christian truth, if more than personal commitment, is less than full truth without it. Orthopraxis can and should mean new awareness, new insight and understanding in theology. And such freshly minted truth cannot in its turn but spur us on to action.

It seems true, then, to say that the Christian believer may not rest content to face the future passively, content to contemplate it as it arrives, but is summoned to face it in terms of committed action, knowing that what lies ahead is of our own determining, our destiny to nurture well or to distort. We do this under parameters set by God, above all in the incarnation and resurrection of Christ. But this means that the future is not only a projection of our present capacities but an adventure with God whose continuing activity in our midst opens up horizons that fill us with hope.

This is no plea to repudiate the past; indeed it is more a plea to be genuinely true to that past by giving it a future in the present. Still, there is need for the risk of involvement, of venturing with faith into uncharted areas, into the wilderness, the dark wood. We can only add "amen" to these words of Robert McAfee Brown: "Let us be prepared to fail a few times, if only that we may persuade the suffering race of man that we desire to stand at their side, sharing their burdens, working on their behalf, bearing their cross."[29] If we believe that God is with us then the absence of God of which we hear so much should perhaps be looked upon as a cultural phenomenon that offers an opportunity to stress in new ways the hidden modes of God's acting in history, and the importance of not looking for God in those areas where he is not to be found. Put differently, perhaps this very absence can make us aware of God's own sovereign, underived initiatives — the Spirit breathes where he will. With Heidegger perhaps we can await the call of the gods, the "grace of a better dawn."[30] Yet even now we can be already "on the way." In the end, only God himself assures us that he himself lies in wait for us at the end of all our striving. But already he has shown us his human face in Jesus, enabling us to believe that "God's cause has already been made the human cause."[31]

ELEVEN

Does Divine Love
Entail Suffering in God?

Until the time of Ludwig Feuerbach theological disputes within Christianity focused on such truths as: the nature of justification, the concept of Church, the divinity of Christ, etc. The one Archimedean point never seriously called into question was that concerning God himself. Whether his existence could be demonstrated, and what arguments might succeed in doing so, had been all along matter for discussion, but not the question of God's reality. Beginning with the late eighteenth century, however, even that ultimate certitude was opened to question. By the mid-nineteenth century the question had become one not only of the truth of God's existing, but of the meaning of all language about the transcendent to begin with. Is it possible to give any meaning at all to speech about that which by definition lies beyond empirical experience? Wittgenstein's theory of language games marked a first phase of resolution: speech about the absolute or transcendent was endowed with meaning on the basis of usage; it meant what its users intended it to mean within the parameters of the language game in which they were engaged. The question of truth, of granting reality to what was the trans-empirical referent of such talk, was simply beyond the reach of all rational discourse. The meaning acknowledged here was not able to be established publicly, but was mutually agreed upon on noncognitive grounds by those of a given religious commitment.

But if theology is to function, if there is to be any talk about God whatsoever in an attempt at objectivity, then some notion of God has to be presupposed. This leaves theists in the dilemma of having to choose, seemingly, between language that is anthropomorphic on the one hand and agnostic on the other. In the first option, the "infinite qualitative difference" (Kierkegaard) is slighted and God is treated as one more entity of the world, even if the most perfect of all. In the second option, it is acknowledged that human speech does not reach the divine at all, and words applied to God are empty of all meaning.

Curiously enough, recent attempts to surmount this dichotomy, between anthropomorphism on the one hand and agnosticism on the other tend to foster a nuanced version of the first alternative, namely anthropomorphism. This is true in theologies which view religious language as paradoxical (Barth), mythological (Bultmann), symbolic (Tillich), or analogical — either in the sense of process theology which tends to treat analogy as univocal speech, or in the sense of existential theology which is open to analogy on the level of *Existenz*. Religious language in the Christian tradition, largely sacral in tone, has lost its hold on believers who live in an all-pervasive secular world. This secularism, coupled with the atheist critique of the past century, has made it difficult for men and women of contemporary experience to believe in a gracious and efficacious God. Present-day Christian theology, then, is witnessing a massive effort at recovering relevance. The overwhelming tendency is to trim the transcendence once ascribed to God on the grounds that such a God remains remote from and unconcerned with affairs that are human-sized. The thesis of this chapter will be that it is precisely God's utter transcendence of and autonomy from the world that explains his universal and intimate involvement with every finite reality and event; the ground of God's immanence then is precisely his transcendence.

Rudolf Bultmann's God reveals not the holy mystery which he himself is, but the depths of human self-understanding. Herbert Braun carries the demythological project further, seeing the concept of God which underlies the language of the New Testament as merely a cultural inheritance from Judaism. Such language is used purely as a means for conveying a message which overthrows the original meaning of the literature, namely, one affirming an omnipotent creator God. Scriptural references to God as transcendent are not to be taken literally, then. Jürgen Moltmann — and less radically, Wolfhart Pannenberg — advance a notion of deity that replaces eternity conceived as timelessness with a form of primal temporality that has the effect of historicizing God. Process theologians, taking their cue from Alfred North Whitehead, balance off infinity as only one pole of God's nature, with finitude as characteristic of the other pole — adding that only the latter, the finite — accounts for actuality in God. Charles Hartshorne is thus characteristic of process thinkers in developing a concept that gives preeminence to the relativity of God, who needs the world as much as the world needs him. The immutable and so timeless God of classical theism is understood as incapable of entering into a relationship with an ever-changing and temporal world. The assumption is that if God stands outside any temporal series, there seems no way of explaining how that series can matter to him at all. Adrian Thatcher carries the complaint further, asking "How is God personal who cannot experience sorrow, sadness, and pain, i.e., experiences which help constitute us as persons and contribute to our personal growth when we encounter them?"[1]

What is happening in all this is a move away from classical theism in the direction of what is generally understood as panentheism, defined as a doctrine which constitutes divinity as neither identical with the world (pantheism) nor as autonomous from it (classical theism), but as in a state of dependence upon it. What comes to the fore in this kind of thinking is the category of becoming, not as excluding the category of, being but as entering into a dialectical and polar relationship with being, in constituting the divine reality. Nonetheless, a certain ontological priority is ceded to becoming over being — with two important consequences for contemporary Christian theology. One is an emphasis upon the future over past and present, so that even God's being is grasped in terms of futurity; he is "the power of the future" (Pannenberg) or "the promise of the future" (Moltmann).[2] The other is a turn to the subject in its activity as self-enacting and self-positing, so that God is conceived of as the absolute subject.

The most graphic consequence of this theological orientation, however, is felt in the endeavor to explain what is meant by designating God as a God of love. All Christian denominations, from radical neo-orthodoxy to extreme neo-liberalism, share in the consensus that no other concept epitomizes more richly and more ultimately the deity of God. Nor is such understanding limited to Christian thought. For the Christian, it is the mere appropriation of the simple "God is love" of the First Letter of John (4:16), but it has clear grounding in the piety of the Jewish Scriptures. It is entirely lacking, moreover, in both Plato and Aristotle. This is clearly the case in Aristotle for whom any love of the finite and the limited by the first unmoved mover would only detract from the latter's absorption with its own infinite being and goodness. For Plato, if the occasional beneficence of the gods might justly be called a love for humankind, this is only a side effect of divine self love, the *eros* on the part of the gods seeking their own fulfillment in striving to share in the subsistent form of goodness. Both Plotinus and Spinoza encourage us to love God, but caution against being misled into thinking of God as personal — an implicit denial that God himself is capable of any love save a form of self-love.

But this central Christian affirmation — that God is love — faces one well-nigh insurmountable obstacle: the objection lodged by the undeniable existence of evil and suffering in the world. Indeed, in our present state of heightened consciousness and concern, it is not simply the fact of human suffering but an overwhelming abundance and proliferation of it on all sides that challenges taking seriously the conviction that God is nowise a God of evil but entirely a God of love. The dilemma here is well-known and needn't be rehearsed in detail. Either God is powerless against the forces of evil in the world, capable at the most of merely mitigating somewhat its destructive power, and then is not omnipotent and so suffers a diminution of his deity, or he does possess such power but chooses not to exercise it to any significant degree, in which case he no longer qualifies as a God of love.

The resolutions offered historically to this dilemma are multiple and varied, but no one of them can lay claim to being an adequate answer; all of them leave important questions unanswered. In itself evil rises before us as a surd, intractable to rational analysis. Thus, ultimately evil poses itself, not as a problem which can be solved or circumvented, but as a mystery hidden in the designs of God with which we must continue to live. Thus, believers continue to believe in an all-loving God in spite of the unexplained phenomenon of innocent suffering in the world. They refuse to allow the arational specter of evil to count against faith in God. For this reason, atheists and humanists consider belief in God to be without rational grounding.

Organized religions have tended traditionally to share the view that God himself is not the direct cause of evil in creation, but even this position has been challenged — in psychology by Carl Jung,[3] in philosophy by Frederick Sontag. The latter dismisses the all-good God developed in Christian Platonism and writes, "The flaws that lead to man's downfall must find their source in God's nature or else go unexplained."[4] C. E. Rolt does, however, develop the extraordinary position in which evil comes from God in the sense that he refuses to create it. That creative act establishes order out of chaos, and God's exclusion of evil from what he does create leaves that chaos with a positive and ever threatening power vis-à-vis good creation.[5] Cognate to this but less radical is a solution, based on a metaphysical presupposition running through dialectical thinking from Hegel to Tillich, that God is being-itself (*Sein-Selbst*) constantly asserting itself over and against the negativizing influence of nonbeing. Thus, Tillich can write, "It is the nature of blessedness itself that requires a negative element in the eternity of Divine Life."[6] This avoids introducing evil into the interior of God, as something intrinsic to his deity — thus, it absolves God from blame for evil in the world. But it achieves this by locating evil as a surd entirely alien to God, contrary to his will but outside his control. Creation itself is then an attempt on God's part to hold back the powers of darkness, a dynamic striving to overcome them. Process theology is sympathetic toward this outlook to which, however, it gives expression in a totally different conceptual scheme. Here God's dependence upon the world in his consequent nature does not make him the source of evil, but it does render him susceptible to the suffering which the world cannot avoid due to its own radical finitude. Though God transforms all values he derives from the world and rejects all disvalues, still his advance into the future cannot ever be other than finite at any given point. The consequence of this is that though God resists all evil, he does experience in his physical feelings or prehensions, human suffering (which in an indirect way can frequently turn out to be something beneficial). In this way, compassion becomes an attribute of God, so that Whitehead himself can describe God as "a fellow-sufferer who understands."[7]

The *Pathos* of God

The most original and challenging way of dealing theologically with this question of how the loving will of God can be reconciled with the phenomenon of a human world wounded deeply by anguish and suffering is one offered in the provocative thinking of Jürgen Moltmann.[8] His initial presupposition is that we have no grounds for assuming that *in himself* (as what Luther calls the *Deus Absconditus*) God is other than all-good and all-powerful, so that he is neither the source of evil in the world nor is his beingness affected untowardly or diminished by the pain of the world. All such negativity arises, then, from this world, due either to its ontological finitude (this is the risk involved in creation as God "lets be" the world) or (as Moltmann seemingly prefers) due to the negativity of human history culminating in its rejection of God. However, in an act of altruistic love, grounded in his uncreated freedom, God, who apart from such a choice is not a God for humankind, chooses freely to become a God of and for human beings, in a relationship of unconditional love (Luther's *Deus Revelatus*). The voice of Karl Barth can clearly be heard here as an undertone to Moltmann's own, and his (Moltmann's) commitment to Evangelical and Reformed theology becomes manifest, in such themes as revelation, human iniquity, and election — the last of these, however, is given a universality it did not originally possess.

Be that as it may, love by definition is a unitive force in which the lover unites himself or herself with the beloved in the most real and most intimate of ways, entering into and taking upon oneself everything that qualifies the existence of the beloved, whether bettering or worsening that existing. But the beloved in this case exists only in an environment of evil and the all-pervasive suffering that accompanies it. It is here that Moltmann's contribution appears in all the power of its originality. God does not simply act in the world so as to bring to an end the reign of the powers of darkness, offering forgiveness to men and women, and eliminating all suffering. This is reasonably said in light of the undeniable perdurance of both evil and human anguish, perhaps even their intensification today. Without denying that God could have acted in this way, at least diminishing radically the proliferation of negative factors, Moltmann envisages the divine love as inaugurating salvation in a quite different and more profound way. God in effect assumes human suffering into his own being, making it to be his suffering. It is possible to conceive of a world from which all suffering has been precluded simply by God's willing to vanquish and banish from it all evil. But the price of this would be a curtailment of human freedom.

At least the love for God as a totally autonomous act springing from finite freedom would necessarily be compromised. Building on an observation of Albert Camus, Moltmann makes the suggestive remark that human beings can gain ascendency over God in one act — that of freely embracing their own deaths.[9] If tradition has long assumed that such an action is impossible to God, Moltmann wishes to suggest that such is not the case at all.

Moltmann's contention is, in effect, that love constitutes the very essence of God, and that by definition demands the "other" as its object. This cannot be supplied for by presupposing the Christian doctrine of the Trinity in total autonomy from creation because the members of that trinity are not other than God. Thus, God requires a world consummated with the creature that, in freedom, is capable both of receiving divine love and responding to it. This is the motivation both of God's act of creating and of his becoming incarnate. But this "requirement" is not anything demanded by God's nature; it is elicited in total freedom by his love.

> God does not suffer out of deficiency of being, like created beings. To that extent he is "apathetic." But he suffers from the love which is the superabundance and overflowing of his being. In so far he is "pathetic."[10]

At this point, it would seem that Moltmann's thought, by its own inner logic demands something like Luther's distinction between the *Deus Absconditus* and *Deus Revelatus*. Because we cannot know the "hidden God" he must be left free of all engagement in human affairs; it is the "revealed God" who is known to us, and known as involved fully with human misery. This distinction safeguards the gratuity of God's decision to take within himself the suffering of humankind. Eberhard Jüngel approximates this theological view when, after insisting that "God's being is in becoming," he adds that one must not confuse this "with other statements such as, God's being is becoming, or, God's being becomes in becoming."[11] Nonetheless, both Jüngel and Moltmann minimize the implications of this distinction: Jüngel in his claim that there is "no being of God in-and-for-itself without man";[12] Moltmann with the statements "He has to be man and nothing but man" and "the cross of Christ is not something that is historically fortuitous, which might not have happened."[13] What prompts this reservation on the Lutheran distinction is the desire to historicize God's being. Thus an even more explicit assertion of Moltmann's suggests giving up "the distinction made in the early church and in tradition between the 'God in himself' and the 'God for us'..." with the consequence that "the nature of God would have to be the human history of Christ and not a divine 'nature' separate from man."[14]

Still and all, God cannot assume a state of suffering except historically; this is possible only if God is there with human beings and as human. Yet the incarnation is not a contingency plan for redeeming fallen humankind;

rather it is willed for the sake of achieving a full love relationship.[15] A possible misunderstanding must be avoided here. It is not a question of God willing suffering to human beings as punishment for sin, and then taking that punishment upon himself. The Japanese theologian Kazoh Kitamori has put this graphically in noting that God is displeased with our sins but does not suffer because of them; what causes his suffering is his own conflict in choosing to love us even as we remain under his wrath.[16] The point is, however, that the nature of love is such that its full realization is achieved only in passing through suffering. In order to be completely itself, love must suffer, so true is this that "one who cannot suffer cannot love."[17] Similarly, God "has to go through time . . . for . . . it is only in this way that he is eternal."[18] And it is a question of suffering in his very divinity; there is no question here of limiting such suffering to only the humanity which God has assumed. "Suffering is in God's being itself."[19] Moltmann advocates nothing less than a genuine panentheism.

In this process, God identifies himself with humankind so as to stand over against (as it were) his own deity. For this to be intelligible means that God must undergo within himself a process of self-differentiation.[20] For Judaism, this is the differentiation that YHWH effects between himself and his dwelling in the midst of his chosen people, the Shekinah YHWH. For Christianity, this duality becomes a trinity. What are called the trinitarian processions are nothing less than divine history. Somewhat differently stated — the history of the world is taken up into God as his trinitarian history.[21] It means that God undergoes a sundering within himself wherein the Son of God is delivered over to the forces of evil, occasioning suffering (differing somewhat in mode) on the part of both the Father and the Son. Since this rendering within God is motivated by love, it overthrows evil which ultimately is explained as the refusal to love. Thus God's suffering is the transformation of evil into good. This originates the second phase of God's history, one in which the Spirit of that love, in its unitive power, rejoins the Son to the Father. In this, the Son bears with him all of suffering humankind who have become reconciled with the Father through him.

Some General Reservations

Several reservations of a general sort on Moltmann's original and challenging thought here assert themselves rather quickly. One is the not so covert Hegelianism — especially evident in the early Moltmann's choice of the Marxist thinker, Ernst Bloch, as his dialogue partner. The implication of this Hegelian background is that God's freedom is somewhat constrained by a controlling idea of historical process as subject to the dialectic of thought — of affirmation, negation, and then synthesis or sublation (*Aufhebung*). Another is the historicizing of God's being, which has the effect of collapsing the immanent Trinity into the economic Trinity. Third, cognate to these is the emphasis upon futurity as the mode of divine being, which has the effect of emptying out the past and especially the present of any lasting meaningfulness. What will follow here, however, is a specific reflection, critical in kind, on Moltmann's contention that love in God entails by necessity suffering in God.

Divine Love as More than *Pathos*

Moltmann's support for his thesis is that love demands a surrender to the "other" in virtue of which the lover is rendered open and vulnerable. This giving of the self means a vulnerability to possible rejection by the beloved, but also to whatever negative factors may be afflicting the beloved. The unitive power of love is such that whatever evils befall the beloved, also work their negative effect upon the lover; in this sense the beloved is "another self." This is surely true of love as a passion, that is as a psychosomatic phenomenon rooted in bodiliness. But very few religions predicate bodiliness of God. It also can be true of love as volitional, as a free disposition of spirit, but this need not be the case. Genuine compassion, meaning voluntarily sharing the suffering of one's friend in an attempt to alleviate his or her pain, characterizes love as finite, not love as such. The core reality of love as such is the affective union with another or others. The primary manifestation of this is a willing of good to that person, not for one's own sake (unless one is involved only in a love of desire, *amor concupiscentiae*, which is love in an utilitarian sense), but for the other's own sake (which is a true love of benevolence, *amor benevolentiae*). If the beloved is in a state of anguish, then the impulse of love is directed toward alleviating that anguish to the extent of its powers. Only when its resources are exhausted due to its finitude, is it content with compassion for the friend in a loving endeavor to lessen this misery by sharing it in a vicarious and sympathetic way. Compassion, then (as opposed to mere pity) characterizes love, not as such but in its finite modes.

But divine love is omnipotent, capable of overcoming whatever evil befalls humankind. This means that God enlists himself on the side of humanity, and in support of the human cause, ranging himself against all forms of evil and suffering. For such love to be operative, however, does not demand that God be a co-sufferer in his divine nature. Tillich's reservation here is well taken when he writes that such a view "brings God down to the level of the passionate and suffering gods of Greek mythology."[22] It is this uniqueness of divine being, whereby God does not and cannot suffer in himself, that explains why he can love unfathomably, in a totally altruistic way, why divine love can be what the New Testament calls *agape* rather than only the self-fulfilling *eros* of Greek rational thought.

For God to love another is to will good creatively and efficaciously to that other, insofar as God is a creator and redeemer transcending all finite reality. This is not a mere sympathetic and compassionate but ultimately impotent love; it is more than the divine *pathos* of which Moltmann speaks. To maintain this is to acknowledge the immutability of God in the sense that, as the creative source and ground of all that is, God is already the fullness of being. Any change in his being means either the acquisition of something previously lacking, or the loss of some perfection previously possessed. But this is to say no more than that God is not susceptible to change *in the way that creatures are*. Immutability remains a negative concept, denying to God all forms of creaturely alteration; though it does intend to designate a positive divine attribute, this is something that we can neither know nor represent in itself. Moltmann's view that God suffers in himself is, in effect, to have God will to be something less than God; even the Christian belief that God became man does not gainsay this since the incarnation does not imply a metamorphosis of divinity into humanity.

The point of all this is that God can love without suffering, even granting the state of humankind as one of misery. If he does in fact choose to suffer, then the reason for this is not any inner logic of the attribute of love itself, but God's utter freedom in willing for humankind a role in its own reconciliation with himself; the reasons lie on the human side rather than God's. So, it is one thing to deny that God can suffer *in his divinity*, and another to acknowledge that he does suffer *in and through* the humanity he has made one with himself. Christian piety and theology have nearly always maintained that the truth cannot be captured in the expression that "the humanity which God has made one with himself suffers"; it has with some consistency maintained that "it is God himself who suffers, though in and through his humanity." This is not to forget that this understanding came to the fore rather gradually, and that many of the pre-Chalcedonian Fathers, especially those of the school of Antioch, resist the suggestion that God himself suffers and dies, and that some even go so far as to deny that the humanity of Christ suffers in any genuine sense of the word, e.g., the monophysites and the followers of Apollinarius. The former position exaggerates the distinction of the two natures in Christ and slights thereby the unity; the latter position assumes the opposite stance and so exaggerates the unity to the point where any admission of suffering on the part of the humanity is tantamount to admitting suffering on the part of the Logos of God. The Arians and Adoptionists believed that the undeniable suffering of the humanity argued against predicating divinity of Christ in any proper sense. Ultimately, however, it is the bolder language of the New Testament that prevails: it is the "author of life" who is killed (Acts 3:15); it is "the Lord of glory" who is crucified (1 Cor. 2:8); it is he whose "state is divine...who...empties himself....even to accepting death" (Phil. 2:6ff.). Such language is adopted without being trimmed by any philosophical doctrine of God's impassibility, by Irenaeus, Tertullian, Origen, Anthanasius, Hilary, and others. After Chalcedon it becomes unchallenged in orthodox circles.

It is not a question, either, of *saying* that God suffers and dies, but meaning that really it is only the humanity united to him that does so. Rather God himself undergoes such agony — but in his humanity and not in his divinity. Medieval theology explained this in terms of the well-known *communicatio idiomatum*, a theory maintaining that attributes of divinity predicated of the Logos, and attributes of divinity predicated of the man Jesus — due to the unification of the two natures as enhypostatic in the person of the Word. Though this theory concerned itself with matters of speech, it was understood as grounded in the state of affairs prevailing in reality.

If this be true, it follows that the suffering which God truly experiences, and in the profoundest way, does not result in any qualitative change or diminution of God's nature. Thus it seems possible to safeguard divine immutability and impassibility, without denying the incredible truth of revelation that God wills to suffer in and through the suffering of his people.

Process theology prefers to locate both impassibility and passibility within the divine nature itself — the former in the primordial nature, the latter in the consequent nature. But if that distinction of natures is real, it jeopardizes the divine unity and simplicity. If it is a rational distinction on our part (as would seem to be the case) then it only calls attention to the truth that God transcends both our concepts, that of passibility on the one hand, and its negation (impassibility) on the other. If so, we need to employ both notions in speaking of God who lies beyond our understanding of ontic immunity from suffering and yet opens himself voluntarily to the ravages of suffering.

The problem, then, is one of how to relate these conflicting concepts of deity in some dialectical fashion. H. P. Owen has attempted to put this truth into words by noting that to deny that God *changes* is not to deny that he *responds* to evil in the world; indeed, it is because he is changeless that he is capable of responding perfectly.[23] He makes another attempt at this in allowing that "God suffers on account of finite evil [but] his sufferings do not modify his perfection."[24] Other authors have striven to capture the intentionality behind some such distinction as this. In every case what is involved is the awareness that love can be predicated of God only analogically. And analogy only seeks a qualified similarity between entities radically different from one another. Karl Rahner, for example, insists that God changes and suffers, not in himself but in his other — meaning in the humanity of Christ, though it is God himself who changes.[25] The distinction is perhaps an overly subtle one and may appear as merely a verbal solution to the problem. But it does allow God to be involved in human affairs, including the negative ones, without sacrificing the idea of God as pure actuality. W. Norris Clarke offers help in denying that God can change in the sense of "moving to a qualitatively higher level of inner perfection" while granting that "God's inner being is genuinely affected, not in an ascending or descending way, but in a truly real, personal, conscious, rational way by his relations with us."[26] Another possibility is to argue from the irreducibility of the distinction between the notions of nature and person or persons in God. This might enable one to say that in his nature God remains ever changeless, while in his personhood he is capable of altering in virtue of the fact that the latter category is understood as a pure relation to other persons, divine and created.[27] The advantage here lies in not viewing God's becoming human as a union of two natures, divine and human (even understanding this as a *hypostatic union*, i.e., a unification in hypostasis or person), but as a unity wherein the person of the Son of God is the ultimate subject of the human nature (perhaps better called a *hypostatic unity*). When finite entities change, God knows and loves them in their changed situation, thus it has to be granted that the divine knowing and loving change at least on the part of their terminative objects. God then knows and loves something new *in the world* and though he gathers this novelty into himself, this need not mean any increment to his own plenitude of being which already pre-contains everything that is or possibly could be. Hans Urs von Balthasar approaches the question in explicit terms of what is really conveyed by the statement that it is God who suffers. Death means a radical severing of all ties with God (thus its ominous character). If one is to speak of the death of God, then, this cannot be reduced to a transaction between God and the man Jesus. Rather there occurs a genuine abandonment of the Son by the Father, so that it is God himself who experiences the God-forsakenness of death.[28] "God did not spare his own Son but gave him up to benefit us all" (Rom. 8:32). Some similar version of this solution is espoused by Eberhard Jüngel, Hans Küng, and Heribert Mühlen, among others within conceptual schemes of their own.[29]

The conclusion, then, is: first, that God remains immutable and impassible in his own intrinsic godhead, so that his genuine love for creatures cannot entail suffering within divinity as such; but second, that God does choose to enter personally and relationally into the heart of humankind's suffering in his transcendentally free and loving response to it. God truly suffers, not (as Moltmann would have it) in his very deity, but in and through his humanity which is one with the humanity of all men and women.

This, however, leaves us with one enormous question: Why? One solution that continues to urge itself is some adaptation of that first proposed, somewhat primitively perhaps, by Anselm of Canterbury.[30] At the root of human suffering (as opposed to natural evils such as floods and earthquakes which God wills indirectly for the sake of that gradation in being and dynamic interaction of forces which characterizes the cosmos as a physical whole) lies malice and rebellion, made possible by the freedom to gainsay God, which is the one power over God possessed by human beings. In the Judeo-Christian tradition, this is conveyed by the symbol of "sin." Suffering which is not sin because it touches the innocent as much as the perpetrators of evil, nonetheless follows a certain connaturality in the wake of sin. Suffering, thus, is not moral evil, but evil of natural defect as such has its negative effect upon the human person who is able to register it in a conscious way. This disruption of order and tranquility arises from some primordial act or acts of malice, one which is universal in affecting indiscriminately the entire human family. It is totally reconcilable with an evolutionary theory concerning human origins, since it can be conceived of as occurring at some given moment on the evolutionary scale. In response to this, however, God's love takes upon itself freely a modality whereby the powers of darkness are overthrown, not by an act of divine omnipotence, but by God himself becoming the subject (*hypostasis*) of an act of human love which negates dialectically that primordial human act which was the refusal to love, i.e., an act of resistance to God's loving will.

God chooses not to cancel out human malice by himself on the ontic plane (thus malice continues to work negatively in the world today) but rather to inaugurate a divine-human act of love wherein human beings themselves enter into the heart of evil by accepting the suffering which is the residue of moral evil, and overthrowing that evil from within. This is in order that human freedom, responsible for its alienation from God in the first place, of which suffering is a sign (it is not a question of suffering as a punishment for sin) might be involved in its restoration with God. Anselm called this "satisfaction," a term laden with forensic implications, many of them deriving from twelfth-century feudalism. Aquinas, taking this thought over from Anselm, moderates it by transposing it from the order of strict justice on God's part to the domain of divine love and mercy.[31] What Anselm intends, however, is that only human beings are obliged whereas only God is able — an expression which indicates the redemptive power of all human suffering undergone in response to God's "becoming sin for our sakes" (2 Cor. 5:21). What all of this amounts to is a genuine Christian panentheism, wherein God who lies beyond suffering in his divinity, chooses freely to suffer as human for humankind.

PART III

PREACHING AND THE SEARCH FOR GOD

TWELVE

Preaching the Word: The Theological Background

A Pre-Note

The Christian, we may take it, is one who "repents and believes [that] the kingdom of God is at hand [in Jesus of Nazareth]." This relationship to God acting in Christ can best be categorized in terms of "discipleship" toward Christ. Discipleship is not ministry, but the latter is radicated in the former, flows from it necessarily and spontaneously, and is inseparable from it. It is to witness to Christ and constitutes, in this basic sense, ministry of the word — taking word here in its Old Testament sense of *dâhbar*, i.e., as meaning primarily deed and only secondarily speech as interpretative of deed. All other Christian ministries are particularizations of this basic ministry of the word, and in a general sense they fall into two categories: official ministries of the word and charismatic ministries of the word. The latter are spontaneous and unstructured in kind, and as varied as the changing circumstances of life of those who form the Church; moreover, they are indispensable to the Church.[1] The former are radicated in church order, i.e., in occupying a distinctive order within the organic and therefore structured Church, which founds a determined relationship of the minister to others.[2] It should perhaps be noted parenthetically that such distinction of order holds true only of the hierarchical Church, i.e., of the Church viewed as the totality of the *means* of salvation; viewed as the people of God, as the community of the saved, no such distinctions prevail, as for example that between priest and faithful. This official ministry, founded in orders, was original to the apostolic college, and is a derived ministry in all others. As expressly formulated in the Second Vatican Council this is threefold; (1) the presbyter — bishop, (2) the presbyter — priest, and (3) the non-presbyter — deacon.[3] The purpose of this introductory note is the need to delimit what this brief chapter will attempt. "Preaching" here will mean the activity of the official minister rather than charismatic proclamation, i.e.,

167

the activity of presbyters and deacons. The reasons for this are that the latter is so broad that it is not readily tractable to theological systematization in a treatment as brief as this one, and that charismatic preaching can be more richly dealt with from a prior, less imprecise, notion of preaching.

Preaching as Charismatic

Having said this, it is now necessary to note that ministerial preaching is itself charismatic. That is, it is a grace of God, an unexacted gift of the Spirit; it cannot be delivered by any amount of theological endeavor. Genuine preaching occurs only when the Holy Spirit (in St. Paul's phrase) "lays fast hold upon"[4] the faith-consciousness of the one called to preach. But the Spirit is invisible, intangible, ineffable; he comes shrouded in anonymity and his identity remains elusive. The Spirit brings the action of God to visibility — or better, to audibility — not in himself but in the *Logos*. He hides himself, if we may so speak, behind the Word — who is not his Word but the Father's. Needless to say, this is not our word, yet the *Pneuma*, evoking in us the response of faith (St. John speaks of the "anointing of the Holy Spirit")[5] affords us accessibility to that Word — so that it is now the Father's Word uttered *in us*.[6] What has thus far been described is, of course, common to all believers; preaching is rather the articulation in the preacher's own words of the uttered Word of God, it is the coming to expression of the eternal Word in the form of the apostolic word. Nevertheless, the Father's Word (and I think it crucial to retain here the trinitarian aspect) can be truly spoken to human beings only in a human way; that is to say, within a consciousness that is simultaneously historic and historical. This means two things: (1) that God's Word to us is *present address*, (2) that such utterance must have objective focus *in given events of history now past*.[7]

Preaching as Medium of God's Present Address

The proclaimed word, then, is the means of rendering present and operative God's Word to humankind — present at this moment of time and in this segment of space, and in a way that is at once human and proper to the order of faith. This Word of God occurring originally in creation, then later in the prophets of Israel, is spoken to us in these latter days finally and definitively in Jesus of Nazareth. As present address, however, we have to do not with the Jesus of history but with the risen Jesus made glorious at the right hand of the Father. There is, perhaps, an important corollary to this: namely that Christ in glory has formed the Church into his body of which he is the head, so that the ecclesial reality which is the Church is not only spoken *to* by Christ but is mysteriously made to be with Christ a *source* whence the Word comes to believers.[8]

Preaching is thus Christocentric insofar as it is a prolongation of the action of God upon humanity, which is only in and by way of Christ as *Kyrios*. As such it renders the Christ-Word present and operative in a saving way. As with any word, one can distinguish the *content* of what is said from an *invitation* always implicit in the speaking; beyond the mere conveying of information the speaker seeks to elicit from the listener some kind of response that will constitute genuine human communion.[9] Here, the latter is precisely God's offer, through the proclamation, of salvation and reconciliation. Thus the proclaimed word is *itself* a saving word; it is more than the mere occasion for salvation, precisely because it is itself the divine word in the form of the apostolic word. Human beings are symbol-making creatures and their symbols are the embodiment, the incarnation of meaning, the emergence of meaning within materiality and bodiliness, on which basis the meaning occurs, comes to pass, arises in availability. It is the proclamatory act that achieves, symbolically and so humanly, the actual encounter with the living Word of God — at which very moment that Word itself convinces us of sin, summons to conversion, uproots us from our world, overthrows all human kingdoms, judges and challenges us in our existence. For this reason, Bultmann would seem right in insisting that the preacher must allow for a response on the part of the congregation that is one of rejection. To the extent that the preaching is genuine, to the extent that it is not the preacher confronting the people, but God — there can be no neutral response, since the demands of God upon us are unconditional.

At the same time, if we have to do here with genuine address, then the human response is drawn up into and becomes part of that address, even when such response is the resistance of sin. This is only to say that the preaching act has about it a dialogic character, which is made actual in the preacher. It is concrete and existential in kind, demanding that preachers realize in their own consciousness the existential faith-situation of the people if they are to mediate the Word of God to their needs. Perhaps, another way of saying this is to note that if it is the Word itself that is effective — "more effective than any two-edged sword" — then it should cut into the very soul of the preacher.

There is a corollary to this: if the address which the preacher renders present and actual is a saving address, then it occurs, ideally, within the content of worship. With this it becomes clear that the proper context for ministerial preaching is the sacramental one. In the case of six sacraments, that context is inchoative in kind, viz., ordered to the central and consummate sacrament which gives meaning to all the rest, the Eucharist.[10] At this point, the teaching of the Second Vatican Council on the "many presences" of Christ within the integral Eucharistic act does much to enrich an understanding of what preaching is meant to be.[11] Basically, these presences reduce to three: (1) in the gathered community, (2) in the proclaimed word, and (3) in the consecrated bread and wine. The first means that the Church pre-exists those who make it up; it is the Church that forms them into people capable of hearing the saving and reconciling word proclaimed by the preacher. The "real" presence (so-called from Scotus's time) is the subsequent realization in new symbols (viz., bread to be eaten and wine to be drunk) of the saving presence of Christ already realized in the proclamation. Obviously, this is no denial that the third presence of Christ is *secundum substantiam*, but it does highlight the fact that it is the proclamation which conveys the meaning and the purpose of that presence. So, ideally, the preacher is at once the minister of the Eucharist, the priest. Karl Rahner, among others, has attempted to relate these two roles more richly by viewing the presbyter — priest as one whose role or function is: first of all, to preach the Word, second, to do so in virtue of office or orders, rather than charismatically, and third, at the highest level of sacramental intensity of that Word, namely in the anamnesis of Christ's death and resurrection.[12]

Objective Focus in History

One cannot do full justice to the Word of God by seeing it as only present address to humankind; it is also a word in the sense of bearing content, a delivered word. Over and above being something active, the source of preaching, it is also something given, the object preached. This is so because God's revealing-saving act is not only existential and historic (*Geschichte*), it is also historical (*Historie*); human beings transcend time only in the sense that events of their past become real for them in the present by way of opening the future. Granting then this human historicity, God's address to humankind finds objective focus in certain deeds of God within history, deeds which retain their once and for all character, and which supply the objective data from which the preaching act originates. There is one sole link with these mighty deeds of God and that is the inspired literary record of them which constitutes the books of sacred Scripture, especially the New Testament. This remains normative for all preaching; what that record means can be gotten at with the help of the sciences of exegesis and hermeneutics. The sole other norm is tradition — articulated as the dogmas of the believing community, exposed and illumined somewhat with the help of the sciences of dogmatic and systematic theology. As one integral source of preaching, these two can perhaps best be brought together in the phrase suggested by the First Vatican Council "the Gospel read in the Church."[13]

But what do we find in Scripture to be preached? First of all, not dogmas; the basis for dogma is there, yes, but not dogma as such. These are rather definitions, authoritative in kind, that serve as guideposts and as limits to the sense in which Scripture can be propounded. The preacher must know the dogmas; they do not, however, as such constitute the themes of his preaching. Second, not doctrines; these are undefined truths developed by the theologian speculatively, with a certain degree of abstraction, and rendered into a particular conceptual system. The activity here is rational in kind and its prime instrument is the science of logic.

What is found in the biblical record is a people's experience of God's action toward them within the context of their actual history; in a word, *Heilsgeschichte* (salvation-history). The task of the preacher is to render that salvation-history present and operative in the world today. One caution on this comes quickly to mind: this should not be misconstrued into the attempt to reconstruct the earthly history of Jesus of Nazareth for the purpose of providing a model for Christian living in a psychological or moral sense.[14] What one seeks to realize are rather the "mysteries" — e.g., the trinitarian truth (that the *Logos* and the *Pneuma* are *homoousion tō Patri*) and the christological truth (that Christ is *homoousion* with us) — not as theological doctrines, but as (and here I borrow a phrase of Ratzinger's) "modes of our Christian existence."[15] This is the way the mysteries of the Trinity and Christ are proclaimed to us in the New Testament, and thus it is not bold to say that the model for preaching is the Bible itself. We need to do for our age what, e.g., Paul and John did for theirs. One difference, of course, is that our experience has its objective focus in the reading of the New Testament whereas theirs was immediate.

The Specific Task of "Kerygmatic Re-interpretation"

But all of this only brings us down to the precise question facing us: *how* does the preacher do this? Not by a mere representation of what is found literally in the scriptural texts themselves, though that may well be a starting point! A positive clue may be uncovered in Heidegger's understanding of hermeneutics. Hermes (Heidegger writes) is the messenger or herald of the gods.[16] Human historicity is such that when we go back to a text that recounts an experience of our common past, we unavoidably bring to it out of our cultural milieu questions which force the text to yield answers not heard before.[17] Something genuinely new comes to light, and granting that this occurs only within human subjectivity, it is not subjectivistic because it comes from the text itself, which (in this case) is God's own objective Word. What is meant here is not any "accommodated" sense of Scripture (one given by the interpreter to fit his or her own purposes) but something closer to the *sensus plenior*, a sense that God himself intends beyond the explicit sense of the words. For one who stands in the Catholic tradition, this cannot be carried to the extremes of Bultmann's radical demythologization or of Tillich's spontaneous religious symbolization.[10] The latter dismiss out of hand any literal meaning or objective historical referent; the newness of meaning for them derives exclusively from religious subjectivity. On the other hand, to merely repeat the traditional formulas of the past is to run the risk of failing to grasp the *meaning* as intended by God here and now.

If this task of "kerygmatic re-interpretation" is not done by the preacher then the consequence in the people addressed is very apt to be incredulity — and the whole purpose of the sermon is, after all, to arouse faith. Either what is said will be dismissed as utterly irrelevant, or it will be "believed" as a mere notional affirmation that remains sealed off from concrete and real life — in neither case will there be a hearing of the Word of God. At this point, two examples, one doctrinal and one moral, may serve to show why this task is necessary. First, the miracles of Christ: these are not peripheral to the New Testament; in Mark's Gospel alone, one-third of the verses recount miracles, thus they must be preached. But is real service done to the religious force of these accounts if they are presented simply as instances of God's dominion over nature or to establish Christ's divinity or perhaps confirm his message or present Christ as a compassionate faith-healer? In the Gospels themselves the miracles are not motives for belief but the very opposite; they occur within a human context in which Christ first of all challenges his listeners, confronting them with the possibility of faith out of the existential and moral situations of their own lives. For those disposed to believe that God is at hand, the miracle occurs as a kind of bringing to expression symbolically (i.e., in the figures of earthly realities) of that faith. Thus only those who believe "see" the miracle, the others go away unchanged. It would seem that the miracle stories can be "translated" so as to confront contemporary human beings with the question of what exactly it does mean to believe in God in the radically altered life-situations of today. Other similar examples abound: Is it true preaching to represent God as a cosmic deity, a sort of Zeus manipulating human affairs in arbitrary fashion — is not this in fact to encourage looking upon God as in Proudhon's phrase, "the Intruder, the Antagonistic One at odds with man's endeavors"? — or to present the infancy narratives as literal history which mythologizes the Christ-event and seemingly puts it at a considerable remove from anything possible to present experience; or to preach the resurrection as if it were an empirical event, something like the resuscitation of a corpse rather than revelation? Of course, one may fail not only by neglecting to re-interpret but by re-interpreting falsely or badly: by preaching a God despoiled of his godness, or reducing the infancy narratives to mere poetry, or viewing the resurrection as only the inner experience of having decided for Christ. A further cautionary note: faith is surrender to the unconditional claims of God involving the overthrow of the will's sovereignty, indeed of all human kingdoms and institutions. No amount of demythologization, then, renders the faith act merely spontaneous and automatic. J. B. Metz for one (against some overzealous disciples of Rahner) has drawn attention to this by insisting upon the unbelief which always lies at the heart of belief and needs to be constantly overthrown.

A second example — this time in view of preaching that is moral rather than doctrinal: does not preaching issue in incredulity if the demands of God upon us are presented without reference to human historicity and the fact that human freedom exists only as culturally conditioned? God's present summons to Christian love in the domain of sexuality is not heard today by us as it was by Augustine in the early fifth century for whom the attendant pleasure was in itself illicit and justified only for the sake of procreation, nor as it was by Aquinas in the thirteenth century for whom the pleasure is in itself good, but only to be sought in a prior intending of the procreative act. The contemporary preacher must make credible how the living out of one's sexuality can be in fact the loving of God, as well as how in fact it can fail to be such. Once again, is it true moral preaching to fail to make clear in, for example, the areas of world peace and social justice (and surely *not* to preach these is to fail the demand made on the minister of the gospel by the Sermon on the Mount) that morality is not individualistic in kind, that the Church does not have ready-made solutions and in some cases has only provisional ones, that those who make up the Church are nowise untouched by the scars of sin?

The Origins of Re-interpretation

How, in actual fact, should the preacher approach this task of kerygmatic re-interpretation? I have only two clues — one intellectual, the other religious: first, in dependence upon theology; second, by undergoing personal conversion. Preaching is a charismatic act and not a theological act, still theology remains constitutive for preaching, something more than a prerequisite. If faith is impossible without hearing, hearing is impossible without understanding, which is to say God's Word to humanity is intrinsically intelligible. First of all, there is the necessity of acquaintanceship with the tradition. If, as the theologians of hope would have us say, the voice of God comes to us out of the future, still that can only be by way of the past. To not know the tradition is the easiest way of running the risk that the Word of God collapses into what are only human words. More than this, God's Word is unitary and has about it a "logos" character, it is necessary to establish the objective continuity between that Word as articulated in the past and its distinct resonances in the present. Much more proximate to the preacher's task, however, will be theology in a quite distinct phase, one which after having sought enlightenment in the way the Word was spoken in the past, now seeks to witness to it in direct confrontation with the religious issues of the day. This means speculative theology, not in the sense of dogmatics (which explores meaning), or systematics (which structures such meaning into synthesis) but as pastoral theology. But it is hardly audacious to say that this today remains a *terra incognita*, and stands in serious need of development. Possibly this could be begun along the lines of what Lonergan calls the eighth functional specialty of theology: "Communications."[19] Here the proper work of theology is the derivation of categories which will allow the kerygma to come to rich expression as present reality. This would mean far more than the mere coinage of new words, which after all would be nothing more than novelty; it would be more a putting of ancient words and concepts into a new context from which there arises genuine newness of meaning. But this derives from a new appropriation by understanding of the mysteries themselves as present soteriological reality, as "modes of Christian existence." Also, this will mean less the appropriation of existing language to communicate what is already understood in a prior act than the spontaneous emergence of language as the embodiment of experienced meaning. Clearly, this activity will have a strong empirical basis; its matrix will be the direct experience of God at work among the people he forms as his own. Preachers should live among and close to those they are called to serve, without losing their identity as those "set apart for the Gospel."

Granting the work of the Holy Spirit, which remains anonymous, there is a religious dimension to the experiences of all human beings, which experience is spontaneously articulated into language. But the contemporary Western world is radically secular and so affords on every side language which has the effect of supplying an interpretation of the experience in an irreligious and godless way.[20] Thus, the preacher of the gospel is called upon to supply language categories which enable believers to interpret their concrete life situations as instances of God's working within them. The Church can be viewed dynamically as self-constituting — indeed constituting itself as the *communitas Verbi*, as those who hear the Word — and the ministers of the gospel then are catalysts in this process, they are those in whom the process becomes conscious. Practically speaking, there is no question here of any sort of technical language; the concern is rather with ordinary language, but a religious use of ordinary language. Left in its secularity, ordinary language simply lacks "carrying power" for the Word, and in many cases must be rejected as banal. This concern with living language raises the question as to whether, in his formal capacity as "those sent" to announce the good news, preachers should give expression to their own opinions and seek to motivate programs of social and political action. Seemingly, these are better left as resonances of the Word within believers themselves, after the self-communication of God in proclamation — i.e., resonances of the Word as it is addressed to their freedom as responsible Christian members of society in the making.

Second, there is the need for conversion. By this is meant not justification, i.e., the turn from sin and acceptance of first grace, nor the special type of once and for all conversion such as that undergone by Newman in 1816, but an ongoing and continually renewed surrender to God's love operative in the world. It is religious in kind and will quite naturally give rise in its turn to moral conversion, but what is more significant here, it can very well be the source of intellectual conversion as well, as Lonergan contends in his most recent writing.[21] Here the love of God, which is always a grace, moves the heart first, occasioning a shift of religious horizons, and creating a world of personal decision and existential commitment, out of which the intellect is led to understand, in an intuitive act of insight, something hitherto undisclosed. Spontaneously, this seeks to come to expression as proclamation. Thomas gives theological expression to his own version of this in his teaching on the intellectual gifts of the Holy Spirit, i.e., in terms of the docility of the intelligence to the illuminative power of the *Paraclete*, by way of the prior union of charity.[22]

At this point, perhaps a cautionary distinction should be made: if ministers of the word feel themselves not to be fully converted to the love of God, if they are aware of their own failure to live up to all the injunctions of the gospel, that does not mean that under plea of unworthiness they are justified in not preaching the gospel in its entirety, in all the demands it makes. To think otherwise is to be guilty of a subtle form of Donatism. This is not inauthenticity, which would rather be to preach without sincerity, to preach that of which one is not fully convinced — this would, of course, rob the proclamation of its saving efficacy.

Ideally then, a theology of preaching should coalesce these two elements, the intellectual and the religious, into a conscious reflection on how in actual practice (i.e., within the existing, culturally conditioned, religious situation) meaning "comes to pass," and incarnates itself in the words and deeds of the preacher. Preaching is thus the release of a twofold efficacy that is indigenous to meaning itself — for meaning is at once communicative and constitutive. It is communicative, that is to say its occurrence has the effect of drawing others into the ambit of meaning achieved. And it is constitutive in the sense that it structures community founded on the common understanding (of goals etc.) made available. Thus viewed, preaching induces conversion in its hearers whereby they surrender to the building power of the Word, achieving in this way self-transcendence — or contrariwise, allowing for the refusal of conversion, and thence alienation, and the deterioration of authentic meaning into ideology. Once again, the concern is less *how* to preach than *what* to preach.

The Word we preach is God's answer to the question posed by human existence. Yet we speak much of the silence of God in these latter days, and this is certainly true at least in the sense of a cultural eclipse of God. This may be due partly to God's will that those called to preach be delivered over to experiencing the sinful condition, one resistant to the Word — as the incarnate Word was "made sin" for our sakes and delivered over to the cross. It may also be God's way of urging upon us the mission of the Church, i.e., the re-appropriation of the saving dimensions of that Word for ourselves and our generation.

THIRTEEN

Preaching as a "Moment" in Theology

One indispensable element in the varied endeavor which is preaching comes to light in viewing it as a terminal moment in what is properly the theological act. So conceived it originates within the womb of theology, is nurtured there, and retroactively redounds back upon theology itself in an act of enrichment. More radically, of course, proclamation arises out of faith — but to be effective it must come from a faith mediated theologically, from a *"fides quaerens intellectum."* Otherwise, preaching can come to be viewed as the mere rhetorical propagation of a tradition.

The hallmark of Christianity is historicity: its origin lies entirely in God's break into our history and his incarnation; his assumption of that history as henceforward *his* history. On such grounds Christianity distinguishes itself from, e.g., Buddhism. History is not mere cosmological time, but time as a dimension of human reality. What this means is that Christian speech as historical cannot be mere repetition but must be some kind of creative transformation, yet in a way proper to being human. It is difficult to see how this can be done effectively other than by way of that sort of reflective thinking mediated by theology.

If theology is a science, it is a "life science" — *Lebenstheologie* or *Geschichtstheologie* — for its subject is God's action in history, an action by way of deed and interpretative word that is at once historical and historic (for Germans, who have words for distinctions such as these, it is both *Historie* and *Geschichte*). God's revelatory act is thus simultaneously past historical event and present address. If God does not address us today and if Jesus the Christ is not living and present in the Church as the focus of that summons — then, quite simply, there is no such thing as Christianity.

Again, as science, theology has an empirical base; it is empirical in two ways: first, in its origins, namely the action of God within history, and, second, in its fruition, its termination. This is only to say that theology originates out of past historical experience but terminates in present historical experience. This latter is an experience of the saving Word rendered real, present, and operative — interiorly in human hearts, and exteriorly in that community and institution which is the Church. This, however, does not occur apart from the proclamation of the Word. Moreover, the proclamatory act is not a mere practical adjunct to theology as theoretic inquiry, but a genuine moment within theology itself.

The Preacher Is Communicator

This notion can be pursued in various ways. An illuminating instance is Bernard Lonergan's explanation of theology as an ordered dynamism that moves through various "functional specialties" (there are eight in all), the culminating one of which is called "communications."[1] Communications concerns itself with the effort to unleash God's Word into the tissue of human life and society. I would simply add that the presbyter-priest in his formality as proclaimer of the Word is the prime instrument of this; that preaching then is a privileged moment within "communications." But this can occur only after: (1) the meaning of the Word is grasped in understanding; (2) its truth affirmed in judgment; and (3) its summons responded to in responsible decision. Only then can that saving Word be sedimented in human hearts and societies. This is to say that the preaching act arises out of the theological specialty "communications." Why is this so?

God's revelation to humankind is something real, it occurs within the domain of the real with all the implications of objectivity. But the humanly real is the intelligible, what is found in a world of meaning. Meaning occurs only within consciousness, but always as embodied in the word. Words are bearers of meaning and there is no such thing as wordless meaning (this is true even of the inner trinitarian life of God). Still, words have no life, no meaning of their own; they gain such only as they live within consciousness. In the dictionary, for example, we find meanings only in the lexical sense, which are only denotations that mark limits to the way in which we can use words; it is the use that endows them with the full power of meaning. Meaning only "comes to pass" within consciousness, as what is meant, what is humanly intended. Thus linguisticality is a code word for the human person; the person who suffers from aphasia — the complete inability to speak — we recognize as suffering from a grave defect. In this sense, words are events; they happen as do other events and in happening they change, for better or for worse, the course of history. In words, Being itself finds its voice (Heidegger).

By way of putting this into a Christian context and perhaps making it more graphic: resurrection lies at the very heart of Christianity in its origins. But this is not simply or exclusively the pure historical event itself in time and space. It is that above all: "If Christ has not been raised then our preaching is in vain" (1 Cor. 15:14). But it is also that event as perduring, as it continues to happen, to be really present, really effective of redemption and salvation, within the faith-community as a human and therefore historical reality. The Anglican exegete, Reginald Fuller, has drawn attention to the truth that "...in the early community, resurrection was not narrated, it was preached."[2] Without the preaching there is no way the resurrection could be made present and operative in a human way, that is, in a way accessible to human consciousness. It is in this sense that theologians understand God's revelatory act as continuing, as constituting present address.[3] Another theologian of the resurrection, C. F. Evans, confirms this in viewing the resurrection as a reversal by God of the cross which ends Jesus' historical life: "Jesus' messianic Lordship is established by God *in the experience of the Church*, which is the point of access to Christ's continuing and effective presence" (emphasis supplied).[4]

One Must Choose

The point here, at any rate, is that preaching is a highly privileged instance of a "word-event," which event, as something specifically human, is the occurrence of *meaning*, which itself summons human beings to *decision* in the face of what is meant. That is to say, grasping the meaning (or to speak more properly, being grasped by the meaning) is to stand before the saving intentionality of God, in such wise that one cannot remain neutral. The dynamic of human conscious life means commitment, at least implicitly, to the value that has come to appearance in availability — or, conversely, refusal of that value. One must choose to live authentically or in failing such, choose to live inauthentically.

But there is one further step. The meaning embodied in words seeks spontaneously to embody itself further in actions, in gestures and deeds. This cannot be denied without denying that bodiliness is essential to the human condition. In the context of the eucharistic celebration, for example, the saving intentionality of God is brought to symbolic expression: (1) first of all in the proclaimed Word articulated in the homily, but then beyond this, (2) in the further earthly symbols of bread and wine, and (3) lastly, within Christians themselves.[5] This is only to say that just as meaning sets the stage for decision, decision in its turn consummates itself in action. This action is, in its common instance, the building up of the authentically human and, in its specifically Christian instance, the building up of the kingdom of God.

If God works through his Word, and if that Word signals the occurrence of meaning within human consciousness, then there is a real sense in which human beings are bestowers of meaning when they speak. Or, at least, they are coconstitutors of meaning since they must presuppose the raw materials which they interpret meaningfully — in Christian religion these raw materials are God's acts in history. Here it becomes clearer that true preaching must emerge out of the matrix of theology. This is even truer in light of the present shift from what used to be called dogmatic theology to what is more frequently today called hermeneutical theology.

Without suggesting that all theology can be collapsed into hermeneutics, the present situation is less one of explaining a once and for all meaning already in the dogma, than one of listening anew to the dogmas to hear what God has to say through them to us today. Obviously enough, our bestowing of meaning is not to be regarded as an act on humanity's part apart from or over against God. The initiative is always the unexacted grace of God, the anointing of the Holy Spirit. And the focus remains the normative expression of God's Word, namely, the New Testament read in the Church. But that is a living Word, and contemporary believers bring to it contemporary questions. This means a certain newness of meaning, but one that comes out of the text; it is not subjectively imposed on the text because it is the text itself that yields it up. On the basis of this continued emergence of newness of meaning in history, it is even possible to say: God realizes himself in human history — not in the sense that he comes to realization in his own intrinsic being, but that he chooses to realize himself in this world only in and through the endeavors of men and women.

Meaning Is Realized Humanly

Put somewhat more succinctly: the meaning realized is God's meaning, not merely human meaning. But as realized in a human way (and apart from that we can only say it is not realized at all), it must be mediated in a way indigenous to the workings of human intelligence. The meaning is there to be understood, and the truth is there to be affirmed. But both of these, understanding and affirmation, are adequately done only as acts of theology. The faith from which preaching arises is a *fides quaerens intellectum*.

Preaching thus unleashes the power inherent in God's Word, a power identified as the meaning of God's saving intentions. What preachers do when they preach is mediate God's meaning. But the question forced upon us now is: What precise functions does meaning have? What in fact does it effect? To borrow again from Lonergan, the function of meaning is fourfold: it is *cognitive;* it is *constitutive;* it is *communicative;* and it is *effective.*[6] Each of these needs to be explained.

It is first of all *cognitive;* it is not just emotive or performative but truly informative. It intends what is real and what is true; it moves one out of a world of arbitrary subjectivity into the objective world of what is real and true. This calls for a stance of openness toward a revealing God. It underlines the truth that the real problem for the preacher is not *how* to preach but *what* to preach. The preacher must know what it is that offers itself for belief, that calls forth belief.

Second, meaning is constitutive. That is to say it constitutes the very reality of the phenomenon which is proclamation, and so of the preacher. The latter does not merely transport mechanically a meaning from the New Testament to the congregation. Preachers let the text come to meaning in their own intentionality on which basis they are formally constituted as those who are now enabled to announce the message of Christ. This meaning, precisely as it occurs, constitutes the revelatory and saving act of God. At the same time, it constitutes the preacher as "one who saves" — in however deficient and instrumental a way. Thus as meanings alter in the one who speaks, so does the very reality of the speaker.

The Preacher Builds Community

Third, meaning is *communicative*. That is, the meaning intended by the individual speaking becomes common meaning constituting thereby community. For communities are founded upon shared meaning. Where commonness of meaning is lacking, the consequence is misunderstanding, distrust, suspicion and ultimately violence. The preacher is thus a builder of community through inducing a shared meaning in the hearers, as the meaning intended by the preacher sediments itself in those gathered to hear the Word. Specifically, of course, this means the Church — but as that community which is structured not only by the inner gift of grace (which is due to God's initiative alone) but also by the outer word which is the meaning thematized by the preacher. Aquinas renders this by saying that faith comes *"ex auditu,"* quoting Romans 10:17, that is, by a hearing *"verborum significantium ea quae sunt fidei,"* which is *"quidem exterius inducens"* in faith, in contrast to the *"causam interiorem quae movet hominem interius,"* namely, the *"interiori instinctu Dei invitantis."*[7]

Lastly, such meaning is *effective*. It spontaneously issues in action, action at once personal and communal which alters the course of events. Without the communication of common meaning action tends to be at cross purposes and any building of the kingdom of God on earth becomes an impossibility. On this level, meaning is not simply shared so as to constitute community, it is released as a historical force, as making history, as becoming a lived tradition that is handed on to others, something that over-arches the generations.

Vis-à-vis this fourfold function of meaning, special attention should be given for our purposes here to the second and third of them, to the insight that meaning plays a constitutive and a communicative role. If meaning occurs simultaneously in the conscious intentionalities of the one who speaks and those who hear (by which is meant not the mere registering of sounds but the grasp of meaning), then meaning constitutes the preacher as the instrument of the saving Word and the congregation as the place where that Word takes root, only in virtue of a conversionary act. If meaning truly happens, those to whom it happens cannot remain unchanged. The Word itself inaugurates the conversion by dismantling existing horizons and structuring a whole new world of meaning. As meanings are enriched, so are the very realities of those who intend and grasp such meaning. This is especially true of that Word which is "alive and active (and) cuts more keenly than any two-edged sword, (which) sifts the purposes and thoughts of the heart" (Hebrews 4:12). Preachers must first of all succumb to the power of the Word within; to the extent that they fail to do so their preaching suffers a diminished effectiveness.[8]

In preaching, knowledge comes to language — but the knowledge in question is at bottom a knowledge born out of the love of God. It is not academic and abstract (in the pejorative sense of non-real) but concrete, personal, historical and existential. It comes always as a grace, which moves the heart first, occasioning a shift of religious horizons, and creating a world of personal decision and existential commitment. Out of this the intellect is led to understand, in an intuitive act of insight, something hitherto undisclosed. This, in turn, seeks spontaneously to come to expression in proclamation. As noted in the previous chapter, in the categories of Aquinas there is an approximation to this in the role assigned to the intellectual gifts of the Holy Spirit. That is, Aquinas views what we are calling here "conversion" as involving a certain docility of intelligence to the illuminative power of the Paraclete, a docility rooted in a prior affective union with God by way of charity.[9]

"What Goes On" Is Important

God is not an empirical entity of our world, available to direct experience. If he is to be found at all, he must be found in human experience. But this is only to say preachers must find a touchstone for this search in the conscious appropriation of their own encounters with God. They must first of all appropriate and affirm themselves as they submit to that drive toward authenticity which the Word itself inaugurates. If the preacher's work is to be credible, it must ring true; to ring true it must square with experience, in this case, of course, of faith-experience.

> Now that my ladder's gone
> I must lie down where all ladders begin
> In the foul rag and bone shop of my heart.
>   (W. B. Yeats)

Hopefully, all of this helps to explain what is meant by referring to preaching as a "moment" in theology — a theology beginning with experience (the encountering of God's action in history) and ending with experience (the communication of that action as it is understood and made presently operative). However, it would do less than service to this way of thinking if it were taken to mean that there is a unilateral or one-directional movement running *from* theology *to* preaching, i.e., from theory to practice. Here I would suggest a broadening out of Lonergan's functional specialty communications into a genuine pastoral theology. Part of the latter's concern would be a reflection upon what is actually going on when the Word is preached in the world today. Preaching would thus redound back upon theology, offering it further data to be interpreted in the search for meaning and truth. Such a theology would be pastoral, not in any narrow sense (for example, confining itself to the *cura animarum*), but in the quite broad sense of seeking theory about practice — yet not practice in the sense of *how* something might be done but in the sense of *what is going on* in the dialogue between God and humankind. Its concern, moreover, would extend to secular disciplines, sociology and other life sciences, for example; its interests would reach to questions of how decisions are reached within societies of responsible persons, policies decided upon, programs inaugurated and implemented, etc."[10] Seemingly, such recourse to secular disciplines is already a reality, at least in the United States. But thus far it would appear to be little more than a material borrowing of techniques or of findings proper to the particular discipline. What is intended here is rather an incorporation of such disciplines within theology where they would become transformed and submissive to theology's own distinctive method and unique subject matter. A pastoral theology in this sense would address such questions as: What are the meanings that God intends for twentieth-century human beings (meanings which will still be understood as coming only out of the normative expression of the Word which is the New Testament read in the Church)? What are the actions to which we are summoned today to build up the kingdom, which can only be built after all in history?

Six Practical Corollaries

1. The preacher needs to remain in dialogue with the scholar-theologian. This is not to say that every preacher must be practicing theologian, but only that the Church in its task of evangelization needs the university. As Fr. Hesburgh has noted, the university is the place where the Church can do its thinking,[11] and if the message is to bear meaning it must be thought through. It is time to put an end to the mistrust and to return to the vision and practice of the Middle Ages when it was the

Church that guaranteed intellectual freedom to scholars, for the sake of guaranteeing relevancy to its own message. By the same token, the theologian has a reciprocal need for the data supplied from the experience of those who preach the Word. At any rate, the day of the theological illiterate is past; nor is it enough to be merely a trained professional. In terms of education, theology has to be continuing, a life-time project, not a four-year stint in a seminary. A sign not to be ignored here is that of Catholic laypersons presently studying theology as a university discipline. This will intensify the scandal of presbyter-priests preaching at a superficial level.

2. Faith today can be effectively communicated only in an ecumenical setting. An exclusively denominational ambience means not allowing a full Christian meaning to the mysteries preached. This does not mean abandoning what is distinctive within a tradition, e.g., the Catholic. On the contrary, it is precisely true ecumenism that demands a strong retention of what is positive in a given tradition. But there is a necessity for deepening one's understanding of what such specificity means — in light of what are unmistakenly "signs of the times" and the work of the Holy Spirit.

3. Communication of faith today seemingly will be effective only if its setting be secularized. The Church exists not in a vacuum but within the world. Communicating the Word, then, does not obey only an inner logic of faith itself, it also attends to the cultural structures and practices in which faith embodies itself. Christianity absorbs whatever there is of truth in, for example, modern science (in a way that Buddhism, by contrast, does not and cannot) — a mode of truth, moreover, not to be found in Christianity itself. This is only to repeat that the hallmark of Christianity is historicity. God has assumed our history as his own in Jesus of Nazareth. Thus the Church in its deepest reality is historical. Without being itself worldly, the Church is set entirely within the world. True — biblical imagery and language remain normative, but not definitive. Some sort of translation appears necessary; in chapter 12 I have suggested that this amounts to what might be called "kerygmatic re-interpretation" or "kerygmatic re-presentation."[12]

4. There remains the need, conversely, for what Edward Schillebeeckx calls "critical negativity" toward secular forms and meanings. If entirely within the world, the Church remains the sacrament to the world of a presence that is transcendent to that world. The spirit of the times (*Zeitgeist*) is not always that of the Holy Spirit. The preacher then has to exercise discernment. Simple accommodation to worldly forms is in fact an abandonment of faith. On the other hand, a merely negative defensive posture seems unworthy of what faith summons us to. What is needed is a response that is at once critical (refusing *all* ideology) and creative. This means continued conversionary surrender to the Word, which is after all a living Word and, moreover, a dialogic one. But the conversion is not only religious, it is

also intellectual; it is a dynamism indigenous to human nature, i.e., it does not unfold other than by way of understanding and judgment.

5. If the crux of preaching is the communication of meaning which embodies itself in words, then there devolves upon the preacher the task of being a catalyst in the emergence of new language. This is not a question of simply coining new words (which would be mere novelty) but of rendering the mysteries present and operative in such wise that they become word-events. This means the preacher must first appropriate those mysteries (that of Christ and the Trinity, for example) not as abstract intellectual formulae but precisely as they constitute present soteriological reality — or, to borrow the phrase of Joseph Ratzinger, as they constitute "modes of Christian existence."[13] This is not a matter of creating a new technical language but of developing a religious use of ordinary language. It means using ordinary language descriptive of common experience in such wise as to bring to awareness a religious dimension to that experience, a dimension that our present languages tend to obscure. Our existing Western languages are markedly secular and in their secularity they already amount to an interpretation of human existence that renders any reference to a transcendent God superfluous and not credible.[14] We undergo our experiences then in ways already interpreted as irreligious and godless. Left in its secularity, ordinary language simply lacks "carrying power" for any word about the transcendent. It falls to the preacher then to supply language categories which enable believers to interpret their concrete life situations as instances of God working within them. Which is only to say the preaching act must have its nurture someplace in the womb of theology.

6. Lastly, if Christianity is historical, so is Christian proclamation. Proclamation is the unleashing of the Word which, in a way proper to itself, makes the saving acts of God in the past to be present realities. But history means a present that is the continual dawning of the future. Thus, it is the very presentiality of God within our time that thrusts human beings boldly into the future. This means both the meta-historical future to come, i.e., the *eschaton*, and the this-worldly future which is the task of men and women, the future they themselves are called upon to build. Contemporary Catholic theology is insisting upon a continuity between the two; eternal life with God is not viewed as discontinuous with Christian life on earth but as the consummation of the latter, granting the transforming act of God. But the point is that the kingdom beyond time seemingly awaits the achievement of the kingdom of God in time. The proclamation of the Word, then, bears within itself this sort of urgency. The preacher needs to make credible that the prime agent in the making of the future is the transcendent God who has already revealed, proleptically, in Christ, what that future is to be. Human beings make the future but only with God as the Lord of history. Theology already recognizes this eschatological dimension to human existence; it is less obvious that preaching as yet does.

One final cautionary remark: the Word, which is the bearer of God's life and meaning for us, incarnates itself in human history, midway between the one who utters it and those who listen. But we must take seriously the fragility of the *human* situation here. God's act in history is a *kenosis;* his intentions remain those of setting up the kingdom in and through the weak things of this world. And so, paradoxically, God cannot do without the stammering ways in which we strive to give utterance to that Word. It is part of faith to accept that.

FOURTEEN

What Is Preaching? One Heuristic Model from Theology

What will be attempted here is something quite modest, namely, the raising of the question, "What is the preacher doing when he or she preaches?" The burden of this chapter, then, will be one of theological exploration, and the resolution will be no more than the suggesting of one, tentative and heuristic theory or model as to what may be going on in the act of preaching. This is to acknowledge explicitly that several such theories — all of them viable — are available. One gain in articulating this one is that it might, in a dialectical tension of ideas, suggest other viable theories. This is all the more the case if preaching is acknowledged as more an art than a scientific task (as would appear to be the case), for there are no hard and fast rules as to how the artist sets about creative making.

To cut quickly to the nerve of the question: the preacher can be viewed as one who mediates a saving encounter of the believer with the living God. The locus of the encounter is the Word of God seen as God's utterance toward humankind, constituting God's sovereign and saving initiatives toward men and women. The context is an ecclesial one, for the Word of God is spoken to the Church — not to people as individuals but as persons forming the community of believers. Indeed, God's Word, in its meaning and meaningfulness, is constitutive of that community called Church. Thus, the preacher's word is the Word of God in the form of the word of the contemporary Church. But what is this more precisely?

Some greater precision can be gained in describing preaching or proclamation as "kerygmatic re-interpretation or re-presentation."[1] The kerygma is here understood as the content of God's Word brought to language in a normative way (*norma non normata*) in the New Testament as read in the Church.[2] It is expressed foundationally in Jesus' own message, "Repent and believe for the kingdom of God is at hand" (Mark 1:15),

187

and more proximately in the Church's message that in the life, death, and resurrection of Jesus of Nazareth, God proffered, and continues to proffer today, reconciliation and salvation to humankind. This, then, is the Word of God — the New Testament being not that Word in a self-identical way, but rather the normative literary articulation of it — wherein God, even though he must remain concealed, due to human finitude and sinfulness, nonetheless "unconceals" for us his loving intentionalities toward the world.

All of this is perhaps general enough to be beyond serious controversy. It becomes a bit more problematic with the realization that the kerygma, in spite of representing God's once-and-for-all activity that will never be surpassed, does not confront us with one monolithic meaning that needs only to be transferred unchanged into the present. It is not an objectively finished product that needs but to be translated into contemporary idiom or updated into today's cultural ambiance. The meaning of the kerygma is less something enshrined in the texts than something that comes to pass within the consciousness of the believer who reads the text as God's offer and summons to men and women of today. Such understanding does not occur apart from God's grace, and so it is an understanding indigenous to faith.

But the confession that the kerygma is true cannot be made exclusively on the claims of others. We cannot in human authenticity confess that Jesus is the Son of God merely on the grounds that the writers of the New Testament make this claim or that the Church proclaims it. Someplace in our own consciousness there must be experientially grasped truth (which thereby authenticates itself) on the basis of which the apostolic claims gain credibility and so make humanly possible the interior act of faith. The question that cannot be escaped is that of Jesus to Peter at Caesarea Philippi: "Who do you say that I am?" (Matt. 16:16).

By the same token, the meaning of the Christian "facts" narrated in the New Testament is grasped by us in what is necessarily a process of interpretation. The would-be preacher brings to the text (and unless one starts here, there is no guarantee that the word spoken is indeed God's Word and not the preacher's own) his or her own pre-understanding, which urges on the text questions not identical with those entertained by the original author nor by subsequent generations of interpreters throughout the forging of tradition. Such pre-understanding comes out of a vast matrix of previous experiences with all the images, models, and conceptual structures in which such experiences have been reflectively interpreted, expressed, and so retained. Present experience, then — by which is meant experience of reality as it is given to us by God in both creation and redemption — enables the text to yield up nuances of meaning not explicitly grasped before.

This must be safeguarded from any fall into subjectivism or historicism, from any indiscriminate conformity to a prevailing worldly spirit, which would in effect replace the Word of God with the word of human beings. This is avoided by understanding that all newness of meaning yielded up is controlled by the text itself, in the sense that the meaning is either implicit in the text (then one is doing exegesis) or potentially there, awaiting actualization by the interpreter (then one is doing hermeneutics).

Thus, a dialectical process is at work here: we do not simply confront the past with present experience, but in a critical way we allow the past, which is both the text itself and the understanding it has received throughout tradition, to call into question our present understanding. What transpires is the opening up, not only of a world of meaning behind the text, out of which it emerges, but more. In Luther's phrase, echoed today by Hans Urs von Balthasar, it is not that we are to interpret the Word of God, but God's Word is to interpret us. But it interprets us as our situation before God differs historically and culturally from that of believers in previous epochs. Two additional safeguards might be mentioned at this point: (1) the experiences in question are not simply psychological and emotive in kind but cognitive and critical; (2) we are concerned with experiences that are not private but rather ecclesial in kind, and so subject to the judgment of the Church. They are experiences in the power of the Spirit who "breathes where he will."

Another way of saying this is to note that the Word, precisely as the Word *of God*, overarches all of history and gathers together past, present, and future into the simultaneity, and so the contemporaneity, of the eschatological moment. This means that as the preacher turns to the Word in the lingual expression it has achieved in the New Testament, what should be his interest is not its linguistic form or even specific content, but its character as God's offer and summons to men and women of today to respond in faith to his proffer of salvation. The Scriptures themselves bring this about, less by conveying to us some specific content than by initiating us into dialogue with their own subject matter (to borrow a thought from Hans-Georg Gadamer), which is God in his saving activity. Our disposition in approaching the texts is one of openness to the call of God, which, being oriented to the open future, cannot be predetermined, but which sounds through the received text.

The text is important because at the same time we are dealing with a Word that is spoken to people and as such must be uttered historically — that is to say, from within a given moment of human history — if it is to be humanly intelligible. Thus, salvation for the Christian is focused on the concrete events that constitute the human life and death of Jesus, and on the disciples' experience of his resurrection. These come to us in the narratives of the New Testament, which are already the interpretations by the disciples of their own experience of these events. As the New Testament articulates their experience in its cultural form, so our own understanding is an articulation of our differing experience of these selfsame events.

An important difference, of course, is that our experience is mediated by theirs. But it is possible to say that our encounter with the living God, mediated by the text in its objectivity, occurs not only within experience but precisely as interpreted experience.

At this point a caution must be expressed. The task of the preacher is here viewed as one of reinterpreting the content of God's Word on the basis of present-day experience. This is legitimate, with the understanding that underlying the language of the New Testament are the experiences of the evangelists (including, of course, such writers as Paul), to which they give expression in the religious culture of first-century Palestine and the surrounding Hellenic world. This awareness affords us the hermeneutical key for interpreting our own contemporary experiences, in the cultural categories of the modern world, as instances of God's continuing offer of salvation to us.

This means that the experiences wherein we encounter God are in fact experiences of grace, as were those of the inspired writers. They are not *merely* human engagements with the world (whether of nature or of humankind), which are then interpreted only rationally, and so are no more than projections of finite humanity. They do occur primarily as human exchanges transpiring on a horizontal level of existence, but they constitute an experience of reality that amounts to a basic form of revelation. God manifests his presence and his summons in and through the structures of the real, both cosmic and cultural-historical.

Religious experience is thus not some isolated sphere of experience, but is a depth-dimension to ordinary experience. But such experiences manifest the divine only insofar as they are interpreted experiences. There are no "raw" experiences that amount to direct discoveries of God apart from an interpretive element. By this is meant neither an interpretation that is subsequent to the experience, superimposed on it from without, nor one that works *a priori*, determining in advance the meaning of the data, but an interpretation intrinsic and indigenous to the experience, forming a dimension of the experience itself.

This is the context of revelation, not because of the experiencing as such, but because of *what is experienced* in its objectivity over and against all activity of human subjectivity. It is the phenomena themselves, in their own intrinsic meaning and meaningfulness, as resistant to controlling knowledge on our part, that enables them to mediate God and God's will to men and women. At the same time, this is revelatory occurrence only insofar as it is interpreted, because interpretation in this sense is really a response in faith to God's "unconcealing" of himself through the realities of world and history wherein he draws near to us. This is a faith-act and not one of reason alone, because it is a response to the experience of grace, of God proffering salvation to men and women today. In Schillebeeckx's phrase (to whom much of the thinking here developed owes its inspiration), it is an awareness that runs through whatever we experience, pointing to the fact that God has made the cause of humankind to be God's own cause.[3] It is the surrender to truth that gives itself through human rationality but lies itself beyond the grasp of purely rational processes. However, interpretation of this sort, ultimately controlled by the interpreted, has its own history preserved and passed on in living tradition.

What is at work here, then, is a dialectical process. The confessional historical faith in Jesus of Nazareth on the part of those of us who feel constrained to preach is the enabling factor in our interpretation of present experiences as themselves revelatory. Yet, simultaneously, that interpretive experience enables us to reinterpret the kerygma as God's saving activity toward us today and, in so doing, to add to the narration that constitutes tradition.

The significance of all this for preaching is that experience readily gives rise to conviction and certitude, due to its self-authenticating character. The experiencer spontaneously seeks to give utterance to what he or she has encountered in experience as a witness to it. This is to say that the very experience as something human is bound up with language, indeed becomes itself a speech-event. The experiencer thus becomes a communicator seeking to draw others into the circle of new understanding that constitutes a faith-response to the encounter with God. The experience thus assumes a narrative structure. Preaching is less the explanation of dogmas or doctrines — necessary as the latter are — than the recounting of a narrative, with all the dramatic implications of bringing to the fore what Johann Baptist Metz calls "dangerous memories,"[4] and the urging upon the listener of a decision either for or against Jesus as the Christ of God. Putting this into a larger context, the preacher incorporates the articulation of his or her own new experiences of God's grace into the ongoing narrative that already constitutes living tradition, thereby creatively augmenting that tradition.

This narrative would appear to have two foci, or to unfold in a dipolar way. On the one hand is the christological focus, for the narrative is the recounting of God's rescue of us in the story of Jesus' human life. On the other hand is the pneumatological, for all genuine proclamation is done in the power of the Spirit. By this is meant the Holy Spirit (*Pneuma Hagion*) who is the Spirit of Jesus crucified and raised, yet at the same time is very God dwelling within us as our spirit, when, as in St. Paul's phrase, he "lays fast hold upon us." It is the Spirit who inaugurates our experiences of grace, enabling us to believe — not only in summoning us to belief but also in answering that summons within us.

The Spirit, however, is characterized by a certain anonymity; he has no doctrine of his own but "will remind you of all I have said to you" (John 14:26). He conceals himself, as it were, behind the Word who is personally God's self-expression and who has become visible to us in our own flesh.

The initial disposition, then, of the would-be preacher is one of surrender to the Spirit who must "not be quenched" (1 Thess. 5:19). It is, in short, conversion, in the sense of that about-face which the New Testament calls *metanoia*.

This reception of the Spirit is at once gift and task. It is God's unexacted grace, but at the same time it is, for those in whom it occurs, a summons to the mission of witnessing in word and deed to the saving act of God. Thus, the appearances of the risen Christ in the New Testament — which, however they are explained, occur in the power of the Spirit — are never without this calling of the disciples to a ministry of the word. The ever-new meanings of God's Word, then, to which the Spirit grants entree are, by a dynamic of their own, communicable to others and constitutive of community on the part of those who hear and, in hearing, believe.

This role of the Holy Spirit in forming the community of belief through the Word brings to center stage the work of those who proclaim that Word. What preaching seeks to achieve is not an institutional or ecclesiastical restructuring (necessary as the need for reform may be), not biblical fundamentalism (which fails to take into account the revelatory character of present experiences), not an exclusively charismatic piety (which runs the risk of being merely private, of saying "yes" to Jesus while remaining resistant to the Church as the community of the Spirit); rather, preaching seeks to achieve the ecclesial reality of a Church truly given over to following after Christ, to seeking ever greater conformity to him and the evangelical values lived by him in his human life. Once again, this is something rooted more in praxis than in theory. But for it the Church needs leaders, and it is here that the role of the preacher is defined; it is to this that the consciousness of the preacher lends itself.

From this it would seem that the primary obligation to preach belongs to those who hold office in the Church: bishop, priest, deacon, or minister of the gospel. But Christian proclamation is truncated and impoverished if such ministerial preaching is not complemented by a vital lay preaching movement alongside it.

Significant here is a special obligation, not grounded in office at all but entirely charismatic in origin, on the part of those who belong to religious orders whose work is apostolic and extends in one way or another to proclamation. The character of preaching here assumes a difference at least in mode. All preaching is Christocentric, and all christologies acknowledge in some sense the primacy of praxis over theory. But for those who live according to the vows of the religious life, this primacy takes the form of a radical following after Christ. Such Christians, to take one example, are impelled through a vow of poverty to a solidarity with the poor and to a life of witnessing against the tyranny of possessions and the self-assertiveness that motivates it.

Here a concrete way of following after Christ, to the extent that it is genuine, nuances the preaching that it nurtures. Simply put, such preaching acquires a prophetic character precisely because of the style of life out of which it proceeds — one that seeks to correspond in visible and symbolic ways with the radical demands of the gospel. This characteristic is less possible for the institutional Church, which cannot so easily depart from the standards of the secular sphere. Thus, the various forms of religious life tend to exist on the outer peripheries of the institutional Church, with an unavoidable tension between them and the domesticated Church. By and large, however, this would appear as a healthy tension.

Be that as it may, the present state of preaching seems to be one of crisis, something not at all unusual in times of major transitions. One way of coming to grips with it is to see it as a crisis of credibility, a lack of deep interiorized belief on the part of large segments of the supposedly Christian populace that forms the preacher's audience.

Karl Marx urged his disciples to leave religion alone (by which he meant primarily Christianity), on the grounds that it would soon vanish of its own failed momentum as Marxist societies superseded it. Time has proven Marx to have been very much mistaken. Concern for the God of Jesus refuses to go away. This may point to the fact that the crisis of credibility is not really a crisis of faith but one of culture, that is, one of communicating the Good News in a radically changing cultural context.

I suspect that people *want* to believe but find the form in which the message is preached alien to their own experiences. Thus, the task of preaching becomes one of forging a new language that is appropriate to those experiences in their revelatory power, without neglecting the normative role of Scripture and tradition. Jean Paul Sartre has come close to the mark, perhaps, with the devastating criticism that Christianity discredits itself because it makes no difference in the quality of life. Historically, Christians have been quite as responsible for unleashing evil upon society as have non-Christians. Part of the difficulty, at any rate, may be that the way in which Christianity is presented, the mode of its proclamation, has rendered it meaningless in its power to confront present problems.

God is not dead, but it is hard to deny that God is absent from contemporary culture. It is possible that we have been looking for God in the wrong places. What the preacher seeks to discover and to convey, though it is something specifically Christian, is to be found *within* the world rather than outside of or above it. Is not this where the Spirit operates in seeking out men and women, that is, in this secular world even in its very secularity — granted that what is sought there is the Transcendent, concerning whom clues are discoverable only at a certain depth dimension of such ordinary experience? If so, effective preaching will not take place under the misguided notion of fostering escape from the world, for it is precisely from within the prevailing human situation that one will listen for the voice of the Spirit.

On the preacher's part, this reality means that a certain solidarity with a wounded world bearing the marks of evil and suffering is required. This view of things is confirmed in the faith-act. Experiences are by definition always contemporary, for they are an awareness of something in its very presence to the subject knowing and so responding in love or in the refusal to love. This is faith in a basic sense as trust that truth lies implicit in the phenomena that confront us as reality given by God, especially insofar as such phenomena are not subject to our manipulations. To use an apt phrase of *Gaudium et Spes* from the Second Vatican Council, "God reveals himself by revealing humanity to itself."[5]

The very emphasizing of this truth, however, prompts a caution regarding its understanding and application. Much of the preacher's concern is with restoring life to a Church that has over-adapted to the world and its structures. The life in question here is something specifically Christian: the "new creation" won for us by Jesus in his dying and rising, and lived by us in the Spirit. If this life is mediated to us in no way other than through worldly realities, it cannot be derived nor inferred from human capacities and achievements. It is always life in response to God's unexpected offer of love, which, even while mediated through others, always remains grace from the Spirit. This calls for an attitude of critical negativity toward the structures and the spirit of secular existence, avoiding all conformity to the mores of bourgeois society and conventional piety in the forgetfulness that we are a people of unfulfilled promise. There can be no collapse of faith into ideology, no absolutizing of finite structures of whatever sort, including the ecclesiastical. All such retain a provisionary character.

Another way of putting this is to allow that the prophetic character of preaching bespeaks an element of urgency that attends it. Now is the time, the *kairos;* every moment is potentially the eschatological moment in which salvation is offered us. It is awareness of this that the preacher seeks to awaken in us. And it is what led Luther to view preaching as a sacrament.

We can even say that the preacher functions in imminent expectation of the parousia; there is a sense in which the second coming is already at hand, summoning those who hear God's Word to decision here and now. This forestalls giving to the present order of things a power it does not have. We cannot remain captive to the past, granting our historicity (though it is there in tradition that preachers find their own identity and that of the communities they address), nor so oriented to the future as to empty the present of all meaning other than that of being a stepping-stone to the future.

Christian preaching remains aware of the transitory character of contemporary existence and so seeks the transcending and thus perduring dimension of present life. This is to acknowledge that eternal life is not some mode of duration that merely succeeds temporal duration. Rather, it is the full fruition of what is begun in this temporal existence, the consummation of the self-enactment we are even now achieving in earthly existence. Thus, it is the kingdom of God already inaugurated within our history but unable to reach consummation except beyond the boundaries of history.

One obvious reaction to this way of viewing the preaching act is that it tends to confuse preaching with theology, especially in light of the dominant tendency nowadays to understand theology and its method as basically hermeneutics. Preaching then appears as a sort of short-circuited theological act that moves directly from hermeneutics to communications, from Bernard Lonergan's second functional specialty to the eighth and last of them. To this it must be said that preaching cannot be reduced to a truncated theology. It is much more than a popular presentation of theological views and conclusions. The hermeneutics at work in theology is markedly critical in kind, while that entered upon in service of preaching is more existential and experiential.

The priority of praxis over theory is more obvious in preaching, as is the avoidance of technical language proper to theology. The Christocentric element, while proper to both endeavors, engages the preacher less as a christology of *thinking about* Christ than as a christology of *following after* Christ. I would be reluctant to suggest that ongoing conversion is less necessary for the theologian than for one entrusted with preaching; but conversion for the former serves as reflective understanding, whereas it is more immediately oriented toward witness on the part of the preacher.

One consequence of this is that in an age wherein theological pluralism is a *fait accompli*, the preacher is not constrained to commit himself or herself to any one theological system. For example, he or she can view the experiences of grace as fulfillments of an *a priori* structure to human beingness (as does Karl Rahner), or one can choose to view them as "contrast experiences" of suffering and evil that disclose God as opposing all such abuses of the human (as does Edward Schillebeeckx). The preacher can reflect on incarnational theology, stressing the manifestations of God within the *humanum*, or favor an eschatological theology that prefers to emphasize the hiddenness of God and so the negativities and discontinuities within the human realm. Or the preacher can focus, now on one, now on the other, whichever best serves the point he or she is making.

Nonetheless, granting that preaching cannot be reduced to theology, it remains true that the tie is, or should be at any rate, very close. Quite simply, theology is necessary for preaching — if not in the preacher himself or herself (which would be the ideal case), at least in the ecclesial community. At the very least, theology nurtures preaching and gives it a critical base it lacks of itself. Heinrich Ott, in a surprising synthesis of Barthian theology and later Heideggerian philosophy — has concluded against Rudolf Bultmann, that the continuity here is such that dogmatics constitutes the reflective part of preaching. It might not be claiming too much to conceive of preaching both as a terminal "moment" in theology and as an instance of Christian orthopraxis that serves as a source for theology as theory.

And so I have come to an end, having done no more than I promised, namely to suggest one tentative but viable response to the question "What is the preacher doing when he or she preaches?" Much more remains to be said concerning the varied forms of preaching, the ecclesial context in which it ordinarily occurs, the phenomenon of lay preaching (i.e., on the part of the non-ordained), the context of worship and especially that of the Eucharist, the difference between preaching as service to the Church and as service to the world, the prospects offered by team ministry of the word, the role of prayer in the life of the preacher, etc. The nerve of the theory lies in a re-interpretative act, but one grounded in present experiences insofar as, sustained by and undergone in union with the Spirit, such experiences constitute revelation from God. Since it is grounded in experience, my only hope is that it will serve to stimulate other richer responses in the varied experiences of others.

Notes

Introduction / *Sacra Doctrina* in the Twentieth Century: The Theological Project of William J. Hill

1. John B. Cobb, Jr., "Claiming the Center," *Criterion* 25 (Winter 1986): 3, 6.
2. Gordon D. Kaufman, "Theology as a Public Vocation," in *The Vocation of the Theologian*, ed. Theodore W. Jennings, Jr. (Philadelphia: Fortress, 1985, 60, 65.
3. Ibid., 60.
4. Schubert Ogden, *The Reality of God* (New York: Harper & Row, 1966), 1.
5. Maurice Merleau-Ponty, *Signes* (Paris: Gallimard, 1960), 12, as quoted by Hill in *Knowing the Unknown God* (New York: Philosophical Library, 1971), iii. See Hill, *The Three-Personed God* (Washington, D.C.: Catholic University of America Press, 1982), xi.
6. *Summa Theologiae* I, q.1, a.8, ad. 2.
7. Thomas Aquinas, *In XII Metaph.*, lect. 9: Marietti ed., 599, n. 2566; Rowan ed., II, 901, as quoted in M.-D. Chenu, *Toward Understanding Saint Thomas*, trans. A.-M. Landry and D. Hughes (Chicago: Henry Regnery Co., 1964), 193, n. 51.
8. William J. Hill, "The Theologian: On Pilgrimage with Christ," *Proceedings of the Catholic Theological Society of America* 40 (1985), Appendix B.
9. The term *sacra doctrina* is used here as Hill used it in his teaching (course notes, Introduction to Thomas Aquinas, The Catholic University of America, 1984) and writings (e.g., *The Three-Personed God*, 67, and "Theology," *The New Dictionary of Theology*, ed. J. Komonchak, M. Collins, and D. Lane (Wilmington: Michael Glazier Press, 1987], 1015). See M.-D. Chenu, *Toward Understanding Saint Thomas* and *Is Theology a Science?*, trans. A. H. N. Green-Armytage (New York: Hawthorn Books, 1959); Thomas Gilby, "Sacra Doctrina," and "The Dialectic of Love in the Summa," Appendices 5 and 10 in *Summa Theologiae*, vol. 1, Blackfriars ed. (New York: McGraw Hill, 1964), 58–66, 124–32; Thomas O'Brien, " 'Sacra Doctrina' Revisited: The Context of Medieval Education," *The Thomist* 51 (1977): 475–509; and Walter H. Principe, *Introduction to Patristic and Medieval Theology*, 2nd ed. (Toronto: Pontifical Institute of Medieval Studies, 1982), 272–76. For further discussion of the disputed issues regarding Aquinas's use of the term see G. F. van Ackeren, *Sacra Doctrina: The Subject of the First Question of the Summa Theologica of St. Thomas Aquinas* (Rome, 1952); Francisco Muniz, *The Work of Theology* (Washington D.C.: The Thomist Press, 1953); Per Erik Persson, *Sacra Doctrina: Reason and Revelation in Aquinas*, trans. J. A. R. Mackenzie (Philadelphia, 1970); James A. Weisheipl, "The Meaning of *Sacra Doctrina* in the *Summa Theologiae* I, q.1," *The Thomist* 38 (1974): 49–80.
10. Quoted by Thomas Gilby, "Theology as a Science," Appendix 6, in *Summa Theologiae*, vol. 1, Blackfriars ed., 86.
11. Gilby, "The Dialectic of Love in the Summa," 124–32.
12. Hill, course notes, Introduction to Thomas Aquinas, The Catholic University of America, 1984.
13. See chapter 3. See "Theology," *New Catholic Encyclopedia*, vol. 17, 652.
14. M.-D. Chenu, *Faith and Theology*, trans. D. Hickey (New York: Macmillan, 1968), 30.
15. Hill, "Theology," *NCE* 17, 652.

197

16. Yves M.-J. Congar, *The History of Theology*, trans. and ed. Hunter Guthrie (Garden City, N.Y.. Doubleday, 1968), 139.

17. See Edward Schillebeeckx, "The Concept of Truth," in *Revelation and Theology*, vol. 2, trans. N. D. Smith (New York: Sheed and Ward, 1968), 5–29; "The Non-Conceptual Intellectual Dimension in Our Knowledge of God According to Aquinas," in *Revelation and Theology*, vol. 2, 411–53; and "Faith Functioning in Human Self-Understanding," in *The Word in History*, ed. T. Patrick Burke (New York: Sheed and Ward, 1966), 41–59.

18. Edward Schillebeeckx, *Jesus: An Experiment in Christology*, trans. Hubert Hoskins (New York: Seabury, 1979), 617.

19. Hill, *The Three-Personed God*, 247.

20. Hill, *Knowing the Unknown God*, 111–44.

21. Christopher Fry, *A Sleep of Prisoners*, quoted in the frontispiece of Hill's *The Three-Personed God*.

22. Hill, *The Three-Personed God*, 255.

23. Chenu, *Is Theology a Science?*, 97–99.

One / Seeking Foundations for Faith

1. M.-D. Chenu, *Faith and Theology*, trans. D. Hickey (New York: Macmillan, 1968), 30.

2. See Bonaventure's *Itinerarium mentis in Deum* and his *De Reductione artium ad theologiam*.

3. Bernard Lonergan, *Method in Theology* (New York: Herder and Herder, 1972), 105, 122; on sublating conversion, 243.

4. Karl Rahner, "The Concept of Mystery in Catholic Theology," *Theological Investigations* 4, " . . . knowledge, though prior to love and freedom, can only be realized in its *true* sense when and insofar as the subject is more than knowledge, when in fact it is a freely given love," 43. What Rahner means to say is that human knowing is by way of anticipating absolute being, something achieved by a surrender to it in love as absolute mystery. See also *Hearers of the Word*, chap. 8: "In final analysis, knowledge is but the luminous radiance of love: . . . As an inner moment of knowledge it is both its condition and its ground"; 40 and 41 respectively in the translation by Joseph Donceel in *A Rahner Reader*, ed. G. A. McCool (New York: Seabury Press, 1975).

5. Wolfhart Pannenberg, "Faith and Reason," *Basic Questions in Theology*, vol. 2, trans. G. H. Kehm (Philadelphia: Fortress Press, 1971), 64.

6. Martin Heidegger, *Identity and Difference*, trans. J. Stambaugh (New York: Harper & Row, 1969), 72–73.

7. James M. Robinson, "The German Discussion of the Later Heidegger," *The Later Heidegger and Theology*, vol. 1 of *New Frontiers in Theology*, ed. J. M. Robinson and J. B. Cobb, Jr. (New York: Harper & Row, 1963), 43, who indicated that Heidegger himself introduced this analogy at the 1960 meeting of the old Marburgers, an analogy of which the theological work of Heinrich Ott has made constructive use.

8. Thomas N. Munson, *Religious Consciousness and Experience* (The Hague: Martinus Nijhoff, 1975).

9. Ibid., chap. 3, esp. 80.

10. The misunderstanding turned on the Arabs reading into Aristotle's text from the *Posterior Analytics* II, 1 (89b 33) concerning the difference between knowing "that something is" and "what something is," the quite different distinction between the copulative and the existential functions of the verb "to be." Aristotle himself, however, was not here (or elsewhere) touching on the distinction between essence and existence, but meant merely to differentiate between noting that a subject of inquiry was something in itself on the one hand, and precisely determined as a particular kind of thing as an object of demonstration, on the other. For a detailed consideration of the interpretation of Aristotle by the Arabic commentators, see Leslie Dewart, *The Foundations of Faith* (New York: Herder and Herder, 1969), chap. 3.

11. The implications of this theory of an *objective* dynamism of intelligence have been worked out in detail by the late Dominic M. De Petter; see "Impliciete intuitie," *Tijdschrift v. Philosophie*, I (1939): 84–105. Unfortunately, none of his work is available in English translation. A development of his theory can be found, however, in Edward Schillebeeckx, "The

Non-Conceptual Intellectual Dimension in Our Knowledge of God According to Aquinas," *Revelation and Theology*, vol. 2, trans. N. D. Smith (New York: Sheed and Ward, 1968), 157–206. Jacques Maritain, earlier in *Creative Intuition in Art and Poetry* (Washington: Pantheon Books, 1953), had written of the preconscious life of the intellect wherein "... reason indeed does not only articulate, connect, and infer, it also *sees;* and reason's intuitive grasping, *intuitus rationis*, is the primary act and function of that one and single power which is called intellect or reason," 75.

12. *Summa Theol*. I, q.5, a.2: "Primo autem in conceptione intellectus cadit ens, quia secundum hoc unumquodque cognoscibile est quod est actu, ut dicitur in IX *Meta*."

13. Aquinas uses the term "intuition explicitly of angelic knowing (*Summa Theol*. I, q.58, a.3); human knowing is rational rather than purely spiritual but remains the knowing of spirit in matter and so retains an intuitional element. This is true especially in that what inaugurates the rational process is an immediate awareness of first principles which can only be by way of an intuitional act, which Aquinas attributes to an immediate awareness of real beings insofar as they have being (see *Summa Theol*. I, q.79, a.7), itself an intellectual intuition that spontaneously and pre-reflectively consummates the act of sensing.

14. Wolfhart Pannenberg, *Jesus, God and Man*, trans. L. L. Wilkins and D. A. Priebe (Philadelphia: Westminster, 1968), 175, n. 146

15. The image is that of Sean de h-Ide writing in "Rahner and Lonergan," *Irish Studies*, Spring 1976, 67.

16. James Richmond, *Theology and Metaphysics* (New York: Schocken Books, 1970), xi.

17. Langdon Gilkey, *Reaping the Whirlwind* (New York: Seabury, 1976), 336, n. 4.

18. Walter Kasper, *Jesus the Christ*, trans. V. Green (New York: Paulist Press, 1976), 183.

19. Munson, *Religious Consciousness and Experience*, 82.

20. James P. Mackey, "Divine Revelation and Lonergan's Transcendental Method in Theology," *Irish Theological Quarterly*, January 1973, 17. This grounds Mackey's proposal that theology deal with the past "not in order to read God's mind but in order to receive the spirit by which to build the future" (19).

Two / Rescuing Theism:
A Bridge between Aquinas and Heidegger

1. Martin Heidegger, "Hölderlin and the Essence of Poetry," *Existence and Being*, ed. Werner Brock (Chicago: Henry Regnery, 1949), 289.

2. The more significant of these attempts are: Johannes B. Lotz: *Martin Heidegger und Thomas von Aquin: Mensch, Zeit, Sein* (Freiburg: Herder, 1975); Bertrand Rioux, *L'Etre et la vérité chez Heidegger et saint Thomas d'Aquin* (Paris: Presses Universitaires de France, 1963); and John Deely, *The Tradition via Heidegger: An Essay on the Meaning of Being in the Philosophy of Martin Heidegger* (The Hague: Nijhoff, 1971). Lotz bases his defense of Aquinas on the pivotal notion of *Ipsum Esse Subsistens*, Rioux on the Thomistic understanding of truth, and Deely on Thomas's understanding of *esse intentionale*.

3. Aristotle, *Posterior Analytics*, Bk. II, Chap. 1; 89 b 33.

4. On this reading of Avicenna and his indebtedness to Al-Farabi, see Leslie Dewart, *The Foundations of Belief* (New York: Herder & Herder, 1969) 160ff.

5. Thomas Aquinas, *Quaest. Disp., De potentia*, q.7, a.2, ad 9.

6. John D. Caputo, *Heidegger and Aquinas* (New York: Fordham University Press, 1982).

7. Ibid., 209.

8. Martin Heidegger, "The Thing," *Poetry, Language, Thought*, trans. Albert Hopstadter (New York: Harper & Row, 1971), 165–82.

9. James M. Robinson, "The German Discussion of the Later Heidegger," *The Later Heidegger and Theology: New Frontiers in Theology*, vol. 1, ed. James M. Robinson and John B. Cobb, Jr. (New York: Harper & Row, 1963), 24.

10. Karl Löwith, *Heidegger, Denker in dürftiger Zeit* (Göttingen: Vandenhoeck und Ruprecht, 1953, 2nd ed.) 20; cited by Robinson, "The German Discussion of the Later Heidegger," 13, n. 37.

11. Edward Schillebeeckx, *Jesus: An Experiment in Christology* (New York: Seabury, 1979), 618–19.

12. Thomas Aquinas, *Summa Theol.* 1, qq. 27–29.
13. Karl Rahner, "Grace and Freedom," *Encyclopedia of Theology* (New York: Seabury, 1975), 598; paraphrase is by Robert Hurd, "The Concept of Freedom in Rahner," *Listening* 17:2 (Spring 1982), 140.
14. Søren Kierkegaard, *Concluding Unscientific Postscript*, trans. David F. Sevenson and Walter Lowrie (Princeton University Press, 1941), 220.
15. *Summa Theol.* I, q. 22, a.2, ad 5; q. 23, a.5.
16. Caputo, *Heidegger and Aquinas*, 206.
17. Hans Urs von Balthasar, *Love Alone*, ed. and trans. Alexander Dru (New York: Herder and Herder, 1969); his complete theological aesthetics is found in *Herrlichkeit: Eine theologische Aesthetik* (Einsiedeln: Johannes Verlag, 1961–1969) whose five volumes comprise the first part of a trilogy whose latter two parts constitute a *Theodramatik* and a *Theologik*. The first two volumes of *Herrlichkeit* are available in English as *The Splendour of the Lord*, ed. J. Fessio and J. Riches, trans. E. Leiva-Merikakis (San Francisco: Ignatius Press, distributed by T. & T. Clark, 1982–83, and Seabury of New York, 1983–84).

Three / The Doctrine of God after Vatican II

1. See Karl Rahner, *Spirit in the World*, trans. William Dych (New York: Herder & Herder, 1969); also a theological employment of the theory in *Foundations of Christian Faith*, trans. William Dych (New York: Seabury Press, 1978). Bernard Lonergan, *Insight* (New York: Philosophical Library, 1958) with theological application in *Method in Theology* (New York: Herder & Herder, 1972). Emerich Coreth, *Metaphysik: Eine Methodisch-Systematisch Grundlegung* (Innsbruck: Tyrolia, 1961). J. B. Lotz, *Das Urteil und das Sein* (Pullach bei München, 1957). Helpful also is Otto Muck, *The Transcendental Method*, trans. W. Seidensticker (New York: Herder & Herder, 1968).
2. See Hans Urs von Balthasar, *Love Alone*, trans. Alexander Dru (New York: Herder & Herder, 1969).
3. J. B. Metz, *Faith in History and Society*, trans. David Smith (New York: Seabury Press, 1980).
4. Edward Schillebeeckx, *Jesus: An Experiment in Christology*, trans. Hubert Hoskins (New York: Seabury Press, 1979), esp. 618–19.
5. Langdon Gilkey, *Naming the Whirlwind: The Renewal of God Language* (Indianapolis: Bobbs-Merrill, 1969).
6. Michael Polanyi, *Personal Knowledge: Towards a Post-Critical Philosophy* (London: Routledge and Kegan Paul, 1962), 266.
7. Hans-Georg Gadamer, *Truth and Method*. Translation edited by Garrett Barden and John Cumming (New York: Crossroad, 1982).
8. Wolfhart Pannenberg, "Speaking about God in the Face of Atheist Critique," *The Idea of God and Human Freedom*, trans. R. A. Wilson (Philadelphia: Westminster Press, 1973), 102.
9. Ernst Bloch, *Das Prinzip Hoffnung*, 2 vols. (Frankfort, 1959).
10. Rahner, *Foundations of Christian Faith*, 48.
11. Sidney Hook, cited by Francis Fiorenza in "Dialectical Theology and Hope, I" *The Heythrop Journal* IX:2 (April, 1968), 144.
12. Edward Schillebeeckx, *Christ: The Experience of Jesus as Lord*, trans. J. Bowden (New York: Seabury Press, 1980) esp. 658.
13. Schillebeeckx, *The Schillebeeckx Reader*, ed. Robert J. Schreiter (New York: Crossroad, 1984), 147–48.
14. For a detailed development of this, see Langdon Gilkey, *Reaping the Whirlwind: A Christian Interpretation of History* (New York: Seabury Press, 1976) esp. 188f.
15. Alfred N. Whitehead, *Process and Reality*, Free Press Edition (New York: Macmillan, 1969) part 5, chap. 2, section 5, 410.
16. *Summa Theol.*, I, q. 13, a.7, corp.
17. Jürgen Moltmann, *The Crucified God*, trans. R. A. Wilson and J. Bowden (New York: Harper & Row, 1974), 235f.

18. Rahner, "On the Theology of the Incarnation," *Theological Investigations* 4, trans. Kevin Smyth, 113–14.

19. W. Pannenberg, "Response to the Discussion," *Theology as History*, vol. 3 of *New Frontiers in Theology*, ed. J. M. Robinson and J. B. Cobb (New York: Harper & Row, 1967) 264, n. 74.

20. See K. Rahner, *The Trinity*, trans. Joseph Donceel (New York: Herder & Herder, 1970), 31–33 and 99–103.

21. W. Pannenberg, *Grundfragen systematischer Theologie: Gesammelte Aufsatze*, Band 2 (Göttingen: Vandenhoeck & Ruprecht, 1980), 118; cited by Philip Clayton, "The God of History and the Presence of the Future," *The Journal of Religion* 65:1 (January 1985), 104.

22. See J. Moltmann, *The Trinity and the Kingdom*, trans. Margaret Kohl (San Francisco: Harper & Row, 1981).

23. E. Schillebeeckx, *Jesus*, 597 and 671.

24. Mt. 22:38–40; Mk. 12:29–31; Lk. 10:25–37.

25. J. Moltmann, *The Trinity and the Kingdom*, 23. On question of suffering in God, see chaps. 9 and 11 in this volume.

26. Hans Urs von Balthasar, "Mysterium Paschale," *Mysterium Salutis*, ed. J. Feiner and M. Löhrer, vol. III/2 (Einsiedeln: Benziger, 1969), 133–326; also available in French trans. of *Mysterium Salutis*, vol. 12 (Paris: 1972), 133–326; and in an independent publication entitled *Theologie der drei Tage* (Einsiedeln: Benziger, 1969).

27. See the persuasive argument for this position by Edward Schillebeeckx, *Christ*, 724f.

28. Claude Geffré, " 'Father' as the Proper name of God," *God as Father, Concilium*, vol. 143, ed. J. B. Metz and E. Schillebeeckx (New York: Seabury Press, 1981), 43–50.

29. Jon Sobrino, *Jesus in Latin America*, cited by Juan Alfaro, "Jesus in Latin America," *Theology Digest* 32:1 (Spring 1985), 6.

30. E. Schillebeeckx, *God is New Each Moment*, Conversations with Huub Oosterhuis and Piet Hoogeveen, trans. David Smith (New York: Seabury Press, 1983).

31. W. Norris Clarke, *The Philosophical Approach to God* (Winston-Salem, N.C.: Wake Forest University Press, 1979), 104.

32. See chaps. 4, 5, 6, and 7 in this volume as well as *The Three-Personed God* (Washington, D.C.: The Catholic University of America Press, 1982), 287–89.

Four / Does God Know the Future? Aquinas and Some Moderns

1. Peter Geach, in his 1973 St. Thomas Day Lecture at Blackfriars, Oxford, published as "The Future" in *New Blackfriars* (May 1973), 209.

2. Ibid., 215.

3. Ibid., 217.

4. John Macquarrie, *Principles of Christian Theology* (New York, 1966), 225.

5. Whitehead's usual designation of God is as a "nontemporal actual entity," but he does not mean by this to exclude from God all temporality, but only that kind of time that is perpetual perishing. It is also true that in *Process and Reality* (Macmillan, 1929; Free Press edition, 1969) the initial aims of actual occasions are explained in terms of God's *primordial* nature as the locus of such ideal values. However, the primordial nature has influence only as a principle that is nowise an agent. Moreover, recent interpreters of Whitehead have indicated the logical necessity of appealing to the consequent nature as specifying the precise aim appropriate to each actual occasion; see John B. Cobb, Jr., *A Christian Natural Theology* (Philadelphia, 1965), 176–214; Lewis Ford, "Divine Persuasion and the Triumph of Good," *Process Philosophy and Christian Thought*, ed. D. Brown et al. (New York, 1971).

6. Ford, "Divine Persuasion and the Triumph of Good," *Process Philosophy and Christian Thought*, 298.

7. Charles Hartshorne, *Man's Vision of God and the Logic of Theism* (New York, 1941), 246.

8. Martin Heidegger, *Being and Time*, trans. J. Macquarrie and E. Robinson (New York, 1962), 499, n. xiii.

9. Schubert Ogden, *The Reality of God* (New York, 1966), 162.

10. Jürgen Moltmann, *Theology of Hope* (New York, 1967), 213.

11. See Louis Dupré, *The Other Dimension* (Garden City, N.Y.: 1972), 468.

12. This is Pannenberg's doctrine of God developed in *Was ist der Mensch?* (English trans., *What is Man* [Philadelphia, 1972]; see the review of Pannenberg's *Jesus: God and Man* by John B. Cobb, Jr., in *Journal of Religion* (April 1969), which clearly indicates that this is what Pannenberg means.

13. Such an interpretation, which cannot be eliminated a priori from the work of Moltmann and Pannenberg, would appear to be a recasting of one strand of contemporary Marxist thought in a Christian vocabulary.

14. Moltmann, *Theology of Hope*, 212.

15. Ibid., 225.

16. Ibid., 209.

17. *Summa Theol.* I, q. 14, a. 13, a. 8; see q. 86, a. 4; *I Sent.*, d. 28, q. 1, a. 5; *Contra gentiles* 1, 67; *Quaest. Disp., De veritate*, q. 2, a. 12; *Quaest. Disp., De malo*, q. 16, a. 7; on eternity see *Summa Theol.* I, q. 10.

18. The account of Aquinas's thought that follows owes much to Bernard Lonergan's work in the context of the distinct problem of *gratia operans* in Thomas, published originally in *Theological Studies*, 1941 and 1942, later in book form under the editorship of J. P. Burns as *Grace and Freedom* (New York, 1971).

19. M. M. Gorce, in *Bulletin thomiste* 7 (1930), cited by Lonergan, *Grace and Freedom*, 78.

20. *I. Sent.*, d. 39, q. 2, a. 2.

21. Ibid.

22. *I. Sent.* d. 47, q. 1, a. 2.

23. *De veritate*, q. 6, a. 3.

24. Lonergan locates the definitive repudiation of a semblance of semipelagianism with *Contra gentiles* 3, 149 (*Grace and Freedom*, 39, n. 63).

25. *Contra gentiles* 3, 94.

26. *Summa Theol.* I, q. 19, a. 8: "Non igitur propterea effectus voliti a Deo eveniunt contingenter quia causae proximae sunt contingentes, sed propterea quia Deus voluit eos contingenter evenire contingentes causas ad eos praeparavit."

27. Ibid., q. 82, a. 4, ad. 3.

28. *De veritate*, q. 22, a. 12.

29. "Liberté humaine et motion divine," *Recherches de théologie ancienne et médiévale* 7 (1935), cited by Lonergan, *Grace and Freedom*, 95.

30. *De malo*, q. 6, a. un. "Quantum ergo ad exercitium actus, primo quidem manifestum est quod voluntas movetur a seipsa; sicut enim movet alias potentias, ita et se ipsam movet. Nec propter hoc sequitur quod voluntas secundum idem sit in potentia et in actu. . . . Relinquitur ergo . . . id quod primo movet voluntatem et intellectum, sit aliquid supra voluntatem et intellectum, scilicet Deus . . . (qui) etiam voluntatem movet secundum eius conditionem, non ex necessitate, sed ut indeterminate se habentem ad multa. . . . Sic ergo quantum ad aliqua voluntas ex necessitate movetur ex parte objecti, non autem quantum ad omnia; sed ex parte exercitii actus, non ex necessitate movetur." See also *Summa Theol.* I-II, q. 9, a. 1, where Aquinas is equally strong on reserving to the will active dominion over its own act, not however independently of the divine motion in the will.

31. Ludovicus Molina, *Concordia liberi arbitrii* (Rabeneck ed., Madrid, 1953).

32. Domingo Báñez, *Comm. in 1am partem Summae Theol.* (Urbano ed., Madrid-Valencia, 1934).

33. Báñez, is even willing to acknowledge that *in some sense* the future so determined by God is necessary. The *consequent*, i.e., the thing itself which eventually is chosen by the will, is not such that it has to be; it is conceivable that the will not have chosen it at all, and so liberty is safeguarded. But the *consequence* is necessary, i.e., under the supposition that God premoves the will to a particular choice, that choice will be made infallibly. As premoved by God, the will is not free — but only in the sense that while actually choosing one course of action, the will is not free at the same time to choose an opposite course. Thomas himself more frequently speaks of a conditional necessity in this case ("necessitas ex suppositione") as opposed to an absolute one ("necessitas absoluta"); see *Summa Theol.* I, q. 19, a. 8, ad 1 et 3; q. 26, a. 6, ad 3. At least once, however, he uses the very terms employed by Báñez ("necessitas consequentis," "necessitas consequentiae"); *De veritate*, q. 24, a. 1, ad 13, but

this represents a relatively early phase in his work between 1256 and 1259, and the context of meaning is other than that which it has for Báñez. At bottom, this is the same as the better-known Thomistic distinction *sensu composito-sensu diviso*, the will being necessitated in the first sense, remaining free in the second. In later Calvinist Scholasticism this came to mean that composing the divine premotion with the will's act resulted in the will's not having at such a moment any real potency to the opposite. The Thomist application was quite different and meant that in combination with God's premotion the will retained a potency for the opposite choice but could not actually elect the opposite as long as it continued to exercise in act its original choice.

34. *Comm. in 1am 2ae Summae theol.*, q. 109, a. 1, n. 3 (de Heredia ed. 3, Madrid, 1948).
35. Ibid., n. 2.
36. See, for one instance, J. B. Metz, "The Theological World and the Metaphysical World," *Philosophy Today* 10 (1966).
37. *Summa Theol.* I, q. 3, a. 4, ad 2: "esse dupliciter dicitur: uno modo, significat actum essendi; alio modo, significat compositionem propositionis quam anima adinvenit conjungens praedicatum subjecto": see q. 14, a. 1 and 2.
38. Ibid., q. 3, a. 4; q. 4, a. 1, ad. 3.
39. Ibid., q. 29, a. 4.
40. Ibid., q. 14, a. 13.
41. For Thomas, personhood within divinity is precisely constituted by subsisting relation: *Summa Theol.* I, q. 29, a. 4. For a fuller development of this, see chap. 7 in this volume.
42. This is the express view of Karl Rahner; see "On the Theology of the Incarnation," in *Theological Investigations* 4 (Baltimore: Helicon Press, 1966), 105–20. Rahner's consideration, however, is restricted to the instance of God's becoming other in Christ.
43. This would appear to be a quite legitimate interpretation of Hegel, who understands philosophy as a transfiguration, not a destruction, of faith: "Faith already has the true content. What is lacking in it is the form of thought" (Lectures on the *Philosophy of Religion* 3 [London, 1895], 148), and then goes on in the famous passage from the *Encyclopedia* to indicate how philosophy transfigures the representational form with which religion describes the divine-human relationship, as follows: "God is only God insofar as he knows himself; his knowing himself is, furthermore, a self-consciousness in man and man's knowledge of God that goes on to man's knowing himself in God" (sect. 564 of the *Enzyklopädie;* the above translation is that of Walter Kaufmann, *Hegel* [Garden City, N.Y.: Doubleday, 1965], 275).
44. See n. 12 above.
45. The potency-act principle, e.g., so basic to the thought of both Aristotle and Aquinas, is retained intact here, without however being understood in such wise as to lead to Báñez's conclusions on physical premotion of the will. Originally discovered by Aristotle in the science of physics as a law of natural motion, it was extrapolated by him to metaphysics as a science of separated substances. But the Stagirite's thought about the realm of immateriality lacks any positive understanding of spirituality, of the character of personhood, and of freedom as something more than spontaneity. In the thought of Aquinas these do begin to emerge, due in large part to a Christian influence on his metaphysics, now transformed into a science of being as being. The consequence of this is a gradual awareness of the limitations inherent in Aristotle's categories when it comes to reconciling divine causality with human liberty. Eventually Aquinas comes to view freedom as the will's *active* dominion over its own act. Its potentiality is not then a passivity demanding that it be physically premoved in every instance of operation, but means rather (a) that it reduces itself to act and (b) that it does not do so apart from God's transcendent activity as continuingly creative of finite freedom.

Five / The Historicity of God

1. Martin Heidegger, *Being and Time* (New York: Harper & Row, 1962), 499, n. xiii.
2. Schubert Ogden, "The Temporality of God," in *The Reality of God* (New York: Harper & Row, 1963), 144–63.
3. See Wolfhart Pannenberg, "Dogmatic Theses on the Doctrine of Revelation," in *Revelation as History*, ed. Wolfhart Pannenberg (London: Macmillan, 1968), 123–58; also Pannenberg, "Hermeneutics and Universal History," in *History and Hermeneutic*, ed., Robert

Funk (New York: Harper & Row, 1967), 122–52 (first published as vol. 4 of *Journal for Theology and the Church*, 1967; also available in *Basic Questions in Theology* 1 [Philadelphia: Fortress, 1970], 96–136).

4. Wolfhart Pannenberg, "Redemptive Event and History," in *Basic Questions in Theology* 1, 21.

5. See Wolfhart Pannenberg's "Response to the Discussion" in *Theology as History*, vol. 3 of *New Frontiers in Theology*, ed., J. M. Robinson and J. B. Cobb (New York: Harper & Row, 1967), 264, n. 74.

6. Wolfhart Pannenberg, *Theology and the Kingdom of God*, ed., R. J. Neuhaus (Philadelphia: Westminster, 1969), 56.

7. Wolfhart Pannenberg, *Jesus — God and Man* (Philadelphia: Westminster, 1968), 157.

8. Pannenberg, *Theology and the Kingdom of God*, 63. Because of this contention Pannenberg is able to disagree with Whitehead that "the futurity of God's Kingdom implies a development in God" and to insist only that "the movement of time contributes to deciding what the definite truth is going to be, also with regard to the essence of God" (62). Just how this is consistent with the words in no. 7 above is not clear.

9. "A Theological Conversation with Wolfhart Pannenberg," *Dialog* 11 (1972): 288.

10. Pannenberg, *Theology and the Kingdom of God*, 62: "Eternity is not timelessness.... The very essence of God implies time."

11. Pannenberg, "Response to the Discussion," *Theology as History*, 250–51.

12. See "Analogy and Doxology," *Basic Questions in Theology* 1, 212–38; also "Response to the Discussion," *Theology as History*, 251. Pannenberg's major treatment (and rejection) of analogy is to be found in his unpublished *Habilitationsschrift;* see Elizabeth A. Johnson, "The Right Way to Speak about God? Pannenberg on Analogy," *Theological Studies* 43 (1982): 673–92.

13. See Charles Hartshorne, *A Natural Theology for Our Time* (La Salle, Ill.: Open Court, 1967) esp. chap. 5; also *The Divine Reality* (New London: Yale University, 1948); also "Whitehead's Idea of God," in *The Philosophy of Alfred North Whitehead*, ed., P. A. Schlipp (New York: Tudor, 1941). See John B. Cobb, Jr., *A Christian Natural Theology* (Philadelphia: Westminster, 1965) esp. chap. 5.

14. All the words in quotation are from Alfred North Whitehead, *Process and Reality* (New York: Macmillan, 1929), 524; in the Free Press edition (New York, 1969), 407.

15. Lewis S. Ford, "The Non-Temporality of Whitehead's God," *International Philosophical Quarterly* 13 (1973): 346–76.

16. Whitehead, *Process and Reality*, 73; Free Press edition, 60.

17. Ibid., 64; Free Press edition, 53.

18. Ford, "Non-Temporality," 325f.

19. Ibid., 357–59.

20. In principle, such creative advance into novelty must be capable of failure. Whitehead, however, understands God in the fidelity of his decisions as preserving the creative process from eventual destruction.

21. See Thomas Aquinas, *Summa Theol.* I, q. 3, a. 3. God's essence is his very act of existing, whence it follows, q. 9, that God is immutable, and thus, q. 10, that God is eternal.

22. "Aeviternity" was the medieval term for the measure of the duration of things substantially unchangeable but accidentally subject to change; Aquinas, *Summa Theol.* I, q. 10, a. 5.

23. Boethius, *De consolatione philosophiae* 5, 6 (PL 63, 858); cited in Aquinas, *Summa Theol.* I, q. 10, a. 1.

24. This is Jüngel's premise throughout his recent *Gott als Geheimnis der Welt: Zur Begründung der Theologie des Gekreuziqten im Streit zwischen Theismus und Atheismus* (Tübingen: Mohr, 1977); see also *The Doctrine of the Trinity* (Grand Rapids: Eerdmans, 1976): "And thus one will be allowed to say and will have to say that there is — thank God — no being of God in-and-for-itself without man" (108, n. 16).

25. Practically all commentators on Whitehead are agreed that such is not the case. See, e.g., Barry L. Whitney, "Divine Immutability in Process Philosophy and Contemporary Thomism," *Horizons* 7 (1980): 49–68, who criticizes my suggestion that such might be at least a logical implication of Whitehead's thought. That ambiguity remains is borne out by Whitehead's statement that "The non-temporal act of all-inclusive unfettered valuation is at once a

creature of creativity and a condition of creativity" (*Process and Reality*, 47; Free Press edition, 37).

26. The whole metaphysical system of Aquinas pivots on the real distinction between essence and *esse*, in which the former explaining the nature of something is merely potential toward existence, whereas the latter is its *actus essendi*. *Esse* is thus the first perfection and the act of all acts: "Nothing attains actuality except by way of existing, and the act of existing is thus the ultimate actuality of everything and even of forms themselves" (*Summa Theol.* I, q. 4, a. 1, ad 3; see also *De veritate*, q. 2, a. 3).

27. Whitehead in an oft-quoted phrase refers to God as "the fellow-sufferer who understands" (*Process and Reality* [New York: Free Press edition, 1969], 413). Moltmann writes of creation as " 'an act of God inwardly,' which means that it is something that God suffers and endures.... Creative love is always suffering love as well" (*The Trinity and the Kingdom* [San Francisco: Harper & Row, 1981], 59); the ambiguity lies in the fact that Moltmann at other times views God not as suffering by natural necessity due to the very nature of love as such but only as willingly opening himself to such suffering.

Six / The Implicate World:
God's Oneness with Humankind as a Mediated Immediacy

1. Frederick Ferré, "Science, Religion, and Experience," in *Experience, Reason and God*, ed., Eugene T. Long (Washington, D.C.: Catholic University of America, 1980), 107.

2. David Bohm, *Wholeness and the Implicate Order* (London: Routledge and Kegan Paul, 1980).

3. Rupert Sheldrake, *A New Science of Life: The Hypothesis of Formative Causation* (Blond and Briggs, 1981; J. P. Tarcher, 1982).

4. David Bohm, cited by Renee Weber in an interview in *Revision* 5:2 (Fall 1982), 39.

5. Ibid., 37.

6. The Thomistic texts are well known: see especially, Thomas Aquinas, *Summa Theol.* I, q. 4, a. 1, ad 3 and q. 7, a. 1.

7. David B. Burrell, *Aquinas: God and Action* (Notre Dame, Ind.: University of Notre Dame Press, 1979).

8. Most notably, Karl Rahner, *Spirit in the World* (New York: Herder & Herder, 1968), esp. 215, 224–25.

9. See the interpretation of Aquinas by Jacques Maritain, *Existence and the Existent* (Garden City, New York: Doubleday, 1957), 34–35.

10. *Summa Theol.* I, q. 58, aa. 3 and 4.

11. *Summa Theol.* I, q. 79, aa. 8 and 12.

12. *Summa Theol.* I, q. 13, a. 5.

13. Martin Henry, "Transcendence," *Irish Theological Quarterly* 42:1 (1976.1): 56.

14. Karl Rahner, *The Foundations of Christian Faith* (New York: Seabury, 1979), 35–39, esp. 38.

15. See Aquinas, *Summa Theol.* I, q. 27, a. 1, ad 2.

16. Emil Fackenheim, *Metaphysics and Historicity*, Aquinas Lecture, 1961 (Milwaukee: Marquette University Press, 1961).

17. *Summa Theol.* I, q. 13, a. 7, corp.

18. For a further development of this point, see John H. Wright, "Divine Knowledge and Human Freedom: The God Who Dialogues," *Theological Studies* 38:3 (September 1977), 450–77.

19. W. Norris Clarke, *The Philosophical Approach to God* (Winston-Salem, N.C.: Wake Forest University, 1979), 91.

20. Alfred Whitehead, *Process and Reality* (New York: Macmillan, 1929); Free Press edition (Macmillan, 1969), pt. V, chap. 2, "God and the World."

21. See Lewis S. Ford, "The Non-Temporality of Whitehead's God," *International Philosophical Quarterly* 13:3 (September 1973): 347–76, and Langdon Gilkey, *Reaping the Whirlwind: A Christian Interpretation of History* (New York: Seabury Press, 1976), esp. 307.

22. Edward Schillebeeckx, *Interim Report on the Books "Jesus" and "Christ"* (New York: Crossroad, 1981), 61.

23. One who makes rich use of the phrase is Edward Schillebeeckx in *Christ: The Experience of Jesus as the Lord* (New York: Seabury, 1980), 808–17.

24. Hans-Georg Gadamer, *Truth and Method* (New York: Seabury, 1975).

25. See, e.g., Rom 5:5, "the love of God is poured out within us by the Holy Spirit who is given to us."

26. Clarke, *The Philosophical Approach to God*, 104.

27. *Summa Theol*. I, q. 41, a. 1, ad 1.

28. For opposing views, see Richard Rorty, *Philosophy and the Mirror of Nature* (Princeton: Princeton University Press, 1979), and Gordon Kaufman, *God the Problem* (Cambridge, Massachusetts: Harvard University Press, 1972).

Seven / Does the World Make a Difference to God?

1. Words put into the mouth of Hegel in hell by Engels in his satirical poem "The Triumph of Faith."

2. An excellent, detailed and updated bibliography is available in *Process Philosophy and Christian Thought*, ed. D. Brown, R. E. James, Jr., and G. Reeves (Indianapolis and New York: Bobbs-Merrill, 1971), 475–89. After Whitehead's *Process and Reality* (Macmillan, 1929; Free Press Edition, 1969) which stands at the origin of the present discussion, special mention should be made of the following: Charles Hartshorne, "The Di-Polar Conception of Deity," *The Review of Metaphysics* 21 (1967); W. L. Reese and E. Freeman, eds., *Process and Divinity*, Philosophical Essays Presented to Charles Hartshorne (La Salle, Ill.: Open Court, 1964); H. N. Wieman, *The Wrestle of Religion with Truth* (New York: Macmillan, 1927); Bernard E. Meland, ed., *The Future of Empirical Theology* (University of Chicago Press, 1969); John Cobb, Jr., *A Christian Natural Theology* (Philadelphia: Westminster, 1965); Schubert Ogden, *The Reality of God* (New York: Harper & Row, 1966); Norman W. Pittenger, *God in Process* (London: S.C.M. Press, 1967); Ralph E. James, *The Concrete God* (Indianapolis: Bobbs-Merrill, 1967); Lewis S. Ford, "The Viability of Whitehead's God for Christian Theology," and Robert C. Neville, "The Impossibility of Whitehead's God for Christian Theology," *Proceedings: American Catholic Philosophical Association* (Washington, 1970); Daniel D. Williams, *The Spirit and Forms of Love* (New York: Harper & Row, 1968); Alix Parmentier, *La Philosophie de Whitehead et le problème de Dieu* (Paris: Beauchesne, 1968).

3. In addition to the suggestiveness in much of the work of Teilhard de Chardin, the following studies have recently appeared in English: Karl Rahner, "On the Theology of the Incarnation," *Theological Investigations* 4; Piet Schoonenberg, *Man and Sin* (Notre Dame, Ind.: University of Notre Dame Press, 1965), esp. 50; Martin D'Arcy, "The Immutability of God," and Walter Stokes, "Is God Really Related to the World," both in *Proceedings: American Catholic Philosophical Association*, 1965; John Robertson, "Does God Change," *The Ecumenist* (May-June 1971); Anthony Kelly, "God: How Near a Relation," *The Thomist* 34 (1970); Joseph Donceel, "Second Thoughts on the Nature of God," *Thought* (Autumn 1971); and W. Norris Clarke, "A New Look at the Immutability of God," *God Knowable and Unknowable*, ed., R. J. Roth (New York: Fordham University Press, 1973).

4. Whitehead, *Process and Reality*, Free Press Edition, 405.

5. "The consequent nature of God is the fluent world become 'everlasting' by its objective immortality in God." Whitehead, *Process and Reality*, 409.

6. Whitehead notes that God "saves the world as it passes into the immediacy of his own life ... He does not create the world, he saves it ... with tender patience leading it by his vision of truth, beauty, and goodness." *Process and Reality*, 408.

7. Ibid., 411.

8. John Cobb in *A Christian Natural Theology* gives to creativity in Whitehead's system an infinity similar to that of Aristotle's prime matter (p. 206); the eternal objects (in God's primordial nature) then possess the infinity proper to formal causes, but these are forms lacking all actuality, thus: "The eternal objects express pure possibilities" (209).

9. Thus Whitehead is reluctant to call God "creator," for this as an appeal to the free initiatives of God's will suggests to him arbitrariness; he "prefers to speak of God and the temporal world as jointly qualifying or conditioning creativity." Cobb, *A Christian Natural Theology*, 204.

10. "It is clear that Whitehead himself thought of God as *an* actual entity rather than as a living person." (Cobb, *Christian Natural Theology*, 188, italics are his own) Cobb attempts here to introduce personhood into God by presenting God's consequent nature as "temporal," whereas Whitehead consistently prefers to speak of it as "everlasting." Even if this be a legitimate "correcting" of Whitehead, it still leaves God as a person only in the non-substantive sense in which Whitehead will allow that human beings are persons.

11. J. B. Metz has made rich theological use of this insight in his book *Christliche Anthropozentrik* (Munich: Kosel, 1962). He has developed it further in an article "The Theological World and the Metaphysical World," *Philosophy Today* 10:4 (1966) stating that the thought of St. Thomas "goes far beyond a thematic enrichment of Greek metaphysics. It changes the whole horizon of the understanding of being and self.... Thus we see in the Christian metaphysics of the middle ages the beginning of the great change from Greek cosmocentrism to anthropocentrism, from objectivity to subjectivity, or better from an objectively ontic to a transcendental-ontological understanding of the subject, from nature to history, from abstract to concrete universality, from the static thing in space to the person in time." (p. 259) Leslie Dewart in his book *The Foundations of Belief* (New York: Herder & Herder, 1969) and Richard Hinners in an article "The Future of Belief: A Response," *Continuum* (Spring 1967) view this as only an attempt to fit newer categories of thought into a Hellenic and Thomistic mold. But it would seem closer to the truth and to offer richer promise to view the newer thought structures as emerging out of older ones by a dialectic natural to thought, in which what is new retains continuity with what came before. At least on the point at issue here, newer conceptualities do not so much replace older ones as complement them, and the former gain in intelligibility by retaining the latter as their matrix. This outlook brings to mind Heidegger's "step backward" into the tradition, to discover something that was not said precisely in what was said. As one very general illustration, it would be anachronistic to deny that St. Thomas's doctrine of being is ahistorical; at the same time, his understanding of being (*esse*) as act does point the way to discovering its historicity.

12. Martin Heidegger, *Being and Time*, trans., J. Macquarrie and E. Robinson (New York: Harper and Brothers, 1962), 32–33.

13. *Summa Theol.* I, q. 13, a. 7: "....manifestum est quod creaturae realiter referuntur ad ipsum Deum; sed in Deo non est aliqua realis relatio eius ad creaturas, sed secundum rationem tantum, inquantum creaturae referuntur ad ipsum."

14. Scholastic thinkers preferred to designate these as *"relationes secundum dici"* (e.g., *Summa Theol.* I, q. 13, a. 7, ad 1) to convey that such were absolute entities which, however, could only be defined in terms of their reference or order to something else, e.g., a faculty in order to its formal proper object; these were relative, in other words, in terms of their definability. At least a logical distinction prevails between designating such as "transcendental" and as "secundum dici." Kevin O'Shea has called attention to Rahner's tendency to call "transcendental" what are in fact "predicamental" relations ("Divinization: A Study in Theological Analogy," *The Thomist* [January 1965], 11, note).

15. For the purposes of the present study it will suffice to give express consideration only to predicamental relations that might be founded upon divine causality. Scholastic thought in fact elaborated an intricate treatment of this Aristotelian predicament, founding such relations also upon the accidents of quantity and quality and (somewhat more obscurely) upon the generic and specific similarity or dissimilarity between one substance and another. Indigenous to such understanding was an insistence upon three really distinct elements in every such relation: the subject related, the term to which related, and the fundament of the very relating. The latter might be found in both subject and term, thus accounting for mutually real relations, or only in the subject, in which case the relation would be real there and purely of reason in the correlate. Illustrative of the latter is the knower-known relationship, which is a real perfection in the knower and nothing at all in the intrinsic being of what is known. Aquinas consistently teaches that relations established between God and world are non-mutual, i.e., real only in the latter. Thus, it follows that God's knowing and loving of the world, by contrast to such activity as finite, is, in its creativeness, a perfecting of the creature so known and loved and nowise any enhancement of God's own intrinsic reality.

16. This is the point of Aquinas's insistence in *Summa Theol.* I, q. 29, a. 4 that person in God signifies either relation *"per modum substantiae"* or equally (*"similiter etiam"*) essence *"per modum hypostasis."* He means to say, in short, that relation is not a pure medium between

208 NOTES

two extremes but must inhere in one term even though its formal character consists in a habitude or reference to the other term. When predicated of God, the *esse in* of relation signifies not inherence in the essence but identity with the latter. Thus, when real (namely, trinitarian) relations are said of God, the concept involved is unique in its analogicity and is not the transfer to God of either the concept of predicamental or transcendental relation merely stripped of all connotations of finiteness.

17. Thomas adverts to the distinction in ibid., I, q. 14, a. 9; the science of simple intelligence being God's knowledge of his own essence as imitable in an infinite number of ways, whereas the science of vision is his intuition of those realities he has called into actual existence — past, present, and future.

18. Among Thomists — Capreolus, Cajetan, and Ferrariensis deny that the subsistent relations bespeak perfection logically distinct from that of the divine essence; the opposite opinion is held by John of St. Thomas.

19. Augustine began his *De trinitate* about the year 407 and then around 412 discovered the use of "relation" by Gregory of Nazianzus in trinitarian disputes with Eunomius (also probably similar uses of "relation" by Didymus the Blind). From this time onward Augustine employs two categories in speaking of God: "essence" and "relation," this practice replacing his earlier one of speaking only of "substance" in God. However, he does not work out a doctrine of notional act (this is to be a later discovery of Aquinas), and so the Augustinian tendency is to conceive the divine nature itself as essentially three-relational. Augustine can thus explain distinction within God but is hard put to explain subsistent distinctness, which makes it easier to understand why he tends to be ill at ease in using the category of "persona" which had become traditional since the time of Tertullian. Pseudo-Dionysius, on the other hand, begins with God as Father, the "fons divinitatis," and seeks an explanation of the origin of the Son by the former's generative activity, suggesting that the nature is already subsistent in the Father prior (logically) to his generative act. Paul Vanier in his *Theologie Trinitaire chez S. Thomas D'Aquin* (Montreal: Institute D'Études Médiévales, 1953) has noted the two distinct tendencies in Aquinas's own teaching: a Dionysian influence in the *De potentia* and an Augustinian one in the later *Summa Theol.* Vanier, however, overstresses the difference; there is textual evidence (e.g., the even earlier *Commentary on the Sentences*) to support the view that there is less a development here in Thomas's thought than an effort to reconcile the approaches of Eastern and Western trinitarianism.

20. Durandus understands the trinitarian processions, somewhat in the spirit of Origen, as emanations of the divine nature, prior logically to divine knowing and loving (*In Petri Lomb. Sententias* [Venice, 1571], Lib. I, Dist. 6, Quest. 2). Suarez, with Molina, similarly argues against assigning to the processions the formality of operation in any proper sense and conceives of them in terms of natural emanations on the plane of intellection, i.e., as something resulting *from* operation much as properties issue from essences (*Opera Omnia*, Tome I, Vives ed. [Paris, 1856], *De Trinitate Personarum*, Lib. I, Cap. 5, n. 7 and 8; Cap. 8, n. 5). Scotus, by contrast, agrees with Augustine and Thomas in seeing the processions as immanent actions but differs from them in affirming that, while such activity is of the intellect and the will, it is not knowing and loving as such but distinct activity that is formally productive in kind, namely, *dicere* and *spirare* (*Opera Omnia, Ordinatio*, Vatican ed., C. Balic, 1950, Lib. I, Dist. 2, Pars 2, Quest. 4, n. 326: "dicere non est aliquis actus intelligendi formaliter; est tamen aliquis intellectus"). For Aquinas, the processions do arise from a certain fecundity of the nature, but a nature that is the pure act of subsistent knowing and loving, so that the fecundity is by way of genuine activity that requires persons as originating principles. Intellective and volitional activity in God is itself formally "productive" (see *Summa Theol.* I, q. 27, a. 3 and 5), not causally, however, — the persons are not to be understood as agents of efficient activity — but in the sense of grounding the pure relation of each person to the others; the persons are thus understood as *principles* of *notional* activity. Materially considered, these actions are knowing and loving, common prerogatives of the nature, but formally considered as notional they are acts exclusive to one or another of the three; only in the Father, for example, does "to know" become "to speak the Word" (see ibid., q. 41, a. 5: "Et ideo potentia generandi significat in recto naturam divinam sed in obliquo relationem.")

21. Seemingly, this rests ultimately in the mysterious metaphysics of knowledge as assimilation.

22. *The Trinity* (New York: Herder & Herder, 1970), 113. See p. 101, Note: "We consciously give up here the explicit use of the concept of person...."

23. There can, of course, be only one real consciousness in God. "...The three subjects are aware of each other through one consciousness which is possessed in a different way by the three of them" (B. Lonergan, *De Deo Trino* [Rome: 1964], vol. II, 193).

Eight / In What Sense Is God Infinite?

1. See Alfred Whitehead, *Process and Reality* (New York: Macmillan, 1929), 48, 63f., and 73.

2. Alfred Whitehead, *Adventures of Ideas* (New York: Macmillan, 1933), 333.

3. *Summa Theol.* I, q. 3, a. 4: "sua essentia igitur est suum esse;" also *De ente et essentia*, c. 5. Since human knowing is conceptual and the concept is the mind's grasp of what pertains to essence, the human question about God cannot avoid taking the form of asking "what is God?."

4. *Expositio super librum De causis*, Lib. unicus, Lectio 6: "...causa prima est supra ens inquantum est ipsum esse infinitum, ens autem dicitur id quod finite participat esse, et hoc est proportionatum intellectui nostro cuius objectum est quod quid est....unde illud solum est capabile ab intellectu nostro quod habet quidditatem participantem esse; sed Dei quidditas est ipsum esse, unde est supra intellectum."

5. God "so to speak contains within himself the entire plentitude of being, not contracted to any generic or specific nature" (*De spirit. creat.*, q. unica, a. 1). Some interpreters of Thomas have extenuated his position that God is the pure act of "to be" to mean that God has no essence. A recent instance of this can be found in William J. Hoye: *Actualitas Omnium Actuum* (Meisenheim am Glan: Verlag Anton Hain, 1975): "To say that God's essence is esse is tantamount to saying that God has no essence" (p. 29); God is here represented as "the *indeterminate* pure act of subsistent being" (p. 33 — emphasis supplied). This, in effect, empties out the term "God" of any meaning and makes it impossible to even think of him. Aquinas himself is aware of the temptation to think in this fashion: "Aliquis enim est sicut Deus cuius essentia est suum esse: et ideo inveniuntur aliqui philosophi decentes quod Deus non habet quidditatem vel essentiam, quia essentia sua non est aliud quam esse suum: (*De ente et essentia*, c. 5).

6. "...because, as we have said, the essence of God is to exist, and since this could not be the case with any created form no such form could represent the essence of God to the understanding" *Summa Theol.* I, q. 12, a. 2.

7. David Burrell, *Exercises in Religious Understanding* (Notre Dame, Ind.: University of Notre Dame Press, 1974), 96.

8. "Unde patet quod dico 'esse' est actualitas omnium actuum, et propter hoc est perfectio omnium perfectionum" (*De pot.*, q. 7, a. 2, ad 9); "Ipsum esse est perfectissimum omnium: comparatur enim ad omnia ut actus. Nihil enim habet actualitatem, nisi inquantum est: unde ipsum esse est actualitas omnium rerum, et etiam ipsarum formarum" (*Summa Theol.* I, q. 4, a. 1, ad 3); "Quod autem est in omnibus effectibus perfectissimum, est esse: quaelibet enim natura vel forma perficitur per hoc quod est actu: et comparatur ad esse in actu sicut potentia ad actum ipsum" (III *C. G.*, 66).

9. Whitehead's eternal objects are cognate to Plato's forms though, as in Aristotle, the forms are not actual outside matter but only in those entities which are their "occasions." But Aristotle is as much a philosopher of essence as is Plato; Aquinas's philosophy, by contrast, is one of being, and moreover of being as act. A contributing factor in this innovation by Aquinas was an Arabic misreading of Aristotle, attributable to religious (Islamic) preconceptions (see chap. 1, n. 10).

10. Decision "constitutes the very meaning of actuality....(It is)...the additional meaning imported by the word 'actual' into the phrase 'actual entity' "; Whitehead, *Process and Reality*, 68. Lewis Ford formulates this in the following terms: "The primordial decision whereby possibility is created by demarcating it from impossibility is the infinite, non-temporal act whereby God creates himself."

11. God and world are both "in the grip of the ultimate metaphysical ground, the creative advance into novelty"; Whitehead, *Process and Reality*, 59.

12. This has been persuasively argued by David L. Schindler, "Creativity as Ultimate: Reflections on Actuality in Whitehead, Aristotle, and Aquinas," *International Philosophical Quarterly* (July 1973); his conclusion is that "creativity is finally inadequate as ultimate in Whitehead's metaphysics because, not being itself actual, it cannot ground the actualities of actual entities, in contrast with *esse* in Aquinas, which is concretized in a single source that is supremely actual, God as *ipsum esse subsistens;*" 171.

13. Whitehead leaves the relationship between the two natures in God obscure and undeveloped, leading to the observation that some critics suspect two Gods (see G. Reeves and D. Brown, "The Development of Process Theory" in *Process Philosophy and Christian Thought*, ed. D. Brown, R. E. James, and G. Reeves (Indianapolis: Bobbs-Merrill, 1971), 31. Nonetheless, *Process and Reality* notes that "as primordial, so far is he from 'eminent reality' that in this abstraction he is 'deficiently actual'... His feelings are only conceptual and so lack the fullness of actuality... (and are... devoid of consciousness in their subjective forms," 521. Hartshorne makes clear in *The Divine Relativity* (New Haven: Yale University Press, 1948) and in *Philosophers Speak of God* (Chicago: University of Chicago Press, 1953) that God has two aspects or dimensions to his being; nonetheless the primordial aspect is abstract, absolute, and included in the consequent aspect which alone is concrete, relative, and actual. For a more detailed development of Ford's alternative view, see his "Whitehead's Transformation of Pure Act," *The Thomist* (July 1977).

14. Karl Rahner, "On the Theology of the Incarnation," *Theological Investigations* 4 (Baltimore: Helicon Press, 1966), 113–14, n. 3: "God who is unchangeable in himself can change in another.... But this 'changing in another' must neither be taken as denying the immutability of God in himself nor simply be reduced to a changement of the other."

15. All that this means is that Rahner so emphasizes the essential relationship of finite being to infinite being, that such a polarization to the infinite enters into the very definition of the former; the human being is thus "incarnate spirit" rather than "rational animal." Further, this would appear to be the implication of such a statement of Rahner's as the following: "*esse*, given in sensibility as limited, is apprehended as unlimited in itself in a pre-apprehension attaining to *esse* as such"; *Spirit in the World* (New York: Herder & Herder, 1968), 157.

Rahner's thought develops against the background of a divine dialectic of self-differentiation in which the notion of creation as commonly understood gives way to that of a self-giving on God's part; the difference is that in the latter God establishes the other "as his own reality" ("On the Theology of the Incarnation," *Theological Investigations* 4, 114). This is clearly indigenous to Hegel's dialectic of the concept which becomes identical with itself in the other. Rahner surmounts Hegel at this point by refusing any reduction of God to the mere processes of thought, but he does this simply by insisting that God is "absolute mystery." All this depends upon seeing the structure of human being as an openness to God's absolute being, which openness consummates itself in the event of incarnation. At bottom, however, remains the question as to whether Rahner is not too facile in overcoming the abyss between God and creature.

16. W. Norris Clarke, "The Immutability of God," *God Knowable and Unknowable*, ed. R. J. Roth (New York: Fordham University Press, 1973), 49. See Ford's appreciative response to this approach in "The Immutable God and Father Clarke," *New Scholasticism* (Spring 1975): 189–99.

17. Ibid., 70.

18. For an attempt at further development of the perennial question, see chapters 4 and 7 in this volume. The resolution to which these studies incline is one allowing that God does know the free future but without any causal predetermination thereof. To suppose that God knows all that there is to be known, but that the future is not yet and so remains unknowable except as possible even to God, appears to compromise what it means to say God is eternal. Still, the creaturely self-determination occurs not outside divine causality but precisely within it and because of it; such causality in its analogous and transcendent character, far from opposing human self-determination, is in fact its very condition.

19. A suggestive expression of this view is to be found in John V. Taylor, *The Go-Between God* (Philadelphia: Fortress Press, 1973), 28–30.

Nine / Two Gods of Love: Aquinas and Whitehead

1. This difference can be seen graphically in comparing Aquinas's *Commentaria in Metaphysicam Aristotelis*, Lib. 5, lect. 9 (Cathala ed., 893–97) with Whitehead's *Process and Reality* (New York: Macmillan Free Press, 1969), e.g., pt. II, chap. 1, sect. 3, 57–60.

2. *Summa Theol.* I, q. 3, aa. 4 and 7.

3. Whitehead, *Process and Reality*, pt. 5, chap. 2.

4. Gordon D. Kaufman, *God the Problem* (Cambridge: Harvard University Press, 1972), 85–88, 92, 95–99, 150–51, 169n.

5. Whitehead, *Process and Reality*, 25. A lucid comparison of this view with that of Aquinas is offered by David L. Schindler, "Creativity as Ultimate: Reflections on Actuality in Whitehead, Aristotle, and Aquinas," *International Philosophical Quarterly* (June 1973): 161–71. (See chap. 8, n. 12.)

6. Joseph Pieper, *About Love*, trans. R. and C. Winston (Chicago: Franciscan Herald Press, 1972), 12.

7. *Nichomachean Ethics*, Bk. I, chap. 7; 1087a, 15f.

8. See G. Quell and E. Stauffer, *Love*, a translation from G. Kittel's *Theologisches Worterbuch zum Neuen Testament* (London: Adams and Charles Black, 1949). Also James Moffatt, *Love in the New Testament* (London: Hodder and Stoughton, 1929).

9. See, for example, Luther's *Commentary on Romans* 15:2, *Luther's Works*, vol. 25, ed. Hilton C. Oswald (St. Louis: Concordia, 1972), 512–15. Extensive documentation is supplied in chap. 6 of Anders Nygren's *Agape and Eros*.

10. Karl Barth, *Church Dogmatics*, vol. IV, part II, trans. G. W. Bromiley (Edinburgh: T. & T. Clark, 1958), esp. 788–99.

11. Anders Nygren, *Eros und Agape*, 2 vols. (Gutersloh, 1930, 1937). English translation by Philip S. Watson, *Agape and Eros*, vol. 1 (New York: Harper & Row, 1969).

12. Sermon 368, 1 (Migne: P.L. 39, 1652).

13. Luther writes in the "Disputatio Heidelbergae habita," xxviii, "Amor Dei non invenit sed creat suum diligibile, Amor hominis fit a suo diligibili," (WA I, p. 354, 35f.); Aquinas's version runs, "Amor noster . . . movetur sicut ab objecto . . . Sed amor Dei est infundens et creans bonitatem in rebus" (*Summa Theol.* I, q. 20, a. 2.).

14. *Summa Theol.* I–II, q. 26, a. 4.

15. "God's willing of the end is not the cause of his willing the things that are subordinate to that end, but he does will that such things be ordered to their end." (*Summa Theol.* I, q. 19, a. 5.) The cause of God's willing of the creature is not, then, the willing of his own goodness; there simply is no causality within God.

16. C. S. Lewis, *The Four Loves* (New York, 1960), 11–14, 32–33.

17. *Summa Theol.* II–II, q. 23, a. 1.

18. *De divinis nominibus*, 15, 180; Aquinas's commentary on this is to be found in his *In div. nom.*, 4, 12, no. 455.

19. Whitehead, *Process and Reality*, p. 406.

20. Ibid., 405. See Lewis S. Ford, "The Non-Temporality of Whitehead's God," *International Philosophical Quarterly* (September 1973): 347–76.

21. Whitehead, *Process and Reality*, 410.

22. Ibid., 411.

23. Ibid., 408.

24. Whitehead himself writes of God as "the fellow sufferer who understands," ibid., 413. However, the full implications of this for theology have been developed by such thinkers as: Charles Hartshorne, *A Natural Theology for Our Time* (LaSalle, Ill.: Open Court, 1967), 105; Daniel Day Williams, *The Spirit and Forms of Love* (New York: Harper & Row, 1968), 117f.; John B. Cobb, Jr., *God and the World* (Philadelphia: Westminster, 1969), 97; Norman Pittenger, *Process Thought and Christian Faith* (New York: Macmillan, 1968), 23. (See also the sources in chap. 7, n. 2.)

25. In particular, Jürgen Moltmann, *The Crucified God*, trans. R. A. Wilson and John Bowden (New York: Harper & Row, 1974); e.g., "The justifiable denial that God is capable of suffering because of a deficiency in his being may not lead to a denial that he is incapable of suffering out of the fullness of his being, i.e., his love." (p. 230).

26. William Blake, "Auguries of Innocence," lines 129–32, in *The Complete Writings of William Blake*, ed. Geoffrey Keynes (London: Oxford University Press, 1966).

27. Pieper, *About Love*, 24–25.

28. "Current Trends in Catholic Theology," *Communio*, The Hans Urs von Balthasar Symposium (Spring 1978), 83.

29. "An enduring personality in the temporal world is a routine of occasions in which the successors with some peculiar completeness sum up their predecessors." *Process and Reality*, 412–13. The general argument here against personal love of God for world is taken from E. H. Madden and P. H. Hare, "Evil and Unlimited Power," *The Review of Metaphysics* (December 1966), 285f.

Ten / Christian Panentheism:
Orthopraxis and God's Action in History

1. Oscar Wilde once observed that the fact that someone dies for a cause is no proof of the truthfulness and goodness of that cause.

2. See Langdon Gilkey, *Naming the Whirlwind* (Indianapolis and New York: Bobbs-Merrill, 1969).

3. Langdon Gilkey, *Reaping the Whirlwind* (New York: Seabury, 1976), 247.

4. Ibid., 246.

5. Alfred North Whitehead, *Process and Reality* (New York: Free Press Edition, 1969), 413.

6. Wolfhart Pannenberg, *Jesus — God and Man*, trans. L. L. Wilkins and Duane A. Priebe (Philadelphia: Westminster, 1969), 165.

7. See Johann Gottlieb Fichte, *Attempt at a Critique of All Revelation*, trans. G. Green (Cambridge: Cambridge University Press, 1978), 53. Fichte, while allowing that finite freedom is subject to partial determinations from the laws of nature, wishes to assert that manifest in the operations of the finite ego, is the truth that ultimately " ...flows from the absolute liberty in its act of discursive self-realization." (*Recent Philosophy: Hegel to the Present*, ed. E. Gilson, T. Langan and A. Maurer [New York: Random House, 1962], 11). Things-in-themselves are thus creations of consciousness: only a doctrine of the universality of mind safeguards this against mere subjectivism. Representative of process thinkers on this point is Lewis Ford, "Can Freedom be Created?" *Horizons* 4:2 (1977): 183–88.

8. See Quentin Lauer, *Hegel's Idea of Philosophy* (New York: Fordham University, 1974), 112.

9. Emil L. Fackenheim, "Mythologizing the Jewish Experience," *The Impact of Belief*, ed. G. F. McLean (Lancaster, Pa.: Concordia, 1974), 53.

10. This can be interpreted in a non-theistic way to mean that "revelation is Reason's gift to itself": see Denis J. M. Bradley, "Religious Faith and the Mediation of Being: the Hegelian Dilemma in Rahner's 'Hearers of the Word,'" *The Modern Schoolman* (January 1978), 138; see also Emil Fackenheim, *The Religious Dimension in Hegel's Thought* (Bloomington: Indiana University, 1968), esp. 164.

11. A profound implication of this is that though God is affected by what arises from the creature he does not (as pure act) thereby acquire perfection previously lacking to him; see W. Norris Clarke, *The Philosophical Approach to God* (Winston-Salem, N.C.: Wake Forest University, 1979), 104.

12. Gilkey, *Reaping the Whirlwind*, 306–10.

13. Ibid., 308–9.

14. For Hegelians, at any rate, the God of Christianity is conceived at the heart of a dialectic of Being wherein Infinite Spirit is real only in unity with finite human spirit.

15. Pannenberg, *Theology and the Kingdom of God*, ed. R. J. Neuhaus (Philadelphia: Westminster, 1969), 56.

16. "God becomes man in order to become God,"; Stanley Rosen, *G. W. F. Hegel, An Introduction to the Science of Wisdom* (New Haven: Yale, 1974), 234.

17. Johannes B. Metz, "Freedom as a Threshold Problem Between Philosophy and Theology," *Philosophy Today* (Winter, 1966): 264–79.

18. Aquinas's way of saying this observes that God contains the things in which he is said to exist; see *Summa Theol.* I, q. 8, a. 1, ad. 2.

19. Thomas Munson, "Freedom: A Philosophic Reflection on Spirituality," *Philosophy Today* (Spring 1967), 52.

20. John Macquarrie, *Principles of Christian Theology* (New York: Scribners, 1966), 225.

21. Edward Schillebeeckx, *Jesus: An Experiment in Christology*, trans. H. Hoskins (New York: Seabury Press, 1979), 653.

22. *Summa Theol.* I, q. 29, a. 4; q. 27, a. 1. This distinguishes Aquinas from Eberhard Jüngel's position that "God's being is in becoming"; see *The Doctrine of the Trinity* (Grand Rapids, Mich.: Eerdmans, 1976).

23. Johannes B. Metz, "The Future in the Memory of Suffering," *New Questions on God, Concilium*, vol. 76 (New York: Herder & Herder, 1972) 20.

24. Nicholas Lash, "Eternal Life: Life 'After' Death," *Heythrop Journal* (July 1978): 271–84. A Reply to Lash by Brian Hebblethwaite appears in the same journal for January, 1979, 57–64.

25. Karl Rahner, "Christianity and the New Earth," *Theology Digest* (Winter 1967), 281.

26. Thomas Aquinas, *II Sent.*, d. 1, q. 2, a. 3.

27. *Summa Theol.* II–II, q. 158, a. 2, ad. 1.

28. Gerard Verbeke, "Man as a 'Frontier' According to Aquinas," *Mediaevalia Lovaniensia*, Series I, Studia V (Leuven: University Press; The Hague: Martinus Nijhoff, 1976), 223.

29. Robert McAfee Brown, "Ecumenism and the Secular Order," *Theology Digest* (Winter 1967), 271.

30. See William J. Richardson, *Heidegger — Through Phenomenology to Thought* (The Hague: Martinus Nijhoff, 1963), 641.

31. See Schillebeeckx, *Jesus*, 62 and 670.

Eleven / Does Divine Love Entail Suffering in God?

1. Adrian Thatcher, "Concepts of Deity: A Criticism of H. P. Owen," *Anglican Theological Review* 59:3 (July 1976), 300.

2. See Wolfhart Pannenberg, *The Idea of God and Human Freedom*, trans. R. A. Wilson (Philadelphia: Westminster Press, 1971), 111; Jürgen Moltmann, *Theology of Hope*, trans. J. W. Leitch (New York: Harper & Row, 1967), 143f.

3. Carl Jung, *Answer to Job* (Princeton, N.J.: Princeton University Press, 1969); here Jung's conviction that all life could be grasped only in polar symbols led him to post a principle of evil within divinity.

4. Frederick Sontag, *The God of Evil: An Argument from the Existence of the Devil* (New York: Harper & Row, 1970), 130.

5. C. E. Rolt, *The World's Redemption* (London: 1913, 95; cited by Jürgen Moltmann, *The Trinity and the Kingdom*, trans. M. Kohl (San Francisco: Harper & Row, 1981), 34.

6. Paul Tillich, *Systematic Theology* (Chicago: University of Chicago Press, 1963), vol. 3, 405.

7. Alfred North Whitehead, *Process and Reality* (New York: Free Press, 1969), 413 (p. 532 in original Macmillan ed. of 1929).

8. Jürgen Moltmann, *The Crucified God*, trans. R. A. Wilson and J. Bowden (New York: Harper & Row, 1973), and *The Trinity and the Kingdom*.

9. Moltmann, *The Crucified God*, 222.

10. Moltmann, *The Trinity and the Kingdom*, 23.

11. Eberhard Jüngel, *The Doctrine of the Trinity: God's Being is in Becoming* (Grand Rapids, Mich.: Eerdmans, 1976), 102, n. 155.

12. Ibid., 108, n. 160.

13. Moltmann, *The Trinity and the Kingdom*, 32–33.

14. Moltmann, *The Crucified God*, 239.

15. Moltmann, *The Trinity and the Kingdom*, 46; his exact words are "The incarnation of God's Son is not an answer to sin. It is the fulfillment of God's eternal longing to become man and to make of every man a god out of grace."

16. K. Kitamori, *Theology of the Pain of God*, trans. M. E. Bratcher (Richmond, Va.: John Knox, 1965), 115.

17. Moltmann, *The Crucified God*, 222.

18. Moltmann, *The Trinity and the Kingdom*, 34, citing C. E. Rolt.

19. Moltmann, *The Crucified God*, 227

20. Moltmann, *The Trinity and the Kingdom*, 30.

21. Moltmann, *The Crucified God*, 246.

22. Tillich, *Systematic Theology*, vol. 3, 404.

23. H. P. Owen, *Concepts of Deity* (New York: Herder & Herder, 1971), 145.

24. Ibid., 88.

25. Karl Rahner, "On the Theology of the Incarnation," *Theological Investigations* 4, esp. 113, n. 3.

26. W. Norris Clarke, *The Philosophical Approach to God*, ed. W. E. Ray (Winston-Salem, N.C.: Wake Forest University, 1979), 104.

27. See chap. 7.

28. Hans Urs von Balthasar, "Le Mystère Pascal," *Mysterium Salutis*, tome 3, vol. 12 (Paris: Éditions du Cerf, 1972), 13–264.

29. Jüngel, *The Doctrine of the Trinity;* Hans Küng, *Incarnation de Dieu: Introduction à la pensée théologique de Hegel comme prolégomènes a une christologie future*, trans. E. Galichet and C. Haas-Smets of *Menschwerdung Gottes* (Paris: Desclee de Brouwer, 1973), esp. Excursus II, 640–49; English trans.: *The Incarnation of God: An Introduction to Hegel's Theological Thought as Prolegomena to a Future Christology*, trans. J. R. Stephenson (New York: Cross-road, 1987); Heribert Mühlen, *Die Veränderlichkeit Gottes als Horisont einer zukunftigen Christologie. Auf dem Wege zu einer Kreuzestheologie in Auseinandersetzung mit der altkirch-lichen Christologie*, 2nd ed. (Munster, 1976).

30. Anselm of Canterbury, *Cur Deus Homo?*, ed. F. S. Schmitt (Munich: International Publications Service, 1956).

31. *Summa Theol.* III, q. 48, a. 2.

Twelve / Preaching the Word: The Theological Background

1. Vatican II, for example, speaking of husband and wife as "witnesses to one another and to their children of faith in Christ" (chap. 4, no. 35), designates parents as "the first preachers of the faith to their children." (chap. 2, no. 11), *Dogmatic Constitution on the Church (Lumen Gentium)*.

2. Ministerial preaching is also charismatic in the sense that the call to office is a grace and that graces of office lie at the root of its effective discharge.

3. "Thus, the divinely established ecclesiastical ministry is exercised on different levels by those who from antiquity have been called bishops, priests, and deacons." *Dogmatic Constitution on the Church (Lumen Gentium)*, chap. 3, no. 28.

4. Romans 8:26.

5. 1 John 2:20 and 27; see 2 Cor. 1:21.

6. By way of clarifying the roles of the two persons of the Trinity sent into the soul, it may be helpful to distinguish faith from belief as the cognitive dimension of the former; it is the *Paraclete* who evokes faith in us, but a faith finding its objective and specifying focus in the *Logos*, who both proclaims the message and is himself the content of that message.

7. Seen as total faith response, the division corresponds to Aquinas's distinguishing the "causam interiorem quae movet hominem interius" from the "quidem exterius inducens" in faith (*Summa Theol.* II–II, q. 6, a. 1), The former is "interiori instinctu Dei invitantis" (II–II, q. 2, a. 9, ad. 3), "Instinctus interior impellens et movens ad credendum" (*Comm. in Joan. c.* 6, lect. 5); the latter rather the material objects of faith, the events known "ex auditu" (Rom. 10:17) "verborum significantium ea quae sunt fidei" (II–II, q. 1, a. 4, ad. 4).

8. The Christ in whom all preaching must take its origin today (as at Pentecost and as in Paul's sermons), is not the "Christ according to the flesh," but the risen Christ, the Lord with his body, of which we all are members"; Joseph Ratzinger, "Christocentric Preaching," in *The Word* (New York: P. J. Kenedy & Sons, 1964), 208.

9. See the development of this distinction borrowed from G. Gusdorf (*La Parole*, Paris, 1953) by Edward Schillebeeckx, "Revelation in Word and Deed," in *The Word*, 258.

10. "Hence the Eucharist shows itself to be the source and the apex of the whole work of preaching the gospel," Vatican II, *Ministry and Life of Priests*, chap. II, no. 5.

11. *Constitution on the Sacred Liturgy*, chap. I, no. 7.

12. "What is the Theological Starting Point for a Definition of the Priestly Ministry?" *The Identity of the Priest*, Concilium vol. 43 (1969), 85. Rahner is here developing an emphasis of Vatican II: " . . . priests as co-workers with their bishops, have as their primary duty the proclamation of the gospel of God to all." *Ministry and Life of Priests*, chap. 1, no. 4.

13. Denzinger-Schönmetzer, 3006.

14. See Ratzinger, "Christocentric Preaching," 208.

15. Neither "doctrinal preaching" nor "prophetic preaching" expresses exactly what is meant here; the former tends to confuse preaching with teaching and the latter to suggest private charisms and to neglect continuity with objective revelation. Also, it would be untoward to present the truths of Christianity as "ideology," i.e., as a system alien to reality and dominated by ideas whose content is dependent on factors outside of thought, especially goals. Marxism is an ideology, Christianity is not.

16. See *Unterwegs zur Sprache*, 121, where Heidegger plays on the word *Erscheinen* ("appearing").

17. In this sense, Heidegger's understanding of historicity allows for something genuinely new, in a way that Hegel's dialectic of history as idea does not.

18. Heinrich Fries has noted Barth's assessment of Bultmann as "the error of making existential pre-understanding the measure of the word of God" and his warning to Catholics against an uncritical Bultmannian influence; *Faith Under Challenge* (New York: Herder & Herder, 1969), 93.

19. See *Method in Theology* (New York: Herder & Herder, 1972), esp. 127–32, 355–68. "Applied" theology suggests too much the direct imposition of the conclusions of systematic theology upon the domain of life and practice. "Pastoral" theology carries the connotation of "techniques," i.e., of practical considerations of *how* to deal with people rather than substantive questions of *what* to do and say, especially in the U.S. where pastoral theology tends to diversify into multiple specializations modeling themselves overly much on secular disciplines such as sociology, psychiatry, etc. "Theology of practice" perhaps better conveys what is intended here, i.e., a strictly theological reflection not on texts or doctrines, but on what believers actually do by way of bringing their faith to authentic expression. Such a theology could profitably be considered as belonging within the broader perspective of "Communications," not in the sense of transposing a meaning already possessed, but in the sense of discovering needs and achievements that would provide the starting point for appropriating new practical truth. Such a theology, for example, while necessarily dependent upon systematics, would at the same time put demanding questions to the latter.

20. This thesis has been explored convincingly in detail by Langdon Gilkey in *Naming the Whirlwind* (Indianapolis and New York: Bobbs-Merrill, 1969).

21. *Method in Theology*, esp. 101–24. Some reservation may be legitimately felt here concerning Lonergan's understanding of how the strictly intellectual categories proper to theology can in fact arise out of prior religious conversion, but the preaching act lies much closer to conversion of heart, to the personal appropriation of the gospel, and here no such hesitancy need be felt.

22. *Summa Theol.* I–II, q. 68; II–II, qq. 8, 9, 45, and 52.

Thirteen / Preaching as a "Moment" in Theology

1. See Bernard Lonergan, *Method in Theology* (New York: Herder & Herder, 1972). What is to follow on the role of meaning is taken from this work.

2. Reginald Fuller, *The Formation of the Resurrection Narratives* (New York: Macmillan, 1971), 16.

3. This is not at variance with the statement from Vatican II's Constitution on Revelation (*Dei Verbum*), chap. 1, no. 4: "The Christian Economy, therefore, since it is the new and definitive covenant, will never pass away; and no new public revelation is to be expected

before the glorious manifestation of our Lord, Jesus Christ (see 1 Tim. 6:14 and Tit. 2:13)," which simply means that the once and for all historical action of God in Jesus Christ is not to be superseded.

4. *Resurrection and the New Testament*, Studies in Biblical Theology, 2nd Series, 12 (London, 1970).

5. In the categories of an older theology we used to say the *sacramentum tantum* and the *res et sacramentum* exist entirely for the *res tantum;* the sacraments are solely means to achieve the reality which is grace.

6. See Lonergan, *Method in Theology*, 76–78.

7. *Summa Theol.* II–II, q. 1, a. 4, ad. 4; q. 6, a. 1; q. 2, a. 9, ad. 3.

8. At the same time, it is necessary to distinguish here between a failure to live up fully to the injunctions of the Gospel, and insincerity, i.e., a lack of conviction about the content of what one preaches; it is the latter that robs preaching of its efficacy.

9. *Summa Theol.* I–II, q. 68; II–II, qq. 8, 9, 45, and 52.

10. O. C. Edwards made some valuable suggestions along these lines in the course of reviewing Clement Welsh's book *Preaching in a New Key, Studies in the Psychology of Thinking and Listening* (Philadelphia: Pilgrim Press, 1974), in the *Anglican Theological Review*, January 1976. Among these suggestions are: the use of systems analysis to "see the listener to a sermon as the focal point of a system of communication, one who processes the data with which his culture bombards him in an effort to make sense of his universe" (101); a study of conceptual systems since "the ideas that are most necessary for survival are, because of remoteness, the least certain and the most arbitrary ones we have. Since these are the kinds of ideas with which preaching deals, the preacher needs to know how they are formed" (102); a study of the ability of people to alter their views — since much preaching is directed to changing ideas — ranging from flexibility to rigidity; reflection on the distinction (from Jean Piaget) between *assimilative* thinking (fitting reality to mental categories already possessed) and *accommodative* thinking (adjusting existing categories to render them more adequate to new data and insights), etc.

11. Quoted in "Evangelization in the American Context," by Patrick S. McGarry, *America*, February 7, 1976, 95.

12. See chapter 12.

13. Joseph Ratzinger, "Christocentric Preaching," *The Word* (New York: P. J. Kenedy & Sons, 1964), 208.

14. See on this point, Louis Dupré: "Has the Secularist Crisis Come to an End?" *Listening* (Autumn 1974), who suggests that the present reaction to an all-pervasive secularity marks a flight to subjective powers of transcendence but not to a Transcendent.

Fourteen / What Is Preaching?
One Heuristic Model from Theology

1. See chapters 12 and 13.

2. First Vatican Council (Denzinger-Schönmetzer 3006–7).

3. Edward Schillebeeckx, *Jesus: An Experiment in Christology*, trans. Hubert Hoskins (New York: Crossroad, 1979), 62.

4. J. B. Metz, *Faith in History and in Society*, trans. David Smith (New York: Crossroad, 1980), 200f.

5. Second Vatican Council, Pastoral Constitution on the Church in the Modern World (*Gaudium et Spes*), no. 41.

Index of Names

Anaximander, 37
Anselm of Canterbury, 162–63
Anthanasius, 161
Apollinarius, 160
Aquinas, Thomas, xiii, 2–13, 19, 24–27, 33–48, 51–52, 57–58, 65, 67, 70–75, 78, 86–90, 94–96, 100, 105, 111–16, 120–21, 123–26, 128–30, 134–35, 139, 150–51, 163, 173, 175, 181–82, 202, 203, 205, 207, 208
Aristotle, 2, 4–5, 18, 25, 32 34, 37, 41, 45, 58, 63, 67–68, 71–72, 75, 78, 85–87, 90, 97, 112–13, 115, 118, 120, 132, 135, 143, 145, 154, 198, 203, 206, 207, 209
Augustine, 8, 18, 47, 71, 115, 134, 138, 173, 208
Avicenna, 34, 41, 71,

Báñez, Domingo, 73–74, 98, 203
Barth, Karl, xiii, 7, 19–20, 24, 51, 81–82, 88, 103, 106, 133, 153, 156, 195, 215
Bloch, Ernst, 55, 69, 158
Boethius, 87
Bohm, David, 92–95, 98, 101
Bonaventure, 18–19, 51
Bonhoeffer, Dietrich, xiv, 82
Braun, Herbert, 153
Brown, Robert McAfee, 151
Bultmann, Rudolf, 19–20, 53, 81–82, 153, 169, 172, 195, 215
Burrell, David, 94, 122

Cajetan, Thomas de Vio, 130, 208
Calvin, John, 51

Camus, Albert, 157
Caputo, John, 35–37, 46
Chenu, Marie-Dominique, 5
Clarke, W. Norris, 64, 100, 105, 126, 162
Cobb, John B., 1, 84, 86, 206
Congar, Yves, 5
Coreth, Emerich, 42, 53

De Petter, Dominic, 5, 198
Descartes, René, xi, 18, 24–25, 32, 37, 45, 93, 111, 148
Dionysius, 18
Dubarle, Dominic, xiii
Dupré, Louis, 7, 216
Durandus, 116, 208

Eco, Umberto, xi
Edwards, Jonathan, 128
Engels, Friedrich, 108, 206
Evans, C. F., 179

Fabro, Cornelio, 122
Fackenheim, Emil, 99
Ferré, Frederick, 92
Feuerbach, Ludwig, 33, 38, 51, 55, 152
Fichte, Johann Gottlieb, 99, 111, 144–46, 212
Ford, Lewis, 7, 84–86, 89, 100, 120–21, 123–25, 209
Fry, Christopher, 7
Fuller, Reginald, 179

Gadamer, Hans-Georg, 12, 20, 21–31, 41, 55, 103, 189
Geach, Peter, 67–68

217

Index of Subjects

Absolute/Absolute Being, xii, 42–43, 45, 53, 146, 152, 154, 210
act/potency, 37–38, 44, 64, 72, 74, 86, 89, 94–95, 98, 109, 112–13, 122, 124, 129, 132, 147, 203
actuality, 35–37, 39, 44–45, 67, 84–85, 89, 94, 99, 113, 122–24, 129–30, 162
aeviternity, 87, 203
aletheia (unveiling), 29, 34–38, 40, 44–45, 104–5
analogy, xii, xiv, 2–7, 10, 72–73, 84, 87, 94–97, 106, 113, 115, 117, 126, 128, 130–31, 140, 147–48, 153, 161, 203, 208, 210
Anwesen (presencing), 6, 36, 41–48, 105
apatheia (impassibility), 17, 157, 161–62
atheism, xii, 33, 51–52, 143, 153, 155

Being (*Sein*), xii, 19–22, 26, 29, 36, 38, 40, 84, 96, 104, 111–12, 126, 132, 178, 212. *See also esse* and *ens*
absolute. *See* Absolute Being
and becoming, xii, 44, 77, 84–87, 154, 157
and beings, 19, 29, 34, 36, 104, 126
as event, 37–38, 45, 58
infinite. *See* infinite/infinity
Ipsum Esse Subsistens, 35, 52, 95, 121, 129, 145, 199, 210
itself, 18–19, 34, 42, 72, 121, 129–30, 155
pure act of, 2, 6, 25, 27, 34, 39–40,

76, 87, 91, 112–13, 117, 120–21, 125, 150, 209
subsistent, xiv, 25, 29, 35, 70, 89, 121, 123, 150, 209

causal/causality, 5, 18–19, 36, 39–47, 71–73, 75, 90, 93, 98–100, 103–4, 113–14, 119, 127, 130, 147–48, 203, 210, 211
classical theism, xii, 7, 33–48, 52, 54, 64, 145, 153–54
communicatio idiomatum, xiv, 10, 62, 90, 161
conceptualism/conceptual, xiii, 7, 22, 26–28, 41, 97, 128, 171, 216
creation, xiv–xv, 2, 4, 6, 9, 18, 34, 42, 73, 78, 94, 97–98, 100, 114, 118, 123, 132, 140, 147, 150, 155–56
creativity, 68, 70, 77–79, 89, 93, 100, 106, 113, 123, 130, 143, 146, 148, 205, 206, 210
cross, 9, 59, 62–63, 137–38, 151, 157, 176

Dasein, 22, 26, 28, 34, 36–38, 42, 69, 104, 111

empiricism, 18, 54, 92, 152, 174, 177
Enlightenment, xi, xiii, 18, 54–55, 88
ens, 39, 115, 121. *See also* Being
entitative order, 10, 75, 104, 111, 114
esse, xiii, 25, 35–37, 39, 42, 67, 87, 94–95, 120–23, 129, 205, 210. *See also* Being
essence/existence (in God), xiii, 6, 112, 116, 121–22, 129, 209

221